GOVERNMENT INTERVENTION
IN THE DEVELOPED ECONOMY

Government Intervention in the Developed Economy

Edited by PETER MAUNDER

CROOM HELM LONDON

© 1979 Peter Maunder
Croom Helm Ltd, 2-10 St John's Road, London SW11

British Library Cataloguing in Publication Data

Government intervention in the developed economy.
    1. Industry and state
    I. Maunder, Peter, b. 1943
    338.9'009181'2   HD3611

    ISBN 0-85664-572-9

Printed and bound in Great Britain by
Redwood Burn Ltd, Trowbridge and Esher

CONTENTS

Preface   9

1. Government Intervention in the Economy of Japan
   G.C. Allen   17

2. Government Intervention in the Economy of Australia
   R.H. Allan, J.P. Nieuwenhuysen and N.R. Norman   41

3. Government Intervention in the Economy of the United
   States
   James W. McKie   72

4. Government Intervention in the Economy of Sweden
   H.G. Jones   101

5. Government Intervention in the Economy of the United
   Kingdom
   Peter Maunder   130

6. Government Intervention in the Economy of the Federal
   Republic of Germany
   Eric Owen-Smith   160

7. Government Intervention in the Economy of France
   J.R. Hough   190

Notes on Contributors   215

Name Index   216

Subject Index   218

PREFACE

The aim of this book is to offer a collection of studies on the nature and experience of state intervention in seven developed countries. Of the seven, four are in Western Europe – France, West Germany, Sweden and the United Kingdom. The remaining three countries – Australia, Japan and the United States – are much more geographically disparate but are obvious candidates for inclusion in a text concerned with the relationship between government and industry in some of the world's leading economies. Of course other countries such as Canada, Italy and Switzerland suggest themselves for similar close examination of the influence of the state. Any dividing line is bound to be arbitrary but in defence of the present selection of countries the reader will no doubt appreciate the need for it to have been drawn tightly so as to keep the length of the book within bounds. Secondly, there was the not unimportant point that the book was not one based on a conference where experts on particular countries had been discussing matters of common interest. In such circumstances the greatest difficulty in writing a book with a multi-nation focus is getting a team of authors willing to be participants in an uncertain venture. That formidable task itself acted as a constraint on the geographic coverage of the volume.

I was fortunate in being able to enlist the services of two of my colleagues at Loughborough University, Eric Owen-Smith and Jim Hough, who have, respectively, discussed the West German and French approach to state intervention. Both draw on their country expertise for lectures at Loughborough University on European Economics and their participation in this book of course eased the editorial task. The choice of an author on Sweden was not difficult because of the link with the present publisher and H.G. Jones.[1] The author has written numerous articles on aspects of Swedish industry and made himself an expert in Britain on the subject. The country itself was a compelling choice not just because of its high standard of living but also due to its distinctive political system and industrial environment.

In the case of Japan I was very glad to be able to include the contribution from Professor G.C. Allen, a well-known authority on Japan who has written several books on the country.[2] John Nieuwenhuysen and the editor had been in contact with each other in the earlier nineteen-seventies concerning competition policy. Croom Helm had published several books by John Nieuwenhuysen and his colleagues[3] on that subject and this further link led inevitably to his invitation to participate. For the obvious US dimension I am indebted to Professor Raymond Vernon for suggesting the name of Professor James McKie. I am particularly grateful to James McKie for his assessment of the American interventionist scene. He responded readily to my invitation to contribute even though there had been no previous communication between us.

If the above indicates how the contributions were assembled it is now appropriate to explain what they were asked to write about.

The word 'intervention' is of course itself somewhat loaded in meaning. It can imply to a person on the Right that an economy ought normally to be run on a free enterprise system. The state 'intrudes' for particular reasons. Someone on the Left might argue that the norm is collectivism and private enterprise can be allowed in certain cases to 'intervene'! Lord Ryder, first chairman of Britain's National Enterprise Board, has thus fairly remarked that: 'The trouble with the word "intervention" is that, like "democratic", its meaning varies enormously depending on the political standpoint of the person using it. This does not exactly make for rational debate.'[4]

The editor's bias towards matters of a micro-economic character partly determined that in each country survey the macro-economic dimension would not be the overriding focus of concern. This decision considerably eased the total task. Thus in no way were the authors even attempting a Brookings Institution study in miniature to contrast with the efforts of the American economists concerning Britain[5] and Japan.[6] Rather the aim was to examine state intervention in both labour and product markets at the micro level.

Policies at the micro level are the basis for the achievement of macro-economic objectives. Thus competition policies work to meet the goal of price stabilisation: subsidies and state takeovers try to fulfil the critical goal of maximising employment levels. This is true in any advanced society and it is in the degree of emphasis that variations between nations are to be found.

In a book with a single country focus discussion of policy matters will probably try to identify not only objectives and instruments but also the nature of parameter values in relevant economic models.[7] The space constraints in this seven-country survey did not permit such exhaustive analysis. What is offered is an overview of the changing nature of policies to meet situations as governments have perceived them. The focus is therefore not an assessment of the fundamental macro goals of economic policy or on a detailed examination of policy implementation.[8] Neither does the book try to suggest solutions to conflicting objectives.

What hopefully the book does offer the reader, given these limitations, is a better understanding of the style of government in countries with which he is not familiar. This educational process was shared by those involved in its preparation. The natural tendency of economists to focus interest on their own country means a paucity of short readable accounts of the situation elsewhere. Four of the authors living in Britain have the rather unusual distinction of a broad outlook and contribute their survey on a country in which they have visited and studied. The four countries involved – Japan, West Germany, France and Sweden are indeed those countries that have become frequently cited in recent years as offering the United Kingdom secrets of successful industrial performance and economic growth. The United States too has been held up as a model for the UK to note. All these countries situated in the northern hemisphere which are studied in this book are joined by a developed country south of the Equator, Australia, so as to give a wider examination of the nature of government. The Antipodean style of state influence certainly has distinctive characteristics.

An ambitious undertaking at the end of the country surveys would have been a systematic comparative assessment of policies in the chosen countries. This was felt by the editor a challenge to be faced at a later date. Rather what now follows are some impressions from each account as to the distinctive thrusts of interventionist policy. It is clear that there are differences in policy approach and results.

Japan is an interesting case since, against a background of a relatively small public sector, close links exist between government and the key large industrial groups. Their lengthy dialogue takes place in a long-term planning context with economic growth the natural order of things. This scenario cannot be understood without an appreciation of early days of Japanese industrial expansion and the reluctance of the state, having actively promoted industrial development, to stay at the centre of the stage. With this historical perspective in mind we find at the present time Japan's government keen to prompt and encourage private enterprise. It engages in extensive discussions with the large groups to a point of acceptable mutual compromise. Public corporations do exist in Japan but are essentially not to be found in civil manufacturing industry. The concern about the growing bureaucracy of these corporations parallels that in other countries such as the UK over the ever-growing size of the civil service.

Competition policies have become of growing importance even if as yet they have not been as dramatic in their effects as in say the US or UK. There have certainly been bold regional policies as the Japanese have come to face the issue of what has come to be known as the 'quality of life'. The significance of formal planning in Japan is open to doubt.

In the case of *Australia* the macro-micro distinction is particularly blurred. The macro dimension has been of extreme importance in the regulation of industry. This is because of the impact on firms of oscillating monetary and fiscal measures arising from the changing political nature of the government. But there is also the distinctive effect of the price, wage and competition policy authorities in Australia. The activities of the latter bodies are, arguably, micro interventions to reach macro objectives. The constitutional arrangements for these bodies is of particular interest: for example, the inability of the federal Australian government to directly control prices.

Competition policy in Australia has become somewhat tougher in approach as it relates to a fairly highly concentrated manufacturing sector in a country with a comparatively small market. A key issue in Australian industrial policy has been the extent of tariff protection. It is inevitably one where strong pressure groups emerge when reductions in tariff duties are proposed. As in other developed nations the recession in the world economy understandably has made the preservation of jobs of high priority in the Australian debate on the restructuring of industry. Another significant aspect of the Australian industrial scene is the concern over foreign ownership and capital inflows.

The survey of the *United States* shows how the sphere of government decision-making has grown ever larger in recent years. Anti-trust policies have operated ever since 1890 but in the last decade have been supplemented by legislation on consumer matters. The promptings of Ralph Nader are by now well-known outside the United States. The regulation of natural monopolies as public utilities has been a model for other areas of the American economy which, arguably, were not obvious candidates for such intervention. Certain parts of the economy such as aerospace and defence are indeed so greatly affected by public policy that they are quasi-public in nature. As in Western Europe the general view seems to be that government intervention *is* appropriate to resolve any specific problem that arises. American faith in private enterprise has somewhat faltered. The emphasis on micro policies — grants, taxes, subsidies, etc. to fulfil the goals of the 1976 Full Employment and Balanced Growth Act parallels the attempts being made in the

UK with its so-called new industrial strategy.

Sweden has attracted increasing attention in recent years from those interested in establishing the secrets of its successful standard of living, arguably the highest in Western Europe. The Swedish style of intervention is very distinctive. The country has shown an enthusiasm for creating bureaucracies and ombudsmen. There are several ombudsmen dealing with competition policy, the press and consumer matters. The stabilisation policies pursued by the Labour Market Board have been viewed with increasing interest in Britain, as indeed has its 'national enterprise board' the Statsföretag. The new non-socialist government since 1976 has had to take tough measures to maintain the competitiveness of Swedish industry. As elsewhere in Western Europe subsidies have been given to rescue firms suffering in the world recession. The preservation of jobs has been a higher priority than commitment to political ideology.

During the past decade selective intervention in *United Kingdom* industry has not just been of the occasional, short-term variety as was the case hitherto. True, there is still the rescue of ailing firms like British Leyland but there is now a deliberate attempt to encourage the development of certain whole industries. Indeed intervention at the micro level has become a fundamental part of government economic strategy. Those who believe in the efficacy of macro-economic weapons to secure faster economic growth have been on the defensive while the number of converts to the now micro-based industry strategy have grown. Both main political parties are now in favour of discriminatory selective assistance for industry but still remain divided over an extension of the public sector into the area of banking. They also have divergent views on the role of the National Enterprise Board, but share a concern for effective regional policies.

Legislation on competition policy has been passed in the periods of office of both Labour and Conservative governments. The Wilson administration's enthusiasm for company mergers in the late 1960s now rather contrasts with the growing conventional wisdom that 'small is beautiful' and mergers policy needs to be amended to help prevent a further concentration of British industry. Any new legislation will be an indication of the current activist approach to industrial policy in contrast with the period until the mid-1960s.

The survey on *West Germany* indicates that the belief in the efficacy of competitive market forces, as favoured after, say, 1949 to reconstruct the war-torn economy, has somewhat faded in recent years. Competition policies have not prevented German industry becoming more heavily concentrated. Since 1967 the concept of planning has existed in practical terms and is arguably a reflection of the diminished faith in the virtues of the social market economy philosophy. The provisions in the 1967 Promotion of Economic Stability and Growth Act for selective financial assistance parallel the British approach as laid down in successive Industry Acts. The Federal government's influence in industry is enhanced by its direct participation in many business under- takings. State-owned banks are of great significance. Regional policies have particular relevance in the Federal Republic which has, in effect, an eleventh state in the problem city of West Berlin as well as the long eastern frontier zone. In short market forces have been increasingly supplemented in the task of resource allocation by government inter- vention.

The economy of *France* is markedly influenced by state intervention as a result of both macro and micro policies. The French enthusiasm for indicative planning far exceeds that to be found in any other West European country and even if its mystique in recent times has faded, it remains a relevant and continuing part of French economic policy. At the micro level the French style of intervention is one of direct par- ticipation, ranging from outright nationalisation to limited ownership, in a host of both big and small enterprises. The scale of state owner- ship in France and in particular its involvement in the financial sector have indeed been important underlying aspects of the effectiveness of the French approach to planning.

Competition policy in France has been somewhat soft-pedalled in application so as to permit the greater concentration of production to be brought about as hoped for by the French government. Concern over the small scale of industry in the 1960s saw the French copy Britain's Industrial Reorganisation Corporation and actively promote mergers. Again, as in the UK, France has experienced active labour market policies. French governments have increasingly devoted more attention to policies to meet the problem of regional imbalance.

The contractual arrangements in France between the government and nationalised industry can be seen as an attempt to resolve the tricky problems of the commercial and political responsibilities of state owned undertakings. As in the UK the government has been anxious to reduce the high level of subsidies being received by state utilities brought about by the soaring rate of inflation in the late 1970s.

In none of these seven countries is there clear evidence of a retreat by governments in industrial affairs, rather the reverse is true. Indeed in these and other developed economies state participation is increasing

through more public ownership and industrial planning. The collapse
of large firms, like Rolls-Royce in Britain and Lockheed in the United
States, has been tempered by state-aided rescue schemes. The problems
of regionalism always provide a pressing basis for state support of
depressed areas. The world recession since 1974 has given added
impetus to these problems as governments continue to strive to meet
the goal of full employment. The soaring pace of price inflation in the
1970s throughout the world has also highlighted the problems facing
private enterprise concerning its very survival. The 'crisis of capitalism',[9]
to quote one survey in Britain, is not an understatement of the matter.
'Lame ducks' have been a worry for most governments with advanced
economies. In the older industries like leather, textiles and shipbuilding
the world recession since 1974 has highlighted the existing structural
problem. The long-term need for further plant closures and reallocation
of resources is not in doubt, but neither is the short-term political
requirement to 'do something'. 'Temporary subsidies' or state takeover
have been the favoured immediate solutions. Job creation schemes,
like Britain's Temporary Employment Subsidy, raise the issue of unfair
international competition particularly when countries seek economic
union.

Three of the countries in this book are part of the European Economic Community. The approach to industrial intervention in one
member country is quickly criticised by fellow members if they feel
adversely affected. The development of a common EEC industrial
policy has yet to evolve fully.

The reader should note that in each of the surveys of EEC member
countries — UK, West Germany and France — the discussion is entirely
focused at the national level. The problem of co-ordinating industrial
policies between EEC members is no better illustrated than the proposed
merger between the British firm of Guest, Keen and Nettlefolds (GKN)
and Sachs AG. This merger was prohibited by the West German Bundeskavtellant but authorised by the EEC Commission. GKN later unsuccessfully appealed in the German Supreme Court against the national
decision. The need for a harmonisation of national and EEC competition
and regional policy is clear but discussion of such policies in each of
the three country surveys from a Community standpoint was not felt
appropriate given the wider perspective of the total book.

16   *Preface*

Notes

1. H.G. Jones, *Planning and Productivity in Sweden* (Croom Helm, London, 1976).
2. G.C. Allen's writings on Japan include *Japan's Economic Recovery* (Oxford University Press, London, 1958); *Japan's Economic Expansion* (Oxford University Press, London, 1965); *Japan as a Market and Source of Supply* (Pergamon Press, Oxford, 1967); *A Short Economic History of Modern Japan* (3rd edition) (Allen & Unwin, London, 1972).
3. J.P. Nieuwenhuysen & N.R. Norman, *Australian Competition and Prices Policy* (Croom Helm, London, 1976).
4. 'Meeting the challenge: the Manager's response', The London Business School Stockton Lecture, 10 February 1977, *London Business School Journal*, Vol. 3, No. 1, Spring 1978, p. 12.

   Sir Alan Cottrell, formerly Chief Scientific Adviser to the British Government, has also commented that 'industrial policy' can have varied meanings. Is it 'policy for industry' (for the encouragement of manufacturers and commerce) or 'policy for the control of industry to serve non-commercial ends of a social or political nature?' See 'Grasping the nettles in British Industrial Policy' *Journal of the Royal Society of Arts, Manufacturers and Commerce*, March 1976, p. 172.
5. R. Caves (ed.), *Britain's Economic Prospects* (Allen and Unwin, London, 1968).
6. H. Patrick & H. Rosovsky (eds), *Asia's new giant; How the Japanese economy works* (Blackwell, Oxford, 1976).
7. A British example of this approach is R.M. Grant & G.K. Shaw (eds), *Current Issues in Economic Policy* (Philip Allan Publishers, Oxford, 1975).
8. An excellent text that documents the development of British industrial policy between 1964 and 1972 is S. Young & A. Lowe, *Intervention in the Mixed Economy* (Croom Helm, London, 1974).
9. The title was the basis for a survey in the *Guardian*, 1 July 1975.

1 GOVERNMENT INTERVENTION IN THE ECONOMY OF JAPAN

G.C. Allen

The part of the State in Japan's economic development and its present
functions in the conduct of the economy have been misunderstood in
the West. European and American students have naturally tried to
interpret Japan's policies and practices in the light of their own countries'
institutions and experiences, and they have often failed to realise that
the *modus operandi* of the Japanese economy is in some important
respects unique. So Western observers of the scene find themselves con-
fronted by what seems a paradox. On the one hand, they can find
support for the proposition that Japan, since the Second World War,
has provided the outstanding example of a highly competitive economy
where, it seems, private enterprise can be given the credit for most of
the country's remarkable economic growth. It is acknowledged also that
the size of the public sector and the ratio of public expenditure to the
gross domestic product are much smaller than in any other advanced
country. (In 1974 the ratios were 23.8 per cent for Japan, 44.8 per
cent for the United Kingdom, 41.5 per cent for West Germany and
38 per cent for France.) On the other hand, many Western writers
have made much of the fact that economic policies which affect both
the direction and the rate of industrial expansion have been worked
out in considerable detail by the bureaucracy and the great firms in
concert, and that the activities of industrial enterprises have frequently
been subject to close guidance from the centre of government. Hence
the appellation 'Japan Incorporated' which some American journalists
have chosen as an apt description of the character of Japan's economic
system.

How can this conflict of evidence and opinion about the importance
of the government in the ordering of the country's economic affairs
be explained—and possibly resolved? To begin with, the contrast between
Western countries and Japan in the ratio of public expenditure to the
national income can be partly attributed to disparities in expenditure on
defence and social welfare. Japan's expenditure on defence has been
restricted by the provisions of the Peace Treaty of 1951 and by the
pacifist mood of the people since the collapse of their country's military
ambitions. As to the relatively low rate of public expenditure on welfare,

the explanation is to be found partly in Japan's social institutions (e.g. the family system and paternalistic practices in industry), and partly in the priority given by the whole nation since the war to rapid industrial growth.

From the standpoint of the present inquiry, these differences between Japan and the West are of great importance. In Europe the increase in public expenditure on defence and social welfare has been one of the chief reasons for the advance in the part played by the State in economic life. As to Japan's concentration on industrial growth, there is little doubt that this policy left inadequate resources available for public investment in the infrastructure and welfare. Nevertheless, because the State's role in certain sectors of the national life has been less prominent in Japan than in the West, it would be rash to conclude that, taken as a whole, the government's influence on economic affairs has been weaker. It can be argued more plausibly, that the main contrast lies not in the *extent* of State intervention, but in the instruments used in effecting it. Another difference is to be found in the motives for intervention. In the West social and political doctrine has strongly influenced the policy of most governments in this field and has been decisive in some. The presiding motives of the Japanese, on the other hand, have been expediency and the search for practical solutions to immediate problems. This contrast between Japan and most European countries in respect of both methods and motives is of long standing. Although the part played by the State in Japan's economic development and management has varied from time to time during the last century, one can detect a thread of continuity which may help to explain the paradox referred to in the first paragraph. A glance back to the activities of government at the beginning of the modern era (1868) will illustrate the truth of this assertion.

Government Policy in the Meiji Era

In the early years of the Meiji era (1868-1912), the central government took the initiative in introducing systems of law, education and administration based on Western models and it was responsible for establishing the infrastructure of a modern society. Its entrepreneurial activities extended to commerce, communications, transport, banking and even manufacturing industry. Many new factories, equipped with Western machines and staffed at the beginning with European and American experts and managers, were founded and capitalised by the State.[1] In these pioneering ventures the Meiji government had in mind certain political objectives that influenced all its policies, above all, the enhancement of the country's military power, for it was ambitious to confront Western nations on equal terms. Industrial development, it was realised, was necessary to establish a basis for an effective diplomacy and every means for the promotion of that development had to be seized. Since private entrepreneurs familiar with Western technology and commercial practices were few, the State was obliged to take the lead. But it did not assume this role because of any compelling principle. The new government in the early 1870s faced numerous problems that demanded an immediate solution. It was these problems that compelled action. They included the provision of jobs for the now functionless *samurai*, the supply of certain goods for its own military and administrative needs, and import-saving at a time when its reserves of gold and silver were exiguous.[2]

The attitude of the Japanese government to its own pioneering activities is demonstrated by its anxiety to dispose of its industrial properties to private firms as soon as the new ventures had succeeded in their immediate aims. Most of them were, in fact, sold by the early 1880s, not, it should be emphasised, out of obedience to a proposition that private enterprise was a superior form of economic administration, but simply in order to relieve budgetary difficulties. The empirical attitude of the leaders is revealed by a remark of Prince Matsukata, the architect of Japan's financial system.[3] During the 1890s, when Japan was just entering a new stage of industrialisation, he commented on the means by which success could be achieved. While he acknowledged the theoretical arguments for *laissez-faire* and competitive private enterprise, he argued that the methods that might be apt for the developed economies of the West might not be best suited, without modification, for the ends that Japan had set herself. If it seemed that, on occasion, the State's initiative was necessary to promote economic growth in the direction desired, then theoretical propositions derived from observations of Western society should not stand in the way. On the other hand, there was certainly no bias against private enterprise among the Meiji leaders. Indeed, not the least important among the government's reforms in the early years was the abolition of the institutions, practices and laws which it had inherited from 'feudal' times, and which, if preserved, would have thwarted economic progress. The mere exposure of what had long been a closed economy to foreign trade and other outside influences was, indeed, a condition of progress; the new freedom gave release from the former shackles on economic initiative.

During the whole period from the 1880s until the 1930s, the development of the greater part of industry was left to private enterprise. The chief export industries, raw silk and cotton textiles, fell completely within this category. Even in these industries, however, the State's role was not passive. Private enterprise was subject to constraints and stimuli designed to guide development into ways conformable with what was regarded by the political leaders as the national advantage. For example, while the processes of silk-raising and silk-reeling were left entirely to small, competitive undertakings, government control was imposed at key points. Success in the export market, it was realised, depended on the production of a filament of uniform quality suitable for use on the American hosiery machines. But uniform quality is elusive in industries composed of large numbers of small firms. The government solved this problem by imposing rigid controls over the quality of the silkworm eggs supplied to the cocoon-raisers, and by providing for a conditioning house at Yokohama for testing the goods before they were exported.[4]

The export trade, as a whole, so vital to Japan's economic expansion, was stimulated by the low-interest loans or discounts provided by the semi-official exchange bank, the Yokohama Specie Bank. Other semi-official banks, which raised resources by selling their debentures to the Treasury Deposits Bureau, later known as Trust Fund Bureau (a body in receipt of Post Office savings), furnished long-term loans to concerns judged to be of national importance. In overseas territories, also, (the colonies and the Manchuria Railway Zone) official or semi-official concerns (e.g. various investment banks, the Oriental Development Company and the South Manchuria Railway Company) acted as agents of the government for economic development. Nor did the State hesitate at any time to take the lead in setting up new industries, or to seize control over established industries, when the military or fiscal needs of the country seemed to require such action. Motives of strategy led to the founding of the first modern steel works, which began production in 1901, and to the nationalisation of the main line railways in 1906. The same motives lay behind the decisions to subsidise the shipbuilding and shipping industries during the 1890s. It was for fiscal reasons that the tobacco monopoly came into being in 1906.

The Zaibatsu

Probably the most potent instrument of all for the execution of national policy consisted of the group of great firms ('conglomerates', we should now call them) which formed the spearhead of Japan's economic development in the Meiji (1868-1912) and Taisho (1912-1926) eras. These were the *zaibatsu* (money groups) whose interests extended into almost every

part of the economy, banking and insurance, trade, mining and manufacturing. These concerns, some of which could look back on several
centuries of flourishing existence, rose to eminence largely because of
their role as indispensable agents of the government's economic policy.
They enjoyed close associations with the political leaders and, in return
for their services, many privileges were conferred on them by successive
governments. They were, however, not merely passive agents. As time
went on, they were able to exert a powerful influence on official
decisions, so that the relations between them and the bureaucracy
became increasingly subtle and complex.

Before the First World War the relative size of the public sector in
Japan was comparable with that in Western countries, and its content
differed little from theirs. In 1913 publicly-owned plants provided only
about 12 per cent of total factory employment. But the influence
exerted by the government on private enterprise through the means
described was far greater than that of the contemporary British or
American governments on their economies. During the next fifteen
years the size of the public sector declined. The 1920s were a liberal
era in Japan and, while the public sector remained much as it was
before, private manufacturing industry expanded considerably. By 1930,
it is estimated, government factories provided only about 4 per cent of
factory employment.[5] The government's share of gross national expenditure was then of the order of 15 to 18 per cent; much of it was accounted
for by heavy expenditure on defence and armaments.[6]

The 1930s witnessed in Japan, as elsewhere, a retreat from economic
liberalism and a wide extension of government controls. During the
latter part of the decade the country moved towards a *junsenji keizai*
(quasi-wartime economy) which was marked by the nationalisation of
industries of strategic importance (e.g. steel and electricity generation)
and the setting up of 'national policy' companies to promote the growth
of others in the same category. Public supervision was extended over
various private undertakings and transactions, and new business groups
(*shinko-zaibatsu*)[7] were formed to carry out industrial policies favoured
by the dominant military establishment both at home and in North
Asia. Of course, as in all the belligerent countries, when war came, very
little initiative was left to independent private enterprise.

Defeat meant that Japan was deprived for six years of control over
her economic policy. One of the chief aims of the Occupation Authority
was to democratise the country and to create a liberal market economy;
the measures introduced at the outset were nearly all directed to those
ends. SCAP[8] wished, in particular, to diffuse economic initiative by

destroying both private concentrations of power and also the institutions by which the central bureaucracy had guided economic processes. Hence the break-up of the *zaibatsu* into numerous constituent parts, the de-nationalisation of steel and electric power, and the conversion of the semi-official banks into private concerns. Other laws provided for the setting up a Fair Trade Commission (aimed at preventing the re-emergence of concentrations of economic power), Land Reform which turned the mass of tenant farmers into peasant proprietors, and Labour Laws (modelled on those of the United States) which conferred on Japanese employees the right of collective bargaining and so opened the way for a new trade-union movement and a modern system of industrial relations.[9]

Against this historical background, let us now consider the nature and extent of interventionist policies in the last quarter of a century, that is since 1952 when Japan regained control over her national policy. Was the American attempt to set up a liberal, competitive, market economy successful and enduring? Did Japan, after the disaster of defeat and the frustrations of the Occupation period, turn her back on the system of national economic administration that had prevailed in the first sixty years of the modern era, or can one detect similarities, or identities, between the post-war economic policy and that of the past? In particular, has the intervention of the State in the ordering of eco-nomic affairs been more or less pervasive than in pre-war days? Let us first address ourselves to these general questions before examining in detail the measures of intervention that have been most in evidence in this period.

There is no doubt that some of the most important American reforms endured and had a profound effect on the country's economic system, although many of them were adapted and modified as time went on to serve Japan's own purposes. Others, soon after the end of the Occupation, encountered the forces of what was known as the 'reverse course'. This reversal affected especially the policy of decentralisation. For example, even before the end of the Occupation, it was evident that the dissolution of the *zaibatsu* had stopped short of the intentions of the policy as originally adumbrated. Although the central holding companies of the *zaibatsu* and the controlling organs of the lesser conglomerates were abolished, and the great trading companies dismembered, the *zaibatsu* banks were left intact.[10] After 1952 the former constituents began to draw together again, and the great trading companies were gradually re-created. However, it soon became evident that the new links between the constituent members of the groups were much looser than formerly.

Those placed in charge of the successor companies relished their freedom from central control, and their attitude did much to modify the
character of the post-war *zaibatsu*. At the same time, the new freedom
gave opportunities for alert entrepreneurs outside the privileged groups,
and several of these during the 1950s built up businesses that now rank
among the greatest in Japan. They were particularly prominent in the
new industries.

A factor that favoured the diffusion of enterprise was the change in
the sources of investment finance. In pre-war days much of it had been
in the hands of the *zaibatsu* banks and finance companies, which channelled resources into the manufacturing and trading concerns in the same
group; but in the post-war world these banks lacked the means to supply
the insatiable appetite of industry for new capital. During the early post-
war years the chief source of reconstruction finance was the Reconstruction Finance Bank, a government bank that handled American aid and
procurement funds, and this bank spread its loans over the emergent
industries. Later, a number of new government banks were set up to
furnish loans at favourable rates of interest to firms in those branches
of the economy which, in the government's view, deserved special
assistance because of their importance to future development, for
example, steel and electric power. (Some of these government banks
will be described presently.)

The importance for industry of central sources of finance did not
diminish significantly in subsequent years. Manufacturing industry, in
particular, remained closely dependent on bank loans to carry through
its rapid expansion. Most of the loans had to be supplied by the ordinary,
commercial banks, but these could not have satisfied the demands of
their customers if it had not been for accommodation from the Central
Bank. This relationship between the central monetary authorities and
the needs of industry for new capital gave these authorities a powerful
influence over the policy of firms in the private sector, an influence
exerted by the use of 'window controls'[11] and preferential rates of
interest. Thus one can conclude that, while the institutional reforms of
the Occupation period, reinforced by the post-war financial stringency,
weakened the former great oligopolists, the power of the central government to mould the economy and to guide industrial development was
increased. The term 'guide' is used advisedly. As already indicated, the
Japanese way is to proceed by discussion leading to a consensus, rather
than by coercion or diktat. It should not be supposed, moreover, that
an agreement on a common policy is *always* reached by the interested
parties. Indeed, there have been some notable exceptions to the rule, and

it is possible that, as industry becomes less dependent upon outside loan-capital for its expansion, one of the instruments hitherto employed by the central authorities to persuade reluctant industrialists will become less effective than it was in the 1950s and 1960s.

Apart from these general and specific financial devices, the government has employed many other means for ensuring that the policy of firms should accord with what is conceived to be the national purpose. They may be classified under five heads:

1. direct controls over foreign exchange and foreign trade;
2. controls over, or obligations imposed on, private firms in regard to such matters as market behaviour, location and pollution;
3. formal and informal relationships established between various Ministries and firms (or industries) that are designed to influence or to determine the strategy of those firms (or industries);
4. indicative economic planning as expressed in a succession of national plans from the early 1950s until the present time;
5. government-owned or controlled bodies or corporations set up to undertake specific functions; under this head fall the numerous public corporations which are highly diversified (in scope and purpose).

1. Controls Over Foreign Exchange and Foreign Trade

During the 1950s and early 1960s the weakness of Japan's international financial position and the frequent recurrence of crises in her balance of payments persuaded her government to maintain strict controls over foreign transactions. At that time imports were subject to licensing and all foreign payments supervised by the central authorities. The practice was for the government to draw up a budget which covered the allocation of the available exchange among different uses, and the import licences granted to importers were governed by these allocations. The controls were associated with various devices for encouraging exports which, for many years, lagged behind the recovery in industrial production. For instance, under a 'link' system, import licences for particular materials were given on condition that the licensee exported a specified amount of manufactured goods. The device was equivalent to an export subsidy, since the disparity between the foreign and the domestic prices of the goods imported enabled the licensee to make a profit on the transaction and so encouraged him to subsidise the export on which his licence depended. Various privileges were bestowed on firms that were parties to approved arrangements for the import of foreign technology. Tax discrimination was exercised in favour of exports, and export bills were discounted at low rates of interest through the Bank of Japan. The official Export-Import Bank also provided loans to exporters on favourable terms. These devices enabled the government to influence the direction of the country's economic growth, and it is probable that they permitted the authorities to press forward their expansionist policy with fewer misgivings than they would have had under a liberal trading regime.

During the 1960s most of the controls were abolished. In 1963, under pressure from the IMF, Japan dismantled her restrictions over current transactions, and later, having acceded to the demand that she should adopt Article 11 status under the GATT, she steadily reduced her quantitative controls on imports and modified her methods of stimulating her exports. A few goods, including many foods, remain subject to quantitative restrictions, but in these respects Japan is not out of line with most of her trading partners in the developed world. Foreign importers still complain that some manufactured goods suffer from discrimination which, they allege, now takes the form of administrative controls of baffling complexity, but the Japanese reply that the main fault lies with traders who do not take the trouble to acquaint themselves with the country's methods of doing business. As in the past, the government has encouraged firms engaged in exporting to form associations for regulating the quantity and quality of export goods. In the early 1950s some of these associations organised the dumping of goods abroad, raising levies on sales in the home market for subsidising exports. In recent years, however, their influence has sometimes been exerted in the opposite direction. Japan's increased competitive strength has been displayed in many markets to the detriment of the home producers who have been loud in their call for protection. So, with the approval of the Japanese government, some of the associations have concerned themselves with applying 'voluntary' export quotas to their members' foreign sales with the object of forestalling import restrictions in the customer-countries. During the last decade the restrictions on foreign investment in Japanese industry, which were once widespread and stringent, have been much relaxed. One may conclude by saying that, in the period of reconstruction, the controls considered in the above paragraphs were important instruments of industrial and commercial strategy, but that they were gradually given up as Japan achieved her position as one of the world's largest industrial producers and traders.[12]

2. Controls Over the Market Behaviour and Policies of Private Firms

The Occupation Authority did not consider that its task of economic liberalisation was completed when it had dissolved, or partially dissolved, the *zaibatsu*. It realised that such success as it had achieved would not survive the restoration of full sovereignty to Japan unless the dissolution policy were buttressed by permanent legal restraints on monopolistic practices. So the government was required to pass an Anti-Monopoly Law and to set up, under it, a Fair Trade Commission with the function of curbing the operations of cartels and of countering any future attempts to monopolise. The legal authority given to the Commission was extensive. It covered measures for the elimination of 'substantial disparities' in bargaining power (as by divestiture) and for preventing devices for monopolisation such as inter-locking directorates, mergers, inter-corporate stock-holding, and holding companies. The Anti-Monopoly Law was reinforced by a Trade Association Law which defined the permitted activities of the associations and forbade restrictive practices on their part. These laws were disliked by the business community, and it was not long before efforts were made to emasculate them. As early as 1949 the harshness of some of the original provisions was modified; for example, the power of the Commission to prevent inter-corporate stock-holding, inter-locking directorates and mergers was reduced. The trend became pronounced after Japan had assumed control over her own policy. For instance, in 1953 resale price maintenance was permitted for a limited class of articles, and it became possible to operate cartels to promote rationalisation and to fix prices by agreement in depressions, although the consent of the Commission had first to be obtained.

The subsequent history of the anti-monopoly policy gives the lie to those who affirm that government in Japan is a seamless robe. The large firms, which are associated with the dominant political party and whose interests are usually defended by the Ministry of International Trade and Industry (MITI), have succeeded in curbing the authority of the Commission. Apart from the cases where depression—and rationalisation—cartels have been authorised, firms brought under scrutiny by the Commission have frequently successfully pleaded that they had acted under the 'administrative guidance' of MITI. On occasions, the intervention of the Commission has been blocked by special enactments which have empowered MITI to encourage consolidation or restrictive agreements in particular industries. In this way it has been possible to by-pass the Anti-Monopoly Law without repealing or amending it. Nevertheless, the Fair Trade Commission, though less influential than had once been hoped, has remained a force to be reckoned with, largely because of popular opposition to the attempts to destroy it. Moreover, the effectiveness of cartels has been weakened, and sometimes nullified, by certain characteristics of the economic system. The various powerful industrial groups are probably less inclined to 'collude' with one another than are corresponding groups in many other countries, including Britain. Rapid economic expansion has been attended by fierce rivalry among the several oligopolists for shares in every new product or new market. Further, as already shown, the high ratio of bank loans among corporate liabilities means that in times of recession nearly all companies come under pressure from their creditors to maintain output in order to service their loans. In such circumstances, cartels lead a precarious existence and 'weak sellers' quickly appear with the onset of a period of bad trade. For similar reasons, it has been found difficult to restrain price competition in the retail trade by the usual devices of resale price maintenance. So, the Fair Trade Commission, despite its enemies, has found that many features of the present economic system are sympathetic to its purposes.

During the 1970s it gained new allies. During the long period of comparative price stability and rising real standards of living, public opinion, though favourable to the Commission's activities, was not seriously offended by restrictive practices, especially as many of these proved to be fragile. But, with the appearance of strong inflationary trends in the early 1970s, especially after the steep rise in prices following the oil crisis of 1973-74, the mood changed. There was a popular demand for new curbs of price-fixing and, despite opposition from MITI, the government pledged itself to strengthen the Anti-Monopoly Law. The alleged collusion of oil refiners and distributors in settling prices brought about the most drastic action ever taken by the Commission. It had previously used its power of requiring concerns found guilty of restrictive practices to desist from those practices. Now, for the first time, it went further and, as it was legally empowered to do in serious cases, it asked the public prosecutor to bring an action in the Courts against certain oil companies for violation of the Anti-Monopoly Law. The successful action was brought in 1974.

During recent years several attempts have been made to restore the FTC's power of divestiture which it lost during the 'reverse course' period, and there has been much debate about the definition of monopoly. This, it is argued, should turn on both the size of the undertaking and the proportion of the national output of a product for which a single firm (or two firms) is responsible. Conflict has also arisen in political and business circles about the response to the American suggestion that there should be an exchange of information between the Japanese and the United States governments in regard to firms in both countries that are parties to international cartels. MITI, as always, has strongly resisted any strengthening of the anti-monopoly policy, and the liberal forces, though they may have gained strength recently, have not yet carried the day.

Regional Policy

Rapid industrial growth after the Second World War resulted in a strong concentration of manufactures and population in three regions, all to the south of the main island (Honshu). These were Tokyo-Yokohama, Nagoya and Kyoto-Osaka-Kobe. In 1961 these three great regions provided three-quarters of the total industrial output and held nearly half the population, a much higher proportion than in the years immediately after the war. The chief contributor to the concentration was the Tokyo area (Kanto) where the rate of growth outstripped that of all other regions. As a corollary, some parts of the country that are remote from the main centres of industry suffered an absolute fall in their population, and in them income per head lagged behind that in the rest of the country. In order to correct this imbalance, a Regional Development Programme was introduced as part of the Income-Doubling Plan for 1961-70. The chief purpose was to relieve congestion in the Tokyo area and to direct an increased proportion of new industrial development to the relatively underdeveloped parts of the country. There were precedents for this policy. From early Meiji times the government had made provision for public investment designed to promote the development of the northern island, Hokkaido, and, during the 1930s, when Tohoku (the northern province of the main island) was severely affected by the agricultural depression, government agencies were established to create new sources of income and employment. After the Second World War public funds were again made available for encouraging higher food production in these areas, and in the late 1950s other relatively backward regions (e.g. South Kyushu and Shikoku) received financial assistance from the government for stimulating development.

The effect of these measures was narrowly limited. After the war the government was intent upon giving priority to industrial development, and policies that in any way conflicted with that aim commanded only lukewarm support. Compared with earlier schemes, the Regional Programme introduced in 1961 was bold and ambitious. The country was divided into eleven regions with the object of achieving (to borrow words from the British Barlow Commission) 'a balanced distribution of industry and population'. Three groups of regions were distinguished:

(a) the congested areas which consisted of the Tokyo-Yokohama area (Kanto) and the Kyoto-Osaka-Kobe area (Kinki);
(b) the hinterland of the two above centres together with the Nagoya area (Tokai);
(c) the development areas which included Hokkaido, Tohoku, Shikoku and Chugoku-Kyushu.

The aim was to limit expansion in the first group of areas by restricting the siting of new factories in them and by assisting firms to locate their establishments elsewhere. Further growth in the hinterland areas was also to be 'regulated'. For the rest, a number of points of growth were selected in the under-developed regions and efforts were to be made by public investment in their infrastructures and by financial inducements to entrepreneurs (e.g. tax concessions and loans from official banks) to build industrial cores round which other industrial zones would cluster. In 1963 thirteen such places were selected as the new industrial centres. According to the plan, the proportion of industrial production in Kanto, Kinki and Tokai was to be reduced between 1961 and 1970 from 75.5 per cent to 68 per cent.

The plan failed.[13] The causes were, first, the quarrels among the local politicians about the choice of development centres and, secondly, the resistance of industrialists to interference in their locational choices. Behind these proximate causes, there was the nature of government itself, the high degree of centralisation and the weakness of the local authorities. In the event, the exceptionally fast growth of the economy during the 1960s, especially in the second half of that decade, was accompanied by an even stronger concentration in the Kanto region. By the early 1970s, however, the people were showing signs of disenchantment with economic growth as the sole aim of economic policy, especially as the ebullient industrial expansion had given rise to serious problems of congestion and pollution in the main industrial areas. They were, therefore, ready to listen to Mr Tanaka, who later became Prime Minister, when he launched his ambitious plan for the re-development of the Japanese Archipelago.[14] Government funds, it was proposed, should be provided on a lavish scale to create new rail and road links between the existing main industrial areas and the remoter regions, and there was to be heavy

investment in the infrastructure of the latter as a means of stimulating
their industrialisation. Recession accompanied by a violent inflation
put an end to these extravagant plans; indeed, their chief result was to
set going a boom in land values that brought fortunes to speculators.
However, concentration in Kanto seems at last to be slowing down,
partly because of the unexpected prolongation of the recession, and
partly because the rise in locational costs in that region has at last
begun to offset its advantages.

3. Formal and Informal Relations Between Firms and Government Departments

We now come to what is undoubtedly the most effective means by
which government has influenced the conduct of private industry. It has
been pointed out by a well-informed authority on the Japanese economy
that 'while the government's statutory authority to control business is
less extensive than in most industrial nations', its informal, extra-
statutory powers are very great indeed.[15] These powers have probably
become more important since the abolition of the rigid controls over
foreign trade and foreign exchange transactions which, until the middle
1960s, gave the central authorities a persuasive, if not always a decisive,
voice in the policy-making of private firms.

> The hand of government is everywhere in evidence, despite its limited
> statutory powers. The Ministries engage in an extraordinary amount
> of consultation, advice, persuasion and threat. The Industrial Bureaux
> of MITI proliferate sectional targets and plans; they confer, they
> tinker, they exhort. This is 'economics by admonition' to an extent
> inconceivable in Washington or London. Business makes few major
> decisions without consulting the appropriate governmental authority;
> the same is true in reverse.[16]

From time to time policies for development worked out in discussions between producers and officials have given rise to recommendations
that have been embodied in laws designed to implement them; for
example, the laws for fostering the growth of the machine-tool industry
(1956), the electronics industry (1957) and the aircraft industry (1958).
The investments proposed in the various plans, whether or not they had
statutory authority, were encouraged by the preferential treatment
accorded to the favoured firms in taxation and loans.

At the risk of tedium, it must be stressed again that the government
and its officials do not attempt simply to dictate policy to private industry.

Such an attempt would be as repugnant as the resolution of disagreements by imposing a majority decision, for both would be divisive. The Japanese prefer to arrive at decisions by a process of consultation that normally leads to a consensus; agreed decisions emerge from the tensions and arguments among the various interests. If the bureaucracy guides private industry along paths that it approves, the industrialists likewise influence the policy of the bureaucracy. Nor do all government departments speak with the same voice on particular issues. There are conflicts among them, some of long standing, just as there is keen rivalry among business groups whose interests, it might have been thought, would be served by collusion with one another.

These rivalries are, to a large extent, the outcome of the vertical divisions that are a feature of Japanese society and affect the bureaucracy as well as private business. Just as the employees of a business group expect to remain with that group for all their working lives and can seldom be persuaded to move to a rival, so in the civil service one finds an exclusive devotion to the single department and little mobility of persons among departments. This particularism often leads to inter-departmental rivalry more bitter and extreme than that found in most other countries. It is sometimes responsible for administrative inefficiency and a lack of co-ordination. It can also lead, on occasion, to sharp divisions over policy, so that the Japanese bureaucracy is, in fact, far less monolithic than it is generally made out to be. That an agreed policy should so often emerge from these dissensions (those among government departments as well as those between government and business), can be attributed in large measure to the institutional factors already described. Social tradition obliges individuals to conform to group pressures. 'Once the official line was given . . . expected behaviour could be enforced by sheer pressure of expectation which nobody could escape'.[17]

This assertion may perhaps exaggerate the degree of conformity achieved in practice, but it is reasonable to suppose that the contending parties have usually been brought to a consensus without much difficulty in the Japan of the post-war period, because such disagreements as have arisen have been about means rather than ends. All powerful groups, and indeed the vast majority of the people, have supported the government's policy of giving priority to industrial growth, and the general acceptance of the main purpose of economic and social policy has narrowly limited the area of contention. Nevertheless, the method of consensus does not always yield harmonious results. On several occasions, the conflicts have remained unreconciled. A notable instance was the *Sumikin* case in 1965-66. Firms in the steel industry during a period of recession sought an agreement among themselves on a reduction in output, but failed in their negotiations. MITI then tried to bring about the reduction by 'administrative guidance'; but one company, Sumitomo Kinzoku Kogyo, rejected this guidance and the scheme broke down. Now that the single-hearted pursuit of economic growth commands less approval than during the 1950s and 1960s, it would not be surprising if industry and the bureaucracy found mutually agreed policies or solutions more difficult to arrive at than in the recent past.

4. Indicative Planning

Soon after the Second World War the Japanese government began to systematise its general policy of development by issuing medium-term or long-term plans for the economy. An official body, now known as the Economic Planning Agency, was made responsible for drawing up plans for the ensuing quinquennium or decade, in accordance with what has been a prevailing fashion over much of the world. The various plans have occupied a prominent place in discussions about the country's economic development, although their influence on actual performance is debatable. As elsewhere, the plans have contained forecasts of the gross national product for a succession of years ahead, the output of different sectors of the economy, investment, savings, exports and imports and other items in the balance of payments. The figures are supposed to be guides for the private sector, rather than prescriptions, but the government, in the exercise of its various instruments of control or persuasion, gives heed to the content of the plans. For the public sector the plans do not become targets until the government departments concerned assent to them, and even this assent does not necessarily mean that the departments commit themselves to the planned expenditure.

At first sight a review of the history of the several plans suggests that they have had little or no effect on what was actually achieved. From the beginning they consistently under-estimated the rate of growth. The first plan in the indicative-planning series (1953-58) forecast the real rate of growth of the GNP at 5 per cent per annum. During the first two years of this period the rate of growth was twice that predicted, and consequently another plan, known as the Long-Range Plan, was drawn up to cover the years from 1958 to 1962. This plan was set out in greater detail than its predecessor, especially in regard to the share of national investment that lay within direct government control, that is, investment in the infrastructure (roads, ports, sewage, water supply and publicly provided housing). This 'administrative' investment was distinguished from the private investment over which official influence was less direct. The average annual rate of growth was forecast at 6.5 per cent but again this proved to be much too low, and in the first two years a rate of 10 per cent per annum was reached. The plan for Doubling the National Income issued in 1960 predicted an annual average rate of growth for the decade (1961-70) of 7.2 per cent. It also provided for a much increased share of total investment in the infrastructure, at the expense of investment in manufacturing industry and the private sector in general. In the event, performance seemed to bear little relation to the predictions. The rate of growth reached an annual average of 10.1 per cent between 1961 and 1965 and 12.1 per cent between 1966 and 1970. Private investment in equipment, far from suffering a reduction in its share of total national expenditure, actually increased proportionately, and investment in the infrastructure again lagged behind. This applied also to the outcome of the Social and Economic Plan for 1967-72. Indeed, it was not until Japan entered upon the protracted depression that began in 1973 that the long-term predictions of growth and private investment had to be revised downwards.

The plans have obviously not controlled events, but it would be wrong to deduce that they have been without any influence at all. It is true that some large industrialists have paid little attention to them, but most firms have probably been in some degree responsive to the climate of opinion they have created. For one thing, since the plans reflect the government's economic judgements and intentions at the time when they were drawn up, they have affected the policy of MITI towards different industries and firms and also that of the various official financial institutions towards applications for loans. But the greatest significance of the plans is to be found in their announcement-effect on entrepreneurs. The surge of investment that followed the publication of the Income-Doubling Plan has been ascribed to the fact that firms regarded the fulfilment of the forecasts as, in some sense, guaranteed by the government. From experience firms had observed that the previous national plans had under-estimated actual performance, and they judged in 1960 that this plan would suffer from the same fault and so reacted accordingly. As already indicated, every large conglomerate, being in keen rivalry with the others, was anxious to ensure for itself an 'adequate' share of any growth in prospect, and the predictions contained in the Income-Doubling Plan stimulated all of them in such a way as to ensure their fulfilment. The optimistic response of the Japanese industrialists to their national plans stands in sharp contrast to the scepticism with which British industrialists greeted the national plans of 1962 and 1965.

5. Public Corporations

Finally, we arrive at the public sector proper, that is, the sector directly controlled and wholly or partly owned by the public authorities. This sector has been administered under a variety of jurisdictional and organisational forms. As in many other countries, the public corporation became the favoured instrument of government enterprise, and several undertakings that at one time were operated by government departments were turned over to public corporations during the early post-war years. For two of the chief undertakings, the national railways and the telegraph and telephone service, the transference took place in 1949, and all new public enterprises since that time have been entrusted to one of several types of public corporation. These corporations, of which some 113 existed in 1977, differ widely from one another in function, the degree of central control and financial arrangements. A Japanese economist who has made a special study of them has classified them under several heads.[17] The most important are set out below.

(i) *Kosha*   This term is the normal Japanese equivalent of 'public corporation' and was introduced in 1949 when certain undertakings were transferred from government departments. At present there are four *kosha*, the Japan National Railways Corporation, the Nippon Telegraph and Telephone Corporation, the Japan Monopoly Corporation and the Japan Atomic Energy Corporation. Of these the first two provide most of the employment in all types of public concern, and they have a high share of the aggregate capital assets in government enterprise. The four *kosha* together are responsible for about four-fifths of employment in public corporations. In these enterprises the government appoints the chairman but leaves him free to select his subordinates. The undertakings are supposed to be self-supporting financially although in this respect performance has lately fallen far short of expectations. Their day-to-day management is free from official interference, but government control over finance is very strict, at least in form. The corporations are required to submit annual estimates for Parliamentary approval, and at the end of the year the accounts are subjected to close scrutiny. The Monopoly Corporation and the Atomic Energy Corporation, though classified as *kosha*, are functionally different from the other two. The purpose of the former is to raise revenue, chiefly through the tobacco monopoly, and the commercial functions of the Atomic Energy Corporation lie in the future.

(ii) *Kodan*   This is a public corporation engaged in constructional work.

Legally it is identical to *kosha*, but it differs from the latter in that its function is not that of operating a public utility service but rather the promotion of 'social overhead capital works, including roads, irrigation, water works and housing'. It is thus an instrument for implementing particular economic and social policies. In the more important *kodan* the capital is owned by the Government (as with the *kosha*), but many of them raise a high proportion of their resources by borrowing from official financial bodies, such as the Trust Fund Bureau (which handles postal savings), and from the local authorities in the regions in which they operate.

(iii) *Koko*   This is a public corporation, with capital supplied by the State, formed to engage in financial operations required for carrying out some specific purpose of national policy, for example, for the finance of publicly-provided housing, regional development plans, and assistance schemes for small businesses and agriculture.

(iv) *Kinko and Ginko*   These are both concerned with finance. A *Kinko* is a public financial corporation for providing financial assistance to co-operative societies. The *Kinko* are financed partly by the government and partly by the various local and national co-operative societies which serve different sectors of the economy, manufactures, agriculture, fishing and forestry, and they act as a kind of central bank for the sectional societies. *Ginko* is the ordinary word for bank and covers, besides the banks in the private sector, such banks in the public sector as the Central Bank and the official investment banks.

(v) There are, in addition, a number of mixed enterprises (*Tokushu Gaisha*), which are capitalised and managed jointly by the State and companies in the private sector. They include the Electric Power Development Company, a concern formed in 1951 to promote the development of power resources, the Japan Airlines, which is responsible for Japan's main air services, the Japan Airplane Manufacturing Company and the Tohoku District Development Company.

(vi) Another group consists of *Jigyodan*, semi-dependent government agencies, which are concerned with providing a wide variety of administrative services. These include the price stabilisation of certain agricultural products, the management of welfare institutions, the introduction of new techniques for technical co-operation overseas, measures for dealing with pollution, to name only a few. The *jigyodan* are usually small in size. In some of them the capital is subscribed by the government; in others local authorities or private investors have provided a share.

(vii) Finally, there is a number of local undertakings with responsibilities for water supply, urban passenger transport, gas and electricity distribution and local railways. In many cases these undertakings, though publicly controlled, are privately owned.

It will be observed that the public corporations and other bodies (official or semi-official) established to carry out specific public economic and social policies resemble in many respects those that exist in Western countries. The variety of form that these bodies have assumed is at least as great in Japan as anywhere else. But their scope is more narrowly limited in Japan than in (say) Britain, for, in Japan, public enterprise is almost absent from civil manufacturing industry and has a comparatively small share of public utility undertakings. Here we find an explanation for the low proportion of total employment in the public sector.

One of the most marked contrasts between Britain and Japan in respect of public enterprise lies in the part played, in the past as at the present time, by municipal enterprise. Japan had no experience of 'gas and water' socialism, which, beginning with the local authorities, evolved into the great British nationalised public utilities after the Second World War.[18] Today there are in Japan many public services operated, or controlled, by the local authorities, but in general these came into being much later than the chief national enterprises. For instance, although private tramways were in existence during the last two decades of the nineteenth century, it was not until 1904 that the first municipal tramway was constructed—in Osaka—and it was not until 1924 that Tokyo started a municipal bus service. Nor has there been anything like the co-ordination achieved, for better or worse, by the London Passenger Transport Board. Even today passenger transport in the Tokyo Metropolitan Area is shared by about twelve different bodies, including the municipality itself, the Japan National Railways, the Teito Rapid Transport Authority and several private companies. Where, as often happens, the central government has taken the initiative in setting up a public corporation to provide local services, little scope is left for municipal enterprise. This subordination of the municipalities extends to finance, for the provision of funds needed for the economic activities of the local authorities, as of all public bodies, is highly centralised. In drawing up its budget the government distinguishes between its General Account and various Special accounts. The latter record the transactions of such public corporations as the railways, the telephone and telegraph service and the national housing corporation. In addition, the government makes provision in its annual Loan and Investment Programme for the expenditure of other public bodies, notably those engaged in public constructional work whether undertaken by a national corporation or by a local authority. The nature of these financial arrangements is indicative of the dependence of such bodies on the central government.

Public corporations of all kinds increased considerably in numbers during the first twenty post-war years. This increase reflected the multiplication of the economic responsibilities of the government which it often found expedient to pass on to semi-autonomous agencies. But cynics have found additional reasons. The typical Japanese civil servant, unless he is likely to reach the top rank in his department, is accustomed to retire early, often before he is fifty. He then seeks re-employment, sometimes in private industry, but frequently in a public corporation, a process known as *Amakudari*. It has been suggested that, just as in early Meiji, an important reason for the government's establishment of new enterprises was its anxiety to find jobs for the functionless *samurai*, so the proliferation of new public bodies since the war can be attributed in some degree to the necessity of providing remunerative occupation for officials on their early retirement – the Japanese version of 'jobs for the boys'. As in other countries, the recession in the private sector has brought criticisms of the swollen bureaucracy, and the government has recently committed itself to a policy of administrative reform which is intended to dissolve some of the redundant public corporations, abolish many of the advisory councils and reduce the scope of 'administrative guidance' given to the private sector by the Ministries. These are large promises which are unlikely to excite much alarm in the Tokyo 'corridors of power'.

Appendix: Leading Public Corporations and Agencies

1. *Kosha*

   Japan National Railways Corporation
   Nippon Telegraph and Telephone Corporation
   Japan Monopoly Corporation
   Japan Atomic Energy Corporation

2. *Kodan*

Japan Housing Corporation
Japan Highway Corporation
Tokyo Expressway Corporation
Hanshin Super-Highway Corporation
Water Resources Development Corporation
Japan Railway Construction Corporation
New Tokyo International Airport Corporation
Agricultural Land Development Machinery Corporation
Japan Petroleum Development Corporation
Keihin Port Development Authority

3. *Koko*

People's Finance Corporation
Housing Loan Corporation
Agriculture, Forestry and Fishery Finance Corporation
Small Business Finance Corporation
Hokkaido and Tohoku Development Corporation
Finance Corporation for Local Public Enterprise

4. *Kinko and Ginko*

Bank of Japan
Japan Development Bank
Export-Import Bank of Japan
Central Co-operative Bank for Agriculture and Forestry
Bank of Commercial and Industrial Co-operatives

5. *Tokushu Gaisha*

Electric Power Development Co.
Japan Airlines Co.
Japan Airplane Manufacturing Co.
Tohoku District Development Co.

6. *Jigyodan* (See text)

Source: K. Yoshitake, *An Introduction to Public Enterprise in Japan* (London, 1973), pp. 12-19, 329-33. For financial accounts of the corporations, see Bank of Japan, *Hundred Year Statistics of the Japanese Economy* (Tokyo, 1966); *Economic Statistics Annual*, and *The Japanese Financial System*, July 1970.

Notes

1. Cf. E.H. Norman, *Japan's Emergence as a Modern State* (New York, 1940); W.W. Lockwood, *The Economic Development of Japan* (Princeton, 1954), Ch. 10; G.C. Allen, *A Short Economic History of Modern Japan* (3rd ed, London, 1972), Ch. 2.

2. T.C. Smith, *Political Change and Industrial Development in Japan: Government and Enterprise, 1868-1880* (Stanford, 1955), p. 33.

3. M. Matsukata, *Report on the Post-Bellum Financial Administration in Japan* (Tokyo, 1895), and *Report on the Adoption of the Gold Standard in Japan* (Tokyo, 1899).

4. The retreat of the Chinese silk industry in the face of Japanese competition can be explained in these terms. See G.C. Allen and A.G. Donnithorne, *Western Enterprise in Far Eastern Economic Development: China and Japan* (London, 1954), pp. 66-8.

5. Ministry of International Trade and Industry, *Fifty Years of Industrial Statistics* (Tokyo, March 1963).

6. K. Emi, *Government Fiscal Activity and Economic Growth in Japan, 1868-1960* (Tokyo, 1963), pp. 5, 20.

7. Literally, 'New Zaibatsu'.

8. SCAP stands for Supreme Commander of the Allied Powers and was used to designate both a person (General MacArthur) and the Occupation Administration in general.

9. These reforms are described in G.C. Allen, *Japan's Economic Expansion* (London, 1965), Chs. 2, 5, 10, 11.

10. The chief work on the dissolution of the *Zaibatsu* is E.M. Hadley, *Anti-Trust in Japan* (New York, 1970).

11. That is, moral suasion buttressed by various administrative controls, see Bank of Japan, *The Bank of Japan, Its Function and Organisation* (Tokyo, 1962), pp. 22-31.

12. These topics are dealt with extensively in Hugh Corbet (ed.), *Trade Strategy and the Pacific Area* (London, 1970), pp. 43-109. See also, Peter Rooper, *The Development, Operation and Control of the Japanese Foreign Exchange Market* (Research Paper, Australia-Japan Economic Relations Research Project, Australia National University) and Japan Information Centre, London, *British Trade with Japan* (January, 1977).

13. In 1970 the share of industrial production provided by the three regions was slightly higher than in 1961, according to K. Tanaka, *Remodelling the Japanese Archipelago* (Tokyo, 1972), p. 94. The Economic Planning Agency in 1969 estimated that the belt that stretches from Kanto in the east of Honshu to northern Kyushu in the west and which comprises only 31 per cent of Japan's area held 63 per cent of the population and provided 84 per cent of the industrial output.

14. See, K. Tanaka, *passim.* Tanaka proposed to reduce the share of industrial output provided by the three great industrial regions to 53 per cent by 1985. This was to be achieved by developing great new centres of heavy industry at the extremities of the country and of founding 'industrial parks' as centres of light, labour-intensive industries on new inland sites. A vast public expenditure on roads, railways, bridges, harbours, water supply and on the infrastructure of new cities was necessary to fulfil this plan. Further development in the congested areas was to be hampered by administrative restrictions and by taxation, e.g. a substantial increase in the surcharge on the corporation tax already imposed on companies located in the congested centres. A National Land Agency was set up to deal with the land planning problems.

15. K. Yoshitake, *An Introduction to Public Enterprise in Japan* (London, 1973) is an invaluable source of information about every aspect of Japanese public enterprise. See also, G.C. Allen, 'The Public and Co-operative Sectors in Japan' in *Annals of Public and Co-operative Economy*, April-June 1968 (Liège), pp. 133-56.

16. W.W. Lockwood, *The State and Economic Enterprise in Japan* (Princeton, 1965), p. 503.

17. J. Hirschmeier and T. Yui, *The Development of Japanese Business, 1600-1973* (London, 1975).

18. K. Yoshitake, pp. 63-5.

2 GOVERNMENT INTERVENTION IN THE ECONOMY OF AUSTRALIA

R.H. Allan, J.P. Nieuwenhuysen, N.R. Norman*

Macro-economic Regulation

The macro-economic problems and policies adopted in Australia during
recent years have set the bounds and constraints of intervention in
general, and of the regulation of industry in particular. The development
of principles of intervention, and the emergence of new regulatory
institutions in Australia during the 1970s have been the joint product
of political philosophies and economic circumstances. The period has
been dominated by economic difficulties, in the face of which vigorous
advocacy of more or less government intervention has characterised
economic debate. Consensus about the role of intervention in the management of the Australian economy is difficult, if not impossible, to
achieve; even generalisations about the nature and impact of intervention are hard to form. But it would seem that the bulk of government intervention in the Australian economy in the last few years,
either through macro-economic policies or through the creation of new
institutions and new industrial policies, is much more likely to have
been in response to specific economic difficulties, rather than the outcome of a well considered, well prepared and well tried programme of
government regulation.

At the federal level the two political forces in Australia are the Liberal and National Country Party Coalition, and the Australian Labor
Party. The latter party follows the lines of the British Labour Party in
that its socialist platform upholds the strengthening of labour's role in
a capitalist society. Its attempts at direct nationalism have been ham-
strung by constitutional restrictions. In 1949 it lost office largely on
the issue of bank nationalisation, and since then has enjoyed power
only between 1972 and 1975, when it introduced various social reforms
including a national health insurance scheme. On the other hand, the
Liberal Party and the National Country Party have long stood for
business investment and agrarian interests respectively. While upholding

*The main division of responsibility for authorship is that Dr Allan has written
the portions on government intervention in the capital market and industrial
ownership and control; Dr Nieuwenhuysen those on intervention in labour and
product markets; and Dr Norman, those on macro-economic policy.

41

the basic tenet of free enterprise, they have created a variety of regulatory bodies which have intervened in market processes. The Liberal Party has always been the senior coalition partner, and it remains the most powerful political force in Australia today.

Macro-economic measures and changes in their general direction during the past ten years are of crucial importance for a proper understanding of the impact of government intervention on Australian industry. These changes in direction are closely tied to alterations in the political complexion of the Australian government. After twenty-three years in power, the Liberal Party lost office in 1972. As one journalist noted, Australia then 'voted in the sparkling Labour Party with its exciting new vision of Australia's place in the world, its leader's passion for the arts, Aborigines, ethnic groups and welfare – and its virtual total disdain for economics'.[1] However Mr Gough Whitlam remained in power only until November 1975 when the Governor-General, Sir John Kerr, used his prerogative powers to dismiss the Prime Minister because of the latter's inability to obtain senate approval for the Government's Supply Bill. In the general election which followed a month later, the Liberal-Country Party coalition won the most overwhelming victory in the history of national government in Australia. The constitutional crisis that surrounded these events is not of course relevant to the present account. But the reader needs to appreciate the shifts in Australian macro policy that occurred in the 1970s in conjunction with these political upheavals. The following section offers an overview of changes in economic policy as an essential background to discussion of particular issues of government intervention.

In company with most Western economies in the post-war period, Australia developed a range of monetary and fiscal instruments by which to regulate the level and intensity of demand, so as to maintain, as far as possible, full employment, price stability, economic growth and a healthy balance of payments. With the exception of a brief period of *inflation* in excess of 20 per cent during 1950/51, Australia enjoyed relative price stability until around 1973. From late 1970, the consumer price index began to rise rapidly, moving from a rate of 3 per cent early in 1970 to around 8 per cent by late 1971, and falling to around 4¼ per cent by late 1972. But following rapid expenditure and monetary growth, rising world commodity prices and wage escalation, Australian prices rose very rapidly between 1973 and 1974 to reach an annual inflation rate of some 18 per cent after 1974. By late 1977, it had fallen to about 10 per cent, after a campaign in three successive Federal Budgets of expenditure restraint and general austerity.

Australia's *unemployment rate* was also gratifyingly low during the 1960s. With the exception of a brief period in 1961, the unemployment rate remained below 2 per cent until 1972. Thereafter, the proportion of the workforce unemployed rose to almost 3 per cent during 1972, began to rise very rapidly during 1974, and has remained consistently in the region of 4½-6½ per cent since 1975, after correction for seasonal factors.

Overall, then, the 1960s appear as a period of relative bliss, with little difficulty for macro-economic policy (with the possible exception of the period 1960/61); but by 1977 both unemployment and inflation rates stood at between three and four times the levels that were characteristic during the 1960s, even though the inflation rate had fallen from the peak it had reached during 1974/75. It is against this background that the reader should view the adoption and variation of general regulatory devices (such as government expenditure, tax and monetary policies) as well as other specific institutional changes in industry regulation.

Post-war macro-economic policies in Australia can be illustrated by dividing the period into three main phases, which may distinguish the various degrees of credibility enjoyed by traditional principles of demand management. These three phases seem to be the following:

1. From 1945-1971, when a long period of traditional principles of demand management went unchallenged. Although the principles were generally unchallenged, they were applied with varying degrees of success, but in the context of an economy growing very rapidly and largely immune from the main problems of unemployment and inflation against which the efficacy of demand management problems might otherwise have been tested.
2. A short but dramatic period from early 1972 to mid 1975, when traditional principles of demand management were either questioned, ignored, or subordinated to other considerations that came to dominate the choice and mix of monetary and budgetary policies. During most of this period, the Labor government was in office.
3. A third phase, from mid 1975, under which macro-economic policies were, as in the first phase, dictated largely by traditional principles of economic management, although the principles appeared in a very much revised form and in apparently new circumstances. For the most part, the policies adopted since 1975 have been in accord with monetarist principles of macro-economic regulation, and have been addressed primarily to curbing inflation (at the cost, at least in the short term, of increasing unemployment).

Phase 1

The long period from the late 1940s until the end of the 1960s was an easy one for macro-economic policy makers in Australia. As mentioned above, except for the year 1950/51, the inflation rate remained firmly below 5 per cent; and except for the period 1961/62, unemployment rates remained below 2 per cent. Moreover, whenever problems of un-employment *or* inflation were noticed, they tended usually to occur separately and not together, in contrast to the experience of most of the 1970s. The general determination of governments over this period was therefore to restrain national expenditure through income tax surcharges, increases in indirect taxes, increases in interest rates, and government expenditure restraints, whenever excess demand or inflation was seen as a problem, and to move the same instruments in the opposite direct-ion whenever unemployment seemed of major concern.

This is not to suggest that governments managed to apply these principles with the timing and success which the theory required. In fact the period is studded with examples in which governments moved too late or in the wrong direction, sometimes exacerbating the macro-economic difficulties that were then imminent. During the strong inflationary boom of 1950/51 the authorities were slow to react, and interest rates were not raised until late in 1951 when the worst of the boom was over. Simultaneously, a 'horror' Budget in 1951 intensified the downturn that had already started and which emerged into the 1952/53 recession. A further period of excess demand during 1955 was again met by belated official action, and policies of restraint (especially increases in indirect taxes) were delayed until March 1956. Following a period of sluggish growth in 1958 and 1959, a speculative stock exchange and land boom developed in early 1960, where official monetary action was again belated, although the workings of an 'unused overdraft system' meant that restraints on bank lending were having an unperceived effect of restraining expenditure through the course of 1960 and which (allowing for the delays) would not have justified further restraint action that was taken later in the year. Yet in Nov-ember 1960 the authorities misread the situation and brought down a series of restrictive measures (including increases in interest rates, special accounts held at the central bank, known in Australia as Stat-utory Reserve Deposits) a sharp increase in indirect taxes on motor vehicles from 30 per cent to 40 per cent, and threatened action which carried such an announcement effect as to terminate abruptly that portion of the boom which might then have remained. In retrospect, it is known that the economy was already turning down from September in 1960 and the official reactions served only to intensify the recession that was imminent for 1961. Even the reversal of the increase in sales tax on vehicles in February 1961 was insufficient to halt the depression in confidence, and the deepest recession known in the post-war period up to that stage was encountered through 1961 and 1962. Fears of a 'liquidity explosion', ungrounded in retrospect, delayed stimulatory action to promote a revival in activity until early 1963. At that time, the economy was assisted by favourable export conditions, and by a belated lowering in interest rates and release of funds to the banks. (These policies were quickly and correctly tightened in early 1964 in order to remove excess demand that was then developing. Through the remainder of the 1960s, the Australian economy was exceptionally stable, and when indications were perceived that either excess or deficient demand was developing, the authorities moved quickly and flexibly to remove detected imbalances.)

Phase 2

Inflation rose sharply to nearly a 10 per cent annual rate in 1971. The response of the government was to apply traditional measures of demand restraint: a reduction in the growth in government expenditure, increases in indirect taxes, cancellation of an investment allowance (granted as a concession from company income tax), increases in interest rates and credit restraint. As 1972 unfolded, these measures appeared not to be working: in retrospect, however, it seems that lags in economic reactions and in the production of statistics masked the contribution which these measures of restraint were making to reducing the inflation rate. In the circumstances of the time, however, events were dominated by the election which was looming towards the end of 1972, and the government began to expand the economy, reversing its measures of restraint, and bringing down an expansionary Budget in August 1972. In the event, the government did not retain office; the incoming Labor government assumed power in December 1972, when the economy was recovering very rapidly and the danger was becoming, once more, one of excess demand.

It was, in many ways, unfortunate that a government bent on social reform, and increased welfare and government outlays, should come to power at a time when the problems of excess demand and inflation were paramount. The initial Labor approach confirmed subsequently in the (September) 1974 Budget, was to effect a transfer of resources from the private to the public sector, to redistribute income in a more egal-itarian fashion, and to create a wide range of regulatory institutions and statutory control authorities. During 1973/74, the first fiscal year in which the new government's policies took effect, government outlays rose by almost 20 per cent. Some concern was being expressed in Australia during 1973 that the upshot of this policy package would be a dangerous inflationary spiral. To this the Government replied by two separate appreciations of the Australian dollar (in December 1972 and September 1973), a one quarter reduction in all tariff rates, increases in 'special accounts' (known as Statutory Reserve Deposits) levied by the central bank on the trading banks in April 1973, and pressure to raise interest rates (effective to the extent of about one and a half percentage points in later 1973). None of these measures was immediately or demonstrably significant in curtailing inflation. Using the annual growth in the official consumer price index, inflation had reached more than 13 per cent by late 1973.

The year 1974 was one of the most interesting and difficult for the Australian economy. Inflation approached 20 per cent per annum, yet unemployment also rose, from around 2 per cent early in the year to almost 5 per cent by the end of the year. These conditions of 'stagflation' bred confusion and dismay among policy makers and the electorate alike. Vigorous calls to restrict the growth of government outlays were not heeded, and the 1974/75 Budget, brought down in middle September 1974, foreshadowed a growth in government outlays of over 32 per cent. In outcome, the actual growth recorded in that year was 46 per cent! Notwithstanding this very considerable growth in government outlays in money terms, the real GDP declined over the same period, unemployment remained at about 5 per cent of the work force, and the inflation rate could not be shaken from the 15 per cent range.

By early 1975 it became apparent that the government was losing control, confidence in industry had been undermined, and its profitability had fallen sharply (intensified by partly government inspired wage escalation from 1973, and by the increasing bite of regulatory procedures, as mentioned later). Symptomatic of the serious economic situation developing, and the associated political crises, two Treasurers were dismissed within six months and a new Treasurer believing in more conventional economic wisdom was installed. The scene was now set for belated restraint in government expenditure, and the assumption of policies designed explicitly to reduce inflation.

Phase 3

The new Treasurer, Mr W.G. Hayden, introduced a budget in August

1975, in which the growth of government outlays was halved, some indirect taxes raised, and the deficit in general reined in. Within four months of the presentation of the budget, Labor had been defeated and the Liberal/National Country Party resumed the office it had departed less than three years beforehand. Yet the fundamental thrust of economic policy remained close to guidelines laid down by Labor's Mr Hayden. The Liberal-National Country government budgets in 1976 and 1977 further reduced the growth of government outlays (down to around 10 per cent in the second of those budgets), and substantial stress was laid on the need to reduce the overall deficit in order to curtail the growth of the money supply without strong upward pressure on interest rates. Even then, there were significant departures from the standard monetarist line implicit in this approach, many of them necessary in order to respond to specific circumstances that arose, and many of them well received by the electorate. Five specific responses can be cited. Firstly, a substantial reduction in personal income taxes was announced in May 1976, and further reductions effected from 1 February 1978. There was a devaluation of the Australian dollar by 17½ per cent (later reduced to less than 10 per cent) in November 1976, and the introduction of a managed 'trade-weighted' exchange rate system going some distance toward the operation of a freer foreign market.

A third response was the adoption of a price and wages freeze for a trial period in April and May 1977, which was, however, marked by poor planning and which was scuttled by the Conciliation and Arbitration Commission's refusal to impose an award wage freeze.

Another *ad hoc* measure that can be mentioned was the introduction of a 'stock valuation' adjustment in order to ease liquidity problems of companies affected by the inflationary impact on stock values and its burden on corporate taxation. A final illustration is the taxation relief granted for smaller businesses and farmers, plus the granting of specific and temporary quota, and also tariff and subsidy assistance to import-competing manufacturers. The principles governing these measures had been set down in a White Paper on Manufacturing Industry released during 1977.

Government Intervention in the Labour and Product Markets

The macro-economic policies so far described have for the most part been government responses to specific difficulties, but there is a long tradition in Australia of devolution of responsibility for what are really decisions of economic policy away from the legislature and towards different statutory authorities, such as the Conciliation and Arbitration Commission, the Trade Practices Commission and Tribunal and the Prices Justification Tribunal. Yet, despite this devolution, these areas of authority remain in a sense government initiatives, since the various tribunals are, after all, the creations of the law as enacted by Parliament. We now examine some of the features of this rather peculiar form of policy that has become so much a part of the antipodean tradition, and which has been intimately connected with the macro-economic regulation so far described.

Wages

The oldest established statutory authorities that intervene in the market are the host of tribunals, at the State and Federal levels, concerned with the conciliation of industrial disputes and the arbitration of pay claims. Indeed, the first aspect of the Australian economy of which outside observers are inclined to hear is the wage settlement or arbitration system. The main feature of the Australian wage determination system is the status and authority of tribunals created and empowered by Commonwealth and State laws to make legally binding wage awards. Special importance within the system attaches to the decisions of the Conciliation and Arbitration Commission, particularly in its major or national (mainly quarterly) hearings, which permeate the structure of award rates and are the means of exercising a centralising control (varying in potency from time to time) over wages. The commission's ability to influence wages largely depends on the indirect effects of its decisions on State awards and on wages and conditions in employment areas not regulated by awards. The commission's awards prevail over State awards where there is a conflict between the two, and for this and other reasons decisions of the commission in national wage cases are normally (though not without exception) followed by State authorities.

The procedures for settling 'award' wages in Australia have seemed to provide some of the elements of a national incomes policy, for which many overseas countries have been striving in the post-war period. One of these elements is simultaneity in the consideration of major claims. A difficulty with decentralised systems of collective bargaining has been said to be the 'particularity' of claims, i.e. smaller, separate claims cannot be shown in themselves to be inflationary. But, so it was observed, 'coercive comparisons' spread individual claims across a wider area. In this argument only when claims were centrally considered would their possibly inflationary consequences be more evident. This central consideration is, of course, provided by the national wage hearings before the Conciliation and Arbitration Commission.

Another reason why some observers felt that Australia possessed the skeleton machinery for an effective incomes policy was that there was, in general, a widespread acceptance, and indeed a reliance upon, the arbitration system. However, the 'relativities scramble' so characteristic of overseas collective bargaining was traditionally in the Australian context conducted in a more orderly fashion. As Sir Henry Phelps Brown has said, 'The procedures [the Australian system] had developed for making awards to particular groups on the basis of work value made for a reasoned adjustment of relativities on criteria that should be acceptable to others because they were applicable to the pay structure as a whole. Its hearings on margins provided a similarly reasoned procedure for the orderly adjustment of differentials; the same purpose was served when the margin came to be regulated only implicitly, within the total wage'.[2]

However, the extent to which the Australian arbitration system could be regarded as an effective device for regulating the price of labour in the economy was severely shaken by the growth of direct bargaining in the late 1960s. The extent of over-award payments and earnings drift has been difficult to measure. But however rapid the expansion may at various times have been, there is no doubt that their persistence must have encouraged the wage tribunals to try and match the market rates and thus to seek to protect those who did not receive over-award wages. As Dr J.E. Isaac noted in 1972, 'the attempt to narrow the gap between award and market rates has resulted in award increases being larger than the commission might have wished in the interest of price stability; even so the absolute gap has widened as over-award pay has kept on rising. Therefore, although over-award pay is a comparatively small proportion of earnings, it is nevertheless important for providing the momentum for a faster increase in wages and prices by its interaction with awards'.[3]

Whatever the cause of the growth of over-award payments and wages drift, the period 1968-77 has been one of relatively rapid money wage rises, with a money wage explosion in the years 1973-75. Moreover, the money wage explosion (average weekly earnings rose by 28.6 per cent in 1974) was accompanied by what seemed like industrial chaos (there was an increase of no less than 342 per cent in the incidence of industrial unrest (as measured by working days lost) between the March quarters of 1973 and 1974). At the same time (from August 1974) there was, as mentioned above, a remarkably sudden upturn in unemployment, and a substantial decline in the share of profits as a proportion of gross domestic product. Moreover, when money wages were rising particularly rapidly, so productivity was at times falling.

While it has, as mentioned, sometimes been suggested that the arbitration system provides the basic machinery for an incomes policy, it may come as something of a surprise to note that it in fact presided over the money wage explosion and took very seriously the enthusiasm of the Labor government for substantial wage rises in national wage rises in 1972-73 and 1974, at the same time as it agreed to introduce equal award pay for women. And while substantial award pay rises were being given, direct negotiation under tight labour market conditions in 1973 was also producing substantial money wage increases.

However, whatever their role in 1973-74, the arbitration authorities have moved more firmly to the centre of the stage since April 1975 when a policy of wage 'indexation' was introduced. In 1975, 1976 and 1977 there has indeed under this policy (but not necessarily because of it) been a considerable moderation of wage claims and substantial adherence to the 'guidelines' which the commission has laid down. Under the wage indexation guidelines, the commission has been able to exert its influence to assist conformity among the variety of wage tribunals in Australia, and to encourage observance by unions and employers of the rules attached to the indexation policy. As one survey of the period 1968-76 concluded:

> the indexation experiment guidelines undertaken from 1975 had largely been observed and, at least for the time being, the central strength of the commission was predominant. Under its initiative, employers, unions and government conferences had been called which (however unsuccessful at first) were still regarded by some as the major source of hope, in conjunction with the indexation package, for industrial amity and wage sensibility at a time of economic crisis.[4]

But, despite the coincidence between the introduction of the wage indexation policy and the downturn in the rate of increase of wages and earnings in 1975, the Commonwealth government has in 1975-77 persistently denounced the indexation package. The government has believed that real wages are too high and that the indexation policy is a serious barrier to economic recovery. It has claimed that, in the absence of indexation, wage rises would have proceeded at an even less rapid rate, presumably because, in the government's view, supply and demand forces (as reflected by unemployment levels in 1977 in excess of 6 per cent) are of crucial importance in determining the rate of increase of wages and earnings. Ironically, however, while the paramountcy of the market is at least implicit in this view, the Commonwealth government sought to impose a 90-day wages and prices freeze upon the economy in early 1977. This effort, however, was not carefully planned and the Arbitration Commission, by declining to freeze award wages in the quarter concerned, scuttled the plan's proposal.

Prices Justification

As in many overseas countries, Australia during both world wars imposed a system of price control. This control was, however, instituted through war time (national security) legislation and was State rather than federal government based. The Australian constitution does not permit the federal government direct power over prices, and when the Labor administration sought this power by referendum in November 1973, it was denied. This absence of constitutional power over prices has naturally differentiated the prices and wages policies undertaken in Australia in peacetime when compared with, say, Britain and the United States. In Britain and the US efforts to contain the 'new inflation' of rising prices in the absence of excess aggregate demand have included full circles of policies, graduating from attempts at voluntary compliance up to statutory schemes including freezes, and returning once more to voluntarism. It has been claimed, for example, that the shock of the August 1971 price freeze in the United States (which came after very recent presidential disclaimers on the need for price control) had a very great psychological impact on the community. Would power to freeze prices in Australia not afford similarly desirable scope to the authorities? Economists are divided upon this issue. But while the need for price and wage powers is pressed by many influential voices, it needs to be remembered that — on the prices side — no firm has failed to accept the Prices Justification Tribunal's recommendations.

The Prices Justification Tribunal was established by the Labor government in August 1973. In the Labor Party policy speech prior to the November 1972 federal election, the Labor leader, Mr Whitlam had announced that his party would, if elected, exert its influence over prices:

> We will establish a Prices Justification Tribunal not only because inflation will be the major economic problem facing Australia over the next three years, but because industrial co-operation and goodwill is being undermined by the conviction among employers that

the price of labour alone is subject to regulation and restraint.

Despite these intentions for the Tribunal, its early years of operation coincided with high rates of general price increase and with a marked rise in the incidence of industrial unrest. For the last two years of the Labor administration, it seemed the positive policy of government to encourage wage rises while price surveillance was exercised. (Indeed it was the definitely stated intention of some Labor ministers to effect, by this policy, a redistribution of income away from profits and toward wages.) The tribunal was part of a series of events and influences which served to compress the share of profits as a proportion of national product, demoralise the business community, and adversely influence the investment and employment decisions made during the recession which culminated in 1974.

Greater public and government awareness of the issues in overseas incomes and prices policies might well have avoided the combination of government enthusiasm for wage rises coupled with private sector price surveillance. On the other hand, the usefulness of the tribunal as a standing 'concept' of policy seemed established when the Liberal-Country Party Government decided in 1976 to retain it, despite prior promises of abolition before the 1975 election. And some would say in the tribunal's favour that the centralising changes which it appeared (at least partly and indirectly) to have wrought on the processes of wage bargaining did in fact assist the successful implementation of wage indexation in the April 1975 national wage case.

As with the wage and trade practices authorities, the prices tribunal was fashioned in the long tradition of Australian policy, which has been accustomed down the years to the devolution of responsibility, previously mentioned, from the legislature to independent statutory bodies. Despite its independence, however, the prices tribunal has proved very sensitive and responsive to changing government submissions on the criteria it should employ in its decision making. Although they have been disinclined to specify guidelines for tribunal, both the Labor and Liberal–National Country Party governments have made their views known on the criteria they regarded as appropriate for the tribunal to follow in individual cases. The tribunal, as a statutory authority, has not been obliged to accept or act on government advice or submissions. But the tribunal has proved very malleable to expressions of government opinion, despite its repeated assertions of independence. An outline of the Labor government's directives to the tribunal illustrates how the tribunal's operations moved broadly in line with govern-

ment guidelines suggested during 1973-75.[5] The tribunal is on the
basis of its record perhaps not as autonomous or philosophically independent as always suggested. Even if the government and the tribunal
were reacting to the same economic circumstances and might therefore
be expected to respond in a similar way, it seems that, in 1973-75, the
Labor government's suggestions for guidelines, at the least, reinforced
and hastened the application of policies by the tribunal.

In assessing the general role of the prices tribunal, there are two
major related questions. Firstly, to what extent has the tribunal overridden the forces of the 'market' and, secondly, what influence, if any,
has it exercised in restraining price inflation? It is difficult to know to
what extent the price rise recommendations made by the tribunal
would differ from those which would occur under the 'free' operation
of market forces. At times, it has seemed that the tribunal has simply
been rubber stamping price rise notifications, especially since November
1974, when it was requested by the Labor government to give due
attention to profitable investment returns. Indeed there is some evidence
that the tribunal has been agreeing to price rises which the firms concerned have been unable (in conditions of slack demand) to apply in
the market place. Similarly, in considering the tribunal's influence
upon the rate of increase of prices, the impossible question is raised of
what would have happened if, over the same period, the tribunal had
not existed, and everything else had remained the same. But while the
magnitude of the anti-profit and anti-price effects of the tribunal are
impossible reasonably to ascertain, their directions have been clear at
different periods of the tribunal's history. The tribunal leaned against
the cyclical wind of profits in 1973-74 but when it relaxed its posture
in late 1974, 1975, 1976 and 1977 its ability to influence events was
probably limited by the prevailing conditions of tighter competition
and slack demand. The tribunal's dilemma is partly that it has such
little influence over material and wage costs. By enactment, it has no
influence over public sector prices. There is little it can do to reduce the
size of wage, material and service costs. The chief feature it can influence is the profitability of companies under its purview, an influence
which some alleged was used for legitimising prices and profits higher
than those which might have obtained in the absence of the tribunal.
Finally, there is no way of knowing how product quality has been reduced following pressure on prices from the tribunal.

Equalisation of Standards and Marketing Authorities

In practice, Australian wages, significantly influenced by the arbitration system, shift more or less uniformly throughout the Commonwealth and at a remarkably even level, considering the country's size. In view of the similarity in wage levels and wage movements between the States, it is unlikely that firms or industries in any one State are able to reap the advantages of being a low wage area. In addition to wage fixing there is a variety of other Federal and State government arrangements designed to equalise economic and social standards throughout Australia. Indeed, an important part of the arrangements and understandings which lay behind the establishment of the Australian Federation in 1901 was that living standards and public facilities should be equalised between the States. This equalisation philosophy has the important industrial regulation implication that State governments in the 'less developed' States need to be assured that the advantages of efficiency and growth do not all accrue to the large diversified companies primarily established in Victoria and New South Wales.

As with wage-fixation patterns, the various statutory Federal and State orderly marketing schemes covering primary products also limit the extent to which secondary industries can adapt their cost structures to increased competition. These primary product marketing schemes have the effect of fixing the price of important raw material inputs of some major industries. The schemes may include controls over export sales, guaranteed prices, two-price schemes with pooling and equalisation arrangements, bounties and subsidies, mixing requirements, the operation of a reserve price scheme, protection from imports and substitutes, production controls and selling through a central authority.

At present, Federal statutes provide for eleven commodity boards and corporations for the following industries: wool, wheat, dairy produce, meat, tobacco, dried vine fruits, canned fruits, apples and pears, eggs, wine and honey. An important example here is the Australian Wool Corporation, which buys wool that fails to reach a day-to-day reserve price at auction. To prevent pressure developing on the Corporation the reserve price and wool stocks are not disclosed. No limit is placed on Corporation stocks, though the Federal government is careful in its surveillance of Corporation policy. Clearly, the Wool Corporation – and other statutory authorities for primary products – are important aspects of intervention in Australian industry. In Australia's growing mining industries, there is also intervention by government in pricing policies from time to time (for example, in negotiated mineral export prices) but this is far more spasmodic and piecemeal than in agricultural production.

Competition: (a) Internal

In their attitude to the regulation of trade practices, successive governments have declined to adumbrate specific guidelines for the trade practices authorities to employ in their interpretation of the public interest. For the 1965 Act, the Trade Practices Tribunal was required in weighing the public interest, to consider the needs and interest of consumers, employees, producers, exporters, proprietors and investors. This definition gave no guidance as to the priority, weight or urgency which should be accorded to the various groups composing the public whose interest might be affected by the trade restrictions under consideration. The tribunal (as with the wage and price authorities) was under the 1965 Act given the onus of making decisions which appeared to some to belong more appropriately to the legislature. The more powerful 1974 Act, and its amended version which applied from July 1977, continue this tradition. The trade practices authorities have again been placed in the position of independent arbiters of the public interest. Section 90 (6) of the 1977 Act states that the Trade Practices Commission

> shall not grant an authorization (for an otherwise prohibited practice to continue) . . . unless it is satisfied in all the circumstances that the provision of the proposed contract, arrangement or understanding would result, or be likely to result, in a benefit to the public and that the benefit would outweigh the detriment to the public by any lessening of competition.

But, whatever the means for its implementation, the Australian legislation on internal competition policy is similar in intent to laws of this kind in other countries. It seeks to eradicate as far as possible restrictive practices which have the effect of diminishing competition. While some spokesmen have seen the law as a directly anti-inflationary device, the general intent has probably been to open the door to innovatory efficiency-improving changes in organisational and industrial structures.[6]

Competition: (b) External

Australia enjoys as a trading nation, the advantage of using sources of commodity supply beyond its own doorstep, and can participate in the benefits of international specialisation. It also enjoys the consequential advantage of a greater variety of products than otherwise available. It is, therefore, able from time to time to employ instruments that may change the nature or extent of import competition being experienced by Australian producers.[7] Substantial tariffs have been erected to condition competition from abroad, and large-scale programmes of reform for these tariffs have been proposed by the Tariff Board (now the Industries Assistance Commission) which while an independent authority, reports to government, and does not have the devolved responsibility exercised by the wage and price authorities in their different ways. In practice, tariff reform tends to be a lengthy, and sometimes costly, process. Generally, government tampering with the tariff has (apart from the variation of generally high tariff barriers) been rather piecemeal, and on an industry by industry basis. As mentioned earlier, in 1973 general tariff reductions of 25 per cent across the board were undertaken. The clear intention of these cuts was to curtail the upward pressure on Australian prices by stimulating the flow of imports into this country. But because of the alleged impact of these cuts on employment, it seems unlikely that this form of intervention will be readily attempted again by a Federal government. Instead, one can anticipate continued industry by industry consideration of the level of assistance and protection from overseas competition considered necessary.

Co-ordination of Policy Devices

The definition of the public interest is not spelled out in the legislation creating the wage, price and competition policy statutory authorities in Australia. And an examination of the cases conducted before, say, the wage and prices tribunals shows a substantially varying interpretation of the public interest at different times. Moreover, there is sometimes difficulty in trying to visualise how the objectives of the various bodies are meant to be reconciled. And the areas investigated by the different authorities are often similar, while little effort seems to be made at co-ordinating the collection of data for the separate enquiries. Furthermore, there appear to be different ways in which the price setting mechanism is viewed by the various authorities.

What can be said of the overall importance or relevance to general economic policy deriving from the various authorities on wages prices and competition to which responsibility for basically economic decisions have been delegated in Australia? In the present (1977) administration's view, it is the wage authorities which persistently seem a thorn in the economy's side through the wage indexation 'package'. This policy represents a great mistake in judgement as far as the government is concerned. In a recent submission before the national wage bench, the government submitted that it is 'imperative . . . that the (Arbitration) Commission accept economic considerations as the prime determinant of the level of any (wage) adjustment awarded'. But, as the commission has frequently stressed, it does not have complete power over wages; it has a responsibility to settle industrial disputes; and its decisions are interconnected with the other aspects of economic policy. The government for its part would clearly wish to be able where it chose to regulate all aspects of the economy, especially fixing processes. But despite its great desire to obtain greater wage restraint, it has not moved towards fashioning a new system of wage determination. In this respect it is in a dilemma, for it could move in only one of two directions—towards free collective bargaining or towards State enforcement of wage rates backed by the power of the law. Neither course is attractive to the government. But it is at present seeking to regulate the framework of wage determination by industrial legislation which would attach penalties to strikes and various trade union actions. In the upshot this form of attempted regulation may prove as disastrous politically as would be any efforts to replace the wage tribunals with any direct State controls of wages, in so far as these would be permitted by the constitution.

Government Intervention in Ownership and Control

There are three distinct aspects of government intervention in the ownership and control of Australian industry. Firstly, the impact of foreign ownership and control on industry and the economy; secondly, internal ownership patterns, particularly the concentration of ownership within small groups, the increasing trend towards ownership of large sections of Australian listed companies by insurance companies and superannuation funds, and the divorce of ownership and control; and thirdly, direct government involvement in State-operated industrial enterprises.

Overseas Ownership and Control

Prior to the mid-1960s there had been selective controls on important or strategic sectors of industry. These included the general banking sector, radio, television and civil aviation. But, apart from a general control through currency exchange approvals by the central bank, overseas companies were virtually unfettered in the expansion of their Australian interests. One important reason for this was the extent of the support this capital inflow gave to the balance of payments. The level of overseas investment was equivalent to more than 30 per cent of new capital expenditure throughout the latter half of the sixties, peaking at 51 per cent in the year to June 1969.

The extent of this inflow had clear implications for ownership and control of Australian industry, but action was not taken till May 1965, when a set of guidelines was introduced in the wake of British and United States restrictions on capital inflow. However, the guidelines had little effect, and foreign investment continued almost unabated until 1968 when the first direct (but limited and ineffective) government intervention took place.

One result of the heightened interest in the limitation of overseas ownership and control was the establishment in 1970 of the Australian Industry Development Corporation (AIDC). The AIDC borrowed abroad, using its high credit rating to fund at relatively low rates of interest small firms which were generally unable to do so on their own account.

In 1969-70 there was a fall in net apparent capital inflow caused partly by a temporary lull in the mining boom and partly by a net reduction in government borrowing overseas. During the following two years the contribution of overseas investment in Australia increased, providing the equivalent of 53 per cent and 46 per cent of new capital expenditure by business for the financial years to June 1971 and 1972 respectively. This was a period of surveillance rather than of direct intervention in the field of foreign investment. In November 1972 the *Companies (Foreign Takeovers) Act* was promulgated, providing for individual assessment of foreign takeover bids. This tightening of the position against increasing foreign influence was reinforced by the incoming Labor government after December 1972 and its policy of 'buying back the farm'.[8] This policy was partly nationalistic, but included a desire to ensure stability of the capital account of the balance of payments as well as maintaining control over the money supply in Australia.

The most far-reaching set of foreign investment guidelines to date was announced by Prime Minister Whitlam in August 1975, and is basically a part of the succeeding government's policy. The guidelines covered four main areas of investment:

1. foreigners were in future virtually unable to invest in real estate or property except for immediate residential purposes;
2. all foreign investment in non-bank financial intermediaries and insurance companies was to be screened, including large existing business where the growth rate of assets was in excess of 15 per cent p.a.;

3. all proposals to establish a new business where the foreign investment totalled $1 million or more were to be examined; and
4. there were minimum Australian participation levels required in mining ventures within Australia.

At the time of the establishment of the Foreign Investment Review Board (FIRB) in 1976 these levels required 50 per cent Australian ownership of all future mining ventures except uranium, where 75 per cent Australian ownership was mandatory.

The FIRB's first report, released in November 1977 and covering the first 15 months of its operation to 30 June 1977, gives some interesting insights into the actual effects of these guidelines. During this time the board considered 1,043 applications for approval with only 7 being rejected—although a further 449 were approved with modifications.

Australia has now reached a watershed in its relationship with overseas investment. While there is still an active encouragement of such investment, the guidelines are now set out clearly, and each project is vetted on its own merits. The machinery is now in place for a more rigorous pruning of new overseas investment.

Patterns of Ownership and Control Within Industry Groups

Foreign ownership patterns within Australian industry have been far from uniform, and summary figures mask the real extent of foreign influence in key sectors. Even if one follows the official definition of foreign control as being where a foreign investor or group of investors owns at least 25 per cent of the voting shares of a company, and no Australian individual or group hold an equal or greater share, the extent of foreign control is still large. In 1974-75, 58.9 per cent of the Australian mining industry was foreign-controlled, including 40.6 per cent by US companies and 12.6 per cent by UK companies. While only 34.3 per cent of the manufacturing sector was foreign controlled in 1972-73, much of this was concentrated in such growth areas as chemicals, metals and specialised equipment, and was very low in stagnating industries such as knitting, clothing and footwear. Thus even should ownership patterns remain unchanged, foreign control of output will increase through its concentration in growth industries.

Foreign control is also substantial in areas of financial intermediation. In 1975-76, 54.7 per cent of finance companies were controlled by overseas companies, and the most recent figures for life assurance companies and general insurance companies (1972-73) put foreign control at 19.4 per cent and 45.0 per cent respectively.

While further statistics will assist in providing a clearer pattern of the extent of foreign ownership and control in Australia, the implications of this pattern for government intervention are more difficult to assess. Clearly, overseas investment in the development and growth of Australian industry has had important, if sometimes unquantifiable, advantages. These include access to advanced technology and experience, increased product ranges, the expansion of high-risk industries such as mining and oil exploration and some access to foreign markets. Against these can be listed the potential disadvantages of foreign ownership, most of which stem from the possibility of a discrepancy between Australian and overseas interests. The cost of servicing the debt is a longer term issue, with implications for the balance of payments. In the shorter term it may also allow speculative movements against the Australian dollar, or by the use of reserves and stand-by facilities, increase the operational lag of Australian monetary policy. The loss of control over natural resources has especially perturbed national policy-makers and the tighter controls implemented through the *Foreign Takeovers Act 1975*, the establishment of the FIRB, the 1975 foreign investment guidelines and the continuing role of control on overseas remittances by the Reserve Bank reflect the shift to an item-by-item surveillance of further inflow within a framework of the general acceptance of its continuing importance for Australia.

Ownership and Control Patterns within Australia

An important aspect of economic power and the attitude of government to industry is the manner in which a small number of firms can dominate an economy. This is analytically distinct from market concentration where a small number of firms can dominate an industry. In Australia the nature of market size and concentration has produced a private sector dominated by a couple of hundred large companies. In 1974-75, 441 or 0.42 per cent of companies with taxable income paid 51.3 per cent of all company taxation.

In examining the degree of concentration in Australia as a whole, it would appear that a small number of firms dominate the private sector (see Table 2.1). However, it is difficult to determine who, in turn, owns those companies themselves. A trend noticeable in the United States has been the increasing importance of corporate ownership in the equity of companies, and the separation of ownership and control. In Australia, the trend towards a greater divorce of ownership and control has also been evident, although on a smaller scale. The concentration of control in the hands of corporations, insurance companies and pension

Table 2.1: Concentration, Profitability and Sales: Manufacturing
Sector 1971-72

Industry	Percentage of total industry sales		Operating profit as a percentage of funds employed
	Largest 5 firms	Largest 10 firms	
Food, beverages and tobacco:			
Margarine, oils and fats	95	99	8.0
Other food products	23	37	13.9
Beverages and malt	55	69	16.5
Tobacco products	99	99	30.6
Textiles:			
Textile fibres, yarns and woven fabrics	42	59	9.3
Rope, cordage and twine	99	99	11.9
Floor coverings and other textile products	47	60	12.4
Clothing and footwear (including knitting mills):			
Knitting mills and clothing	16	24	14.6
Footwear	36	50	16.6
Wood, wood products and furniture (except sheet metal):			
Timber milling, veneers and boards	29	40	13.5
Wooden products and joinery	32	37	18.8
Furniture and mattresses (except rubber or wire)	26	32	17.0
Paper and paper products, printing and publishing:			
Paper and paper products	72	91	11.9
Printing and publishing	35	47	17.1
Chemical, petroleum and coal products:			
Basic chemicals	55	70	8.6
Paints, varnishes and lacquers	79	87	17.3
Pharmaceutical, veterinary, cosmetics and toilet products	31	45	22.5
Soaps and other detergents	82	92	30.1
Other chemical and related products	81	91	14.3
Petroleum refining, petroleum and coal products	82	95	9.2
Glass, clay and other non-metallic mineral products:			
Glass and glass products	99	99	10.7
Clay products and refractories	39	51	12.5
Cement, concrete and other products	58	74	15.5
Basic metal products	67	83	5.9
Fabricated metal products	26	43	12.6
Transport equipment:			
Motor vehicles, bodies, trailers and caravans	85	95	7.8
Motor vehicle instruments, parts and accessories	61	73	14.6
Other transport equipment	51	79	10.1

Industry	Percentage of total industry sales		Operating profit as a percentage of funds employed
	Largest 5 firms	Largest 10 firms	
Other industrial machinery and equipment and household appliances:			
Photographic and scientific equipment	49	54	18.9
Household appliances and electrical equipment	34	51	9.8
Other machinery and equipment	15	25	12.4
Leather, rubber and plastic products and manufacturing not elsewhere classified:			
Leather and leather products	55	61	10.1
Rubber products	76	90	6.3
Plastic products	50	64	13.0
Other manufacturing industries	25	36	18.2

Source: Tariff Board, Annual Report, 1972-73, p. 13.

funds is equally high. A break-down of the largest 20 shareholders for the top 60 listed companies in December 1977 indicates a strong concentration of control within these companies. Approximately 43 per cent of the issued capital of the companies was owned by the largest 20 shareholders. These shareholders thus collectively owned in the region of 18 per cent of the total issued equity capital of all ordinary and mining companies in Australia. Of the 43 per cent of issued capital owned by the top 20 shareholders, the bulk was in the hands of other corporations, life assurance companies and pension funds. These three groups owned 26 per cent of the total issued capital of the 60 companies. This percentage is even higher if nominee companies are included. On a wider front, financial intermediaries in June 1976 owned approximately 17 per cent of total shares on issue in Australia.

In summary, Australian industry is dominated by a number of companies which are mainly owned by corporations and institutions, and where control appears to be largely in the hands of management. This concentration of industry is in accord with Australia's comparatively small population and narrow local market. Often growth took place through an initial takeover or merger by overseas interests, which then developed internally to expand within Australia. It is interesting to note from a recent study of mergers in Australia that of the 82 mergers by US companies between 1959 and 1970 only one company recorded three mergers over the period. The remainder were content with either one or two mergers and to expand internally from within these corporate vehicles. In contrast, five UK firms engaged in 66 takeovers or mergers between them over the same period, and British firms in general concentrated on horizontal integration rather than the US pattern of vertical integration.[9]

One extension of Australian government intervention into ownership and control has been in regulating the degree of control which one company can exert over an industry. It is clearly inconsistent to restrict certain practices between companies which are against the public interest yet to permit the same practice through the merger of two companies. As a result the *Trade Practices Act 1974* prohibited both monopolisation (Section 46) and anti-competitive mergers (S50). Although monopolisation is not *per se* an offence, if the company takes advantage of its market position to 'substantially damage' a competitor then that *practice* is prohibited, rather than the actual corporate existence.

The problem has been that in some areas the size of the market dictates that if a firm is to reach satisfactory standards of efficiency then it may exist as a virtual monopolist—especially at the infant stage of any product or industry. In addition, the government should not erect a matrix of controls which prevents the exercising of initiative and competitive skills by efficient managements. The trade-off in this case may be inefficient use of resources through unnecessary market fragmentation or the subsidisation of uncompetitive firms.

An Overview of Ownership and Control

The previous two sections have attempted to examine separately the problems of foreign ownership of Australian companies and the separate issue of ownership and control patterns within Australian industry. The amalgam of the two provides a complex problem in supervision and control for government authorities.

Statistics published in 1976 but relating to data for 1969 showed that 69 firms in Australia each with at least a 50 per cent foreign shareholding accounted for the following percentage of activity in the manufacturing sector: 21 per cent of turnover, 19 per cent of value-added, 14 per cent of employment, 16 per cent of wages and salaries and 27 per cent of fixed capital expenditure.[10]

Thus in terms of its most important participants in the manufacturing sector, foreign-owned firms have been relatively capital-intensive and highly productive in relation to the remainder of the sector. It is also difficult to obtain up-to-date statistics on their activities—with 1969 providing the latest comprehensive coverage. Figures for the services sector, which employs nearly 70 per cent of the workforce,[11] are almost non-existent, although clearly the impact of foreign ownership is far less important than in the manufacturing sector. This is also true of the agriculture sector, where ownership remains widespread and control is often exercised through co-operatives or marketing boards.

The 1975 guidelines on foreign investment are at present the critical considerations for further capital inflow, and the 50 per cent Australian equity requirements for selected industries (plus 75 per cent for uranium) present a variable control which may be tightened or eased as Australia's internal and international trade patterns develop. Certainly the presence of overseas interests is a crucial element in the structure of ownership and control in Australia, but the pattern of government control reflects containment rather than curtailment. Short-run policies have concentrated on regulating the flow of funds through instruments such as currency controls and variable deposit requirements. Longer-run policies remain in their formative stage, but the present guidelines have a built-in flexibility to adjust to structural movements within industry and in terms of the growing ability of domestic industry to finance its own growth and development.

Government assistance in this area through bodies such as the Australian Industry Development Corporation and the Australian Resources Development Bank is able to direct resources to specific industries, but this is of only marginal assistance on a national level. The trend in Australia has been towards an increasing emphasis on domestic control without disenchanting foreign ownership, and policies in the future will probably reflect a growing dependence on Australian ownership and control in the development of industry and commerce.

In controlling the structure of Australian industry the government has however not restricted its activities to trade practices legislation and to more selective control over foreign investment. Apart from bounties and subsidies to industry, there has been direct involvement through the establishment of government-owned industries in juxtaposition with privately owned firms. Of particular note are the Federal government's airline, Trans Australia Airlines (TAA) and its banking firm, the Commonwealth Trading (and Savings) Bank. The establishment of TAA in 1946 followed the defeat of the then Labor government's attempts to obtain, by referendum, sufficient power to nationalise all air services. Today, TAA and another (private) airline share interstate air traffic by working a dual service. In banking, the Commonwealth Bank is the largest of the commercial banks, and exerts considerable influence. Its aim, as with TAA, is to raise the degree of competitiveness in their respective industries. To what extent this is true is, however, open to conjecture. The same comment applies to other fields in which government and private industry have competed – shipping, bus and road transport services.

In addition to activities side by side with private industry, federal and state governments have traditionally, through public enterprise, played an important role in the Australian economy. Public utilities and developmental works are dominated by government enterprise, completely so in transport (railways, tramways, roads, bridges, ports and harbours) and in communications (posts, telegraphs, telephones and telecommunications). Governments also provide all public water supply and sewerage services; they also control water resources, dams, irrigation works and most forests. However, the catalogue of government involvement in the supply of industrial services in Australia, and in intervention in industry, is probably not unduly different from other 'industrialised market' economies.

Government and the Capital Market

The Australian capital market has grown increasingly diversified and complex in the post-war period, and the government's role in shaping this trend has been important, with ramifications for the general economy as well as for those firms involved in and affected by the capital market's changing structure.

The expansion of the capital market was accelerated during the second half of the 1960s by the need to finance Australia's mining boom. This led to a proliferation of intermediaries who were able to provide both working capital and longer-term finance, with the latter constituting about 70 per cent of the demand, given the nature of investment in the mining industry. These intermediaries consolidated their position during the early 1970s and continued to expand even during the credit squeeze of 1974 and the current recession. Those financial corporations covered by the *Financial Corporations Act 1974*[12] controlled assets totalling $25,255 million as at 31 December 1976, compared with $19,532 million controlled by trading banks and $15,834 million by savings banks. The major sources of funds to the capital market over the last decade have been personal accumulation of household saving, retained company profits and depreciation allowances. Between 1964-65 and 1969-70 households accounted for an average of 20.6 per cent of all savings in Australia. This percentage almost doubled to average 38.2 per cent between 1970-71 and 1975-76. While other proportionate shares also changed, this was the most dramatic. Less spectacular have been changes in the use of these funds. For Australia as a whole, 26.3 per cent of Gross National Expenditure was spent on capital goods between 1970-71 and 1974-75 (compared with 27.3 per cent for the previous six year period). Of this 26.3 per cent, three-fifths was in the private sector.

The main function of any capital market is the mobilisation of surplus funds and the transference of these funds to their final users. This has been facilitated by the development of different types of sub-markets and securities, reflecting the diverse demand and supply characteristics or requirements of lenders and borrowers. Yet not all market growth has resulted from the interaction of supply and demand. Within Australia there are substantial market distortions and restrictions which impede the free flow of funds between deficit and surplus users, one example of which is shown by the degree of captiveness in the market for government securities. Trading banks, savings banks, pension funds, life assurance companies and the official short-term money market have minimum levels of Australian government securities which they are required or constrained to hold. As at 30 June 1968 this meant that approximately 40.2 per cent of government securities on issue were in the 'captive' category, with the proportion rising to 49.0 per cent in June 1972 and to 50.5 per cent in June 1976.

Government Non-Bank Financial Institutions

The need to finance economic development has led to the establishment of a number of specialised and directly or indirectly backed government institutions designed to supply the medium- and long-term financial requirements of industry and agriculture. The Australian Resources Development Bank (ARDB) was established in 1969 by the major trading banks in association with the Reserve Bank. The aim was to provide a vehicle for longer-term loan funding partly financed by the trading banks' Term Loan Funds. The ARDB raises finance for use in making direct loans to the mining and manufacturing sectors, as well as for the refinancing of loans through the trading banks. The Common-wealth Development Bank (CDB) was formed in 1960. Its main function is to provide short-term loans for small borrowers in the primary and secondary sectors. It also uses approximately one fifth of its funds for hire-purchase financing. The Australian Industry Development Corpor-ation (AIDC), which is a merchant bank, was set up by the federal govern-ment in 1970, especially designed to assist the manufacturing and mining sectors in obtaining medium- and long-term finance.

Other government intermediaries include the Export Finance and Insurance Corporation, the Overseas Trading Corporation and the

Australian Housing Corporation. Collectively they provide important lines of finance – particularly longer-term finance – for both the business sector and for private housing finance. Each aims at bridging a gap that existed in the capital market in the provision of funds where the social marginal return exceeded the private marginal return, or where the government believed specific assistance to industry was warranted. As the capital market continues to mature, some – for example, export finance and insurance – may be returned to the private sector. In other areas, such as mortgage banking, the government may be in a position to initiate a specialist area in the provision of capital in the future, and in this way continue to exercise a positive role in the capital market.

Of major importance to both long-term and short-term aspects of the Australian capital market has been the government's attitude to overseas capital flows and to overseas ownership of financial institutions. Overseas borrowing outstanding by Australian companies totalled $6,236m at the end of June 1976.[13] Of this total, $4,071 million was borrowed from related overseas companies and $2,165 million from unrelated companies. In addition, the non-bank financial intermediaries had stand-by facilities with overseas companies of $751 million at the beginning of the 1976-77 financial year.[14]

New money raised by listed and unlisted companies in Australia highlights one of the problems of reliance on this source – that of variations in flow. This is partly due to changing demands for funds in Australia, and the cost of funds in relation to overseas markets. However, it also depends on government controls over capital flow. The introduction of an embargo on short-term funds and of Variable Deposit Requirements (VDRs) on other borrowing in 1973 was a major factor in restricting borrowing during 1972 and subsequent years. The VDR regulations required that amounts up to 33½ per cent of borrowings had to be deposited interest-free with the Reserve Bank, making overseas funds prohibitively expensive in most cases, and reducing the flexibility available to Australian companies in funding their projects. This policy, together with change in emphasis of the monetary authorities from direct controls on the banking system, led to a recovery by the trading and savings banks of their relative strength *vis-à-vis* other financial institutions. It also led to a reduction in the growth rate of the money market corporations, or merchant bankers, who nevertheless experienced the most rapid rate of growth of the major financial institutions in the decade to June 1976, averaging 45 per cent p.a. compared to the average of 13 per cent p.a. for all listed institutions.

The restrictions on overseas borrowing, and the exchange control requirements on remittances overseas have shackled Australia's ability to benefit from international interest rate differentials, although they have also largely isolated Australia from speculative capital flows. Perhaps even more significantly, no new banking licences have been issued since the second world war, and general banking remains one of the most protected industries in Australia. In addition, under the *Foreign Takeovers Act 1975* all substantial purchases of interest in Australian companies are required to be approved by the Foreign Investment Review Board. This has further restricted the ability of overseas financial institutions to develop their Australian interests.

In conclusion, in assessing the direction of government intervention in the capital market, there has been a trend to greater control of the markets themselves and a relaxation of controls on securities and interest rates. Since the collapse of the share boom in January 1971, there has been substantial legislative reaction to imperfections within the market. The States passed a series of Acts to control the securities industries in 1971-72, mainly aimed at tightening share issues and market operations, including those of portfolio management firms. In August 1974 the *Financial Corporations Act* was enacted, giving the Reserve Bank the power to control asset ratios and interest rates paid or receivable by these financial intermediaries by the Act. While these powers have not yet been exercised by the Reserve Bank, their existence has greatly increased the leverage of the monetary authorities in influencing the reaction of these intermediaries to government policy initiatives and open market operations.

A second major Bill is at present being prepared by the Federal Government in consultation with the states to bring the securities industry within the ambit of federal regulation. This follows the report of the Senate Select Committee on Securities and Exchange, tabled in 1974, which revealed widespread inefficiencies and malpractices in the share market and related markets. It is proposed that a National Corporations and Exchange Commission, a Ministerial Council, and a research unit be set up to cover company and security legislation. Each State would repeal its existing Acts and pass complementary Acts ensuring a national perspective of the securities and share markets.

In regard to securities themselves there has been a general easing of restrictions. The ceiling on bank negotiable certificates of deposit was raised in 1972 and removed in September 1973, thereby allowing the trading banks the opportunity to be fully competitive in this form of security. There has been greater use of open market operations by the Reserve Bank and the Bank has shown greater flexibility in its use of the last resort rate in relation to the official short-term money market. But in many ways the Australian capital market remains stultified by regulations and direct controls. The government restricts the interest rates policies of the banking sector, their portfolio structure and — most important of all in the long run — both the number of banks and overseas banking competitors. The foreign exchange monopoly of the trading banks is one example of a debatable restriction within the market.

Since the 1950s the Australian capital market has shifted from a domination by the trading banks towards a more specialised but heterogeneous group of institutions. The present areas of growth indicate even further expansion, with both old and new instruments of finance being developed, such as promissory notes and irrevocable letters of credit.

The banks, while remaining of crucial importance, have grown relatively more slowly than the majority of other financial intermediaries. This has been partly due to the advantages of specialisation and increased services offered by these intermediaries. Yet the speed at which finance companies, building societies and money market corporations have been able to expand has also been stimulated by the restrictions placed on trading and savings banks. These include: Statutory Reserve Deposit Accounts (SRDs) which the Reserve Bank may use to freeze a proportion of trading bank deposits; direct control over bank interest rates; portfolio controls on trading banks in the form of the LGS convention (liquid assets plus government securities); minimum holdings of government securities in the case of savings banks; and 'moral suasion', which is a most important weapon of central bank control.

The shift away from discriminatory policy instruments does not imply a reduction in overall control by monetary authorities, as the *Financial Corporations Act 1974* gives these authorities increasing control over intermediaries. Correspondingly, there is an increasing ability within the financial sector to cope with greater freedom of interest rates and overseas capital transfers, and this is an area for future relaxation of government restrictions. It points to an ever increasing emphasis on measures whose major thrust is not restricted to sub-sectors of the capital market. This is one important advantage of a maturing capital market, and one which may be expected to be utilised to an increasing extent in the future.

The scope for non-Australian involvement in the capital market is already large, and growing. The capital market may better perform its function of the mobilisation of savings and the transfer of these savings to those users requiring funds if there was greater freedom externally as well as internally. During the late 1960s and throughout the 1970s the capital market has shown the ability to expand in response to increased demand. However considerable restrictions remain on the interaction between Australian and overseas capital markets. Whilst the trend to easing these restrictions has been encouraging there is a long way to go before Australia can be said to have a fully mature capital market.

Conclusion

Australian industry in recent decades has been subjected to changing macro-economic policies, with stimulants and restraints through a great variety of devices that have sought to manipulate levels of industrial and general economic activity. These policies have been in response, for the most part, to the swiftly flowing tide of events, in which industrial growth has waxed and waned—yielding a ready supply of flotsam and jetsam—along with other sectors of activity. As a backdrop to macro-economic policies there has lurked an important number of statutory institutions created partly to influence the labour and product markets. These bodies, which have operated in the fields of wage awards, private sector prices, and internal and external competition, are continually by their decisions affecting industrial behaviour, structure and, no doubt, performance. In other markets, too, such as the capital market, government instituted (but not always devolved) regulation has been of influence, partly through restrictions on the free operation of the price system. And in the ownership and control of industry—especially patterns of foreign ownership—government has been active in seeking to affect the scene. Perhaps it is the constitutional inhibition of industrial nationalisation that has preserved more pervasive government intervention in industry. It certainly seems clear that governments of differing political hues are disinclined to divest themselves of current involvement in industry. Australia therefore seems likely to largely retain its existing pattern and degree of government intervention in industry.

Notes

1. A. Robinson, 'Few good omens ahead' in survey on Australia, *Financial Times*, 1 September 1977.
2. E.H. Phelps Brown, 'A Social Contract in Australia?' in *Australian Economic Policy*, J.P. Nieuwenhuysen and P.J. Drake (eds) (Melbourne University Press, 1977), p. 86.

3. J.E. Isaac, 'Australian Compulsory Arbitration and Incomes Policy' in F. Blackaby (ed.), *An Incomes Policy for Britain* (Heinemann Educational Books, 1972), p. 130.

4. J.P. Nieuwenhuysen and J. Sloan, *Australian Wages Policy Discussion 1968-1976* (forthcoming).

5. J.P. Nieuwenhuysen and A.E. Daly, *The Australian Prices Justification Tribunal* (MUP, 1977), Chapter 5.

6. The History of Australia's Trade Practices Law to 1975 is set out in Chapters 1 and 2 of J.P. Nieuwenhuysen and N.R. Norman, *Australian Competition and Prices Policy* (Croom Helm, London, 1976).

7. See Nieuwenhuysen and Norman, *Australian Competition*, Chapter 3.

8. See W.H. Arndt, 'Foreign Investment' in J.P. Nieuwenhuysen and P.J. Drake (eds), *Australian Economic Policy* (Melbourne University Press, 1977), Chapter 11.

9. I.C. Stewart, 'Australian Company Mergers 1959-1970' *Economic Record*, March 1977, page 27. One Dutch firm, Philips Industries Holdings Limited, also made eight takeovers.

10. Committee to Advise on Policies for Manufacturing Industry: *Policies for Development of Manufacturing Industry: A Green Paper*, Vol. 3, page 127 (April 1976).

11. K.A. Tucker (ed.), *Economics of the Australian Service Sector* (Croom Helm, 1977), p. 36.

12. Building Societies, Credit Co-operatives, Authorised Money Market Corporations, Pastoral Finance Companies, Finance Companies, General Financiers, Inter-Group Financiers, and Other Financial Corporations (excluding Shareholders' funds).

13. ABS, *Overseas Investment*, 1975-76.

14. ABS, *Financial Corporation Statistics*, December 1976.

3 GOVERNMENT INTERVENTION IN THE ECONOMY OF THE UNITED STATES

James W. McKie

The United States is widely regarded as a free, private-enterprise economy – one of the few remaining in the world. But by the standards of the nineteenth century, or of ideal *laissez-faire* libertarianism, it falls considerably short of that. It is better characterised as a 'mixed' system. The government has an ubiquitous presence and strong influence that reaches into the micro-structure and detailed operations of the system, even though private organisations still make most of the decisions about its direction. The sphere of government decision is enlarging: the sphere of private decision is contracting.

Up to now, the scope of 'intervention' has not followed any grand ideological design which demarcates those economic functions in which the one or the other mode, public or private, must be dominant. It has resulted from a large number of relatively small decisions over a long period of time. Public demands for extension of government control are largely *ad hoc* – they usually result from occasional notable failures of the private system in some essential respect rather than from a dispassionate comparison of the costs and benefits of the two modes of economic organisation. The small decisions by now add up to a very considerable role for the government. It often plays this role jointly with private enterprise rather than displacing it altogether.

Economists, in attempting to attribute some measure of rationality to governmental intervention, frequently cite the principle of 'market failure'. If the operation of private uncontrolled markets fails to achieve some necessary goal of the economy reasonably well, government may intervene to 'correct' the result. We shall examine some of the means used by the government in America in attempts to remedy market failure. (We should not forget the failures of government to achieve these same ends through regulation, or public ownership, or whatever; it is easy to find examples of that.)

A lot of intervention is nothing but the old political game of attempts by people and organisations to use the machinery of the state for their own purposes, and not necessarily in the 'public interest'. Particular groups can be expected to ask for intervention whenever the market system fails to promote their private interests as well as they think the government will.

The two major political parties in the US have taken different official positions on government intervention in the economic system: the Republicans are against it, while the Democrats declare in favour of intervention to deal with a variety of problems. In practice, the extension of government control and influence since the days of the New Deal (1933-38) has proceeded somewhat more rapidly when the Democrats were in power and more slowly when the Republicans could arrest it, but it has not been reversed. Republican administrations have shown repeatedly that they too are willing to promote *ad hoc* governmental responses to specific economic issues as they emerge.

The Government Presence

No economic system has ever lacked a governmental presence, but we will not give our attention to the 'traditional' claims of the government on the economy for administration of justice, education, monitoring claims to property, etc., except as they involve questions of policy in procurement. The gross total of consumption and investment by the government is quite impressive. Out of a total Gross National Product in 1977 of $1,890 billion, total governmental purchases of goods and services were $396 billion, or 21 per cent. The distribution was $251 billion state and local expenditures, and $145 billion Federal.[1]

The sheer size of government consumption or use of resources is so great that it could easily influence the economic system as much through changing the direction of its acquisitions as through many of the regulatory practices to be reviewed subsequently. But most such procurements are regarded as routine: the government enters the market as any other customer, only a much bigger one. The resulting impact on resource allocation and on the infrastructure of roads, public works, land access, waterways, airways, schools, urban amenities, and so on, is often overlooked. In fact, the government has encountered most of its procurement policy issues in the procurement of military supplies, chiefly of weapons and their support, which accounts for nearly one-third of total Federal exhaustive expenditures. A further word is said subsequently about military procurement.

We also exclude consideration of macro-economic policy: those forms of government intervention designed to affect overall levels of activity in the economy—employment, aggregate production, the price level, general taxes, income transfers and the supply of money and credit. These are unquestionably important areas for public policy, but this chapter is confined to those policies of intervention that affect the structure and functional detail of the economy – individual industries or sectors, prices, markets, the allocation of resources among different activities and the economic circumstances of particular groups. Briefly, we are concerned with micro-economic intervention, which admittedly is an incomplete picture of government influence on the economy.

The Ten Thousand Commandments: Corrective Intervention

Government often intervenes in the market not to supersede private ownership but to make markets work better, ostensibly in the public interest but frequently on behalf of particular groups. There are several types of 'corrective' intervention.

The Government as Rulemaker and Proctor: Anti-trust

Perhaps the simplest kind of government intervention in the economic system is to ensure that the private system itself will work satisfactorily, by preserving effectively competitive markets. It is a Deistic kind of intervention: it sets the rules and conditions for the game, and then lets the system run itself. It is quite in accord with the principles of *laissez-faire*, at least in conception.

The United States embarked in 1890 on a policy of restricting monopoly, with the passage of the Sherman Anti-trust Act. (Several states had earlier passed anti-monopoly laws, but these were never very effectual.) This was a period of growing concentration in the US economy. Public opinion had turned against big business because of some flagrant episodes of price-fixing and monopolistic exploitation, and in addition small business – always a potent political force in the United States – demanded protection from the predatory acts of increasingly powerful rivals.

The Sherman Act was not effectively enforced at first against large combinations or 'trusts'. Concentration of the American economy proceeded apace until about 1905. Thereafter the law became a more effective weapon against monopoly. In 1914 the Sherman Act was joined by the Clayton Anti-trust Act and the Federal Trade Commission Act, aimed specifically at anti-competitive practices such as exclusive dealing and price discrimination. There have been numerous small supplements to the basic legislation since then, including a rejuvenation of state anti-trust policy following initiation of a Federal aid programme in 1975.

Anti-trust policy and litigation have been extremely broad and complex. We shall have to summarise the main thrusts of the policy and ignore many details.

Up to now, the anti-trust laws in the United States have attempted
to limit monopoly by preventing certain kinds of conduct; they are not
designed primarily to change the economic structure. The Sherman Act
does not make monopoly as such illegal; it prohibits monopolisation
and attempts to monopolise. The line between the two has dimmed
over time, but it is still there. For this reason the law has found it
relatively easy to prohibit and police price-fixing and other kinds of
conspiratorial behaviour by firms selling in interstate markets. Structural monopoly has been a more difficult target.

A few of the early 'trusts' were found to be illegal combinations
formed with the intent to monopolise, and were broken into more
competitive pieces — notably the Standard Oil Company, dissolved in
1911 into 33 successors.[2] Nowadays any corporation that accounts for
a major fraction of a large industry in the United States can expect an
anti-trust action sooner or later. A really dominant firm — one that
evidently has the power to control prices in a major market and exclude
competitors — can escape a Sherman Act attainder only by showing that
monopoly was 'thrust upon' it or was maintained solely as a result of
its superior efficiency or technological innovation.[3] But few important
industries or markets in the United States are controlled by a single
firm.

A more significant problem of market structure in the United States
is oligopoly — industries dominated by a few rivals. A highly concentrated
oligopoly can jointly sustain monopolistic prices and restrict output if
the firms can maintain barriers to entry. But oligopoly is not illegal
under the anti-trust laws unless the firms overtly conspire or use predatory or deliberately exclusionary tactics against smaller firms or potential entrants to the market.

Anti-trust cases brought by the government against large oligopolistic
firms charging monopoly or conspiracy to monopolise can be very
expensive and protracted. The case against the Aluminum Company
of America (Alcoa), for example, lasted over ten years from start to
finish, and cost both government and defendant many millions of
dollars. The complaint against IBM was filed in January 1969; the trial
began in May 1975; three years later it was nowhere near its end. Other
massive cases were pending in 1978: one against American Telephone
and Telegraph, in which the Department of Justice planned to sue for
divestiture of the manufacturing subsidiary, Western Electric, from
AT & T; and one against eight integrated oil companies, who were
charged with price fixing and exclusion of competition.[4]

Anti-trust policy can and does take effective action against increase of concentration and monopoly through mergers. Present rules are quite strict. No firm with a dominant position in an industry, no firm among the leaders in a concentrated industry, is likely to be permitted to acquire a competitor, or for that matter an important supplier or customer. Even 'conglomerate' mergers of firms or parts of firms in different markets are looked on as potentially dangerous when the merging entities are large. So, while anti-trust policy does not often move to break up existing monopoloid structures, it attempts to prevent extension of monopoly – a policy of containment.

But policy is not consistent. In several important sectors, as we will see, government actually mandates the very things that it prohibits where the anti-trust laws do apply: price fixing, restrictions on entry, limitations on output. It would be hard to determine whether the government's procompetitive intervention outweighs its anti-competitive intervention. There are also exempt sectors where private parties are free to pursue monopoly if they can secure it. Leading these are (1) labour markets, where the government follows a policy of benign neutrality toward labour monopoly; (2) patented articles and processes. Patent holders, as long as they do not conspire with others, are legally empowered to exclude competitors and exact monopoly profits, to the extent that they can, for a limited period (currently 17 years). Naturally patent holders generally try to extend their monopoly beyond the limited grant, and anti-trust law has had to define the boundary of the monopoly privilege rather sharply.

One 'anti-trust' law, the Robinson-Patman Act,[5] prohibits price discrimination which injures *competitors* of the firm charging or receiving discriminatory prices, such as large-volume discounts to chain grocery stores. Critics[6] have sometimes objected that protection of competitors is not always consistent with furtherance of competition, both actual and potential – a goal which may indeed hurt inefficient competitors. Protectionism frequently lurks behind government intervention, and is of course incompatible with a vigorous competitive process.

A word should be said about enforcement of the anti-trust laws. The Department of Justice, the legal arm of the government in ordinary litigation, has exclusive responsibility in anti-monopoly and conspiracy cases under the Sherman Act. It shares responsibility in Clayton Act cases (against mergers and certain anti-competitive practices) with the Federal Trade Commission, an independent administrative body with quasi-judicial functions. The FTC has exclusive jurisdiction over proceedings against 'unfair methods of competition'. It is not surprising that moșt of the criticism for protecting competitors rather than competition has been levelled against the FTC; nevertheless, the Commission is as devoted as the Justice Department to competition as the proper goal of economic policy.

Anti-trust policy has not been unequivocally successful in containing monopoly or maintaining competitive conditions. Concentration in the American economy has been increasing slowly since World War II, after a substantial remission in the inter-war period. Table 3.1 gives information on the drift of concentration in the manufacturing sector as a whole, as measured by the share of the largest corporations in total value added by manufacture. There probably has been a comparable drift in other sectors, some of which (such as public utilities and transportation) were more concentrated than manufacturing to begin with, while others, such as distribution, were less so, though very large firms (e.g. Sears, Roebuck) exist in distribution as well as in manufacturing.

Table 3.1: Share of Total Value Added by Manufacture Accounted for by the 50, 100, and 200 Largest Manufacturing Companies in the United States in 1947, 1958, 1967 and 1972

	Percentage of Value Added by Manufacture by		
	Largest 50 companies	Largest 100 companies	Largest 200 companies
1947	17	23	30
1958	23	30	38
1967	25	33	42
1972	25	33	43

Source: US Bureau of the Census, Concentration Ratios in Manufacturing, Special Report MC72 (SR)–2, 1972 Census of Manufactures (Washington: US Government Printing Office, 1975), p. 4.

But monopoly is more a matter of concentration in individual markets or industries than in whole sectors of the economy. Most industries have enough competing firms to prevent control by one or two sellers, and are not evidently dominated by tacit collusion. In 1967, for example, out of more than 450 manufacturing industries identified by the Bureau of the Census, in only about 25 did the largest four firms account for more than 75 per cent of the value of products shipped by that industry, and in 14 of those industries the four-firm concentration ratio had actually fallen since 1947. Less than 15 per cent of total value added by manufacture in 1967 originated in industries in which the largest four sellers accounted for 70 per cent or more of value added in their industry. Nearly half of manufacturing value was produced in industries in which the largest four firms had less than 30 per cent of the total.[7]

Some monopolies have been overthrown by technological revolution. Anti-trust policy has also played its part, principally through (1) effective discouragement of agreements to fix prices and allocate markets, and (2) stringent limitation of mergers among large firms. Monopolistic performance, aside from a few highly concentrated industries with substantial barriers to entry, is to be found primarily in those sectors of the economy that are exempt from the anti-trust laws or where the government itself has been largely responsible for imposing monopoly in one form or another.

In one major sector of the economy, competition evidently cannot work, and the government has turned to regulation instead of enforcement of competition as its tool of policy.

The Government as Regulator: Public Utilities

In the United States, if the government (at any level) is persuaded that the competitive market has 'failed' beyond redemption, its most common response is to regulate rather than to supersede the private market by government ownership. The oldest and most comprehensive form is regulation of that class of industries known as 'public utilities'.

The meaning of 'public utility' is not precise. Originally it was derived from the law (tracing back to Elizabethan times) sanctioning regulation of activities 'affected with a public interest' such as the operation of wharves and inns; but in the United States it soon acquired a different context. A public utility means a firm offering an essential service (essential in terms of contemporary living standards) that operates under conditions approaching natural monopoly, i.e. where monopoly is irresistibly more efficient than competition. The usual candidates are suppliers of electric power, local distributors of gas and water, natural gas pipelines, and local and switched systems of electric and electronic communications.

The definition is loose enough in practice to encourage extension of the 'public utility' concept to other activities such as milk distribution which do not seem to most economists to fit at all. Moreover, some activities which once might have been classified as public utilities, such as railroad transportation,[8] now do not meet the test of natural monopoly, but are still regulated all the same. Commercial transportation of all types, in fact, is regulated by the Federal government under an imprecise extension of the public utility concept. Other activities are also regulated, even though they may not be natural monopolies, simply because they are supplied by firms that are so regulated; an example is inter-city leased-private-line communications.

What about public utilities does the government regulate? In the 'classic' case, it (usually a state government) sets up a regulatory commission, which has a regular staff and continuing existence. Its first point of attack is usually the rate of return on the utility's invested capital, which in the absence of regulation would presumably be too high, reflecting natural monopoly. But it cannot stop there. The regulatory authority, whether it likes it or not, must set up rules governing depreciation of property and prudent cost, as well as minimum standards of service; otherwise evasion of rate-of-return ceilings would be transparently easy for the regulated firm. It usually also regulates minimum and maximum *rates*, and the degrees of price discrimination among classes of customers. (Thus, electricity for home lighting sells at quite high prices, whereas power for home heating where the customer has an alternative may bear much lower prices under a typical residential tariff.) In fact, the regulatory authority may get involved in complex questions of business management.

Opinions differ, inevitably, about the success of regulation. Some vocal critics have charged that rate-of-return regulation in fact has had hardly any discernible effect on the rate earned by most regulated utilities.[9] Others have asserted that controlling the rate of earnings induces inefficiencies in their use of resources.[10] The charge is often heard that regulatory authorities tend to become the captives of the regulated industry, protecting the monopoly usually granted to it by franchise and acquiescing in its monopolistic price and output policies: or even more strongly, that regulation is simply a protective service bought in the political marketplace by the most powerful economic interests.[11]

One aspect of utility regulation that is universally decried tends to bear out the 'capture' theory: the great difficulty experienced in freeing an industry from regulation once its natural monopoly (or any other aspect of market failure) has ceased to exist. Regulation, it seems, cannot let go if vested interests have meanwhile grown up that depend on it. The worst example is probably transportation of freight. There is no reason why motor freight transportation, for example, cannot be treated like any other competitive industry with freedom for any responsible firm to enter, to decide what routes it will serve and what commodities it will haul, and what rates it will charge. After all, there are over 15,000 common carrier trucking firms in the United States now, and many more are eager to enter. Instead, regulation has created an inefficient cartel, with collusive rates and blocked entry.[12]

Access to the Market

Access to the market by anyone willing to buy or sell would appear to be among the most fundamental attributes of a free economy. The governments of the United States, both State and Federal, have intervened in dozens of cases to restrict access. The most common form is licensing: of taxicabs, beauty parlours, physicians, real estate brokers, establishments distilling alcoholic beverages, electrical contractors, even (in Texas) automobile dealerships. There is almost always a persuasive reason for restricting access to those firms and individuals who are qualified, certified, and responsible: protection of the public health, safety and need, which presumably the unregulated market could not provide adequately. Unfortunately, the very existence of licensing lends itself to cartellisation and guild restrictions to protect the incomes and other vested interests of the 'insiders', who themselves may ultimately control the licensing process. This effect can be seen clearly when a transferable licence itself acquires a market value, which is the capitalised value of the monopoly restriction on entry.[13]

Restrictions on access also accompany other forms of regulation, such as public utility franchises, and certificates of convenience and necessity for inter-state airlines and national banks.

The other major case is Federal control of access to the broadcast band, the most important aspect of which now is television broadcasting. Control of rights in the limited electro-magnetic spectrum is clearly necessary, since free entry would lead to broadcast interference and ultimately would mean that no one could transmit a clear signal. The government decided early in the radio age not to allocate spectrum by allowing potential users to bid for broadcast rights and thus collect the economic rents—a policy that many economists think would be in the public interest.[14]

Though allocation of spectrum is really the only matter requiring public intervention, the governmental presence in television broadcasting (as well as in other forms of radio and TV communication) has inevitably generated public demands for government control of the medium itself. Large segments of the public are not happy with what they hear and see on television. So far the Federal Communications Commission has resisted any responsibility for programme content, but it has at least tried to promote local broadcasting by restricting network programming during evening 'prime time'.

FCC regulation has produced few solutions to the problems of broad-casting; in fact, it may have generated some of them. An example is its policy of allocating spectrum to stations in the VHF band in the early years of television, which left room for only three national networks. Since then these networks have often been charged with operating a joint monopoly. Most TV stations admitted later to the UHF band have never been able to compete on equal terms with the VHF stations. Another example is the restrictive policies of the FCC toward cable television, apparently to protect the pre-existing interests of broadcast television.[15]

Ubiquities and Externalities

So far we have considered government regulation of particular industries: prices, profits and entry. The political process has more recently begun to perceive market failure in a number of problems that seem to be common to many industries and activities. These are still micro-economic in nature, but are not identified with particular organisations. This type of regulation is sometimes called 'new-style' regulation. It also deals with externalities: costs that industrial activity inflicts on the economy at large and benefits that are not captured in the accounts of individual firms. The following are just three examples of 'new-style' regulation.[16]

The Environmental Protection Agency was created in 1970 to develop and enforce Federal standards for clean air and water. It eval-uates environmental-impact statements that most large construction projects must now file, and may intervene to halt or delay such projects: it also regulates toxic chemicals and noise pollution.

The Equal Employment Opportunity Commission and several other agencies, founded in the 1960s, oversee compliance with the Federal Government's various regulations and policies against discrimination in employment on the basis of race or sex.

The Occupational Safety and Health Administration (OSHA), estab-lished in 1971, regulates health and safety conditions in all places of employment except those of the government itself. OSHA has gained renown for its petty and unnecessarily complicated regulations, one of the most famous of which was a 21-page regulation for the design of ladders. After becoming a principal target of criticism of the new regulation, OSHA announced a reform in its methods and policies in June 1977; henceforth it would go after the principal dangers to health and safety and not after trivia.

Protection of Consumers

The government has intervened in the market (1) to ensure that consumers are adequately informed, and (2) to exclude potentially harmful substances, such as those that can cause cancer in unsuspecting consumers. The first such intervention was the Pure Food and Drug Act of 1906, which set up the Food and Drug Administration (FDA). The law has since been strengthened by repeated amendments which have extended controls to such things as cosmetics and pesticides. Very strict rules for testing of drugs were laid down in the Amendments of 1962. The FDA has sometimes been criticised for an excessively cautious approach, allowing the consumer little opportunity to take his own risks; its recent bans on cyclamates (1972) and saccharin (1976), for instance, have been widely attacked. However, the law leaves it little choice. Public opinion generally supports a strict policy on medicines and drugs, and a moderately severe policy to ensure the purity of food.

Policy to improve consumer information is exemplified by the Truth-in-Lending Law of 1971, which has certainly revealed to borrowers the correct prices of credit; on the other hand, there is no evidence that it has made credit any cheaper, as some advocates apparently thought it would.

The Consumer Product Safety Commission, organised in 1972, extends protection to products other than foods and drugs, requiring better labelling and safer product design.

These relatively modest interventions to protect consumers have not entirely satisfied the more ardent consumer advocates, such as Ralph Nader and his associates. They demand more comprehensive regulation. Some critics want a general assault on what they think is business irresponsibility, claiming that corporations, through advertising, create consumers' wants and then ill-satisfy them with shoddy, over-priced, unsafe and unwholesome goods. Others think that it is imperative for the government to save consumers from their own folly, and to deny them the opportunity to spend money on goods and services that the critics think are not good for them. But the American economy still relies chiefly on consumer sovereignty in the competitive market rather than on government regulation to promote consumer welfare.[17]

The Government as Supporter, Promoter, and Operator of Industry

The types of intervention now to be described are somewhat different from the preceding ones. While they too may aim to correct market failure, they have required actual governmental support and operation, not merely rules and exhortations.

Fiduciary Protection and Guarantees of Credit

When financial institutions fail in their fiduciary obligations, they often fail disastrously. Few forms of market failure upset the public so much. The government at first moved into the operations of securities markets, banks and other financial institutions with conventional regulation to oversee their fiduciary relations to the public, or to establish one if the institution was not previously conscious of a trust obligation. Sometimes these extensions of public control have resulted from pressures by the public in a dangerously punitive mood as a result of some financial catastrophe or other. Such was the origin of bank examination by Federal and state governments, of control of entry of banks and savings institutions, of ceilings on interest rates; and, of course, most of the panoply of regulation of corporate securities and securities markets after the débâcle of 1929. Several other types of financial institution, such as insurance companies and pension funds, are highly eligible for fiduciary regulations.

But the government has also appeared on the fiduciary scene in a positive role, as guarantor of last resort of the obligations of private financial institutions to the public. It has assumed this function to forestall failure or the repetition of failure, as in its insurance of bank deposits and savings institutions.[18] It has also promoted the flow of funds in different directions and volumes from those that a strictly private lending system might have chosen. For example, the Federal National Mortgage Institution (Fannie Mae) has provided a secondary market for home mortgages insured by still other Federal agencies, while the Federal Land Banks have provided credit for agriculture. The purpose of these and many other credit programmes was to close a 'credit gap' for some of the government's favourite economic sectors. They have done so successfully on the whole, in fact, some agencies (including the Land Banks and FNMA) have been converted to private ownership.[19]

The Government as Promoter and Supporter

The US government has become a promoter of major activities such as nuclear power, which rests on a government-provided infrastructure of research, development, and production of fissionable fuel. It provides (through NASA) the aerospace support for satellite communication. It constructs canals, ports and waterways which private transportation companies use without compensatory charges. It operates a system of airways communications and controls, gratis to airlines. All of these activities affect relative costs, prices, output and investment.

Perhaps the leading example of Federal help is in agriculture, long a favoured constituency. Since the 1920s, agriculture has benefited from a large variety of promotional and support programmes. Government credit was mentioned above. The government has supported prices of some staple crops at levels ostensibly designed to bring farmers' purchasing power closer to that of the non-agriculture sectors, by direct and indirect purchase whenever the market prices fall below support levels. It has limited planting for the same purpose of maintaining prices. The surpluses that often result from price supports have been stored, given away, or distributed under subsidy. Farmers have been encouraged to set up their own systems of price support and production controls; these have been most effective in milk markets and in fruit markets. Total direct outlays for these purposes have been enormous over the years, and consumers have paid additional costs in higher prices for food and fibre. The government has several times attempted to reduce the scope of its intervention and to restore market forces as the primary determinants of agricultural prices and production—most recently under Secretary Earl Butz in the 1971-76 period. But the agricultural slump of 1977-78 elicited new controls, reversing the previous policy.

International trade policy for the US, as for almost all countries, is promotional and protective. The effects of protective tariffs and quotas are too familiar to require discussion. All we can say is that the US economy is far less 'protected' against foreign-produced goods than it used to be, under the benign influence of GATT and the several post-war rounds of tariff protection. But the battle for favoured status goes on, and in the mid-1970s the automobile, steel, shipping, electronics, agricultural and clothing industries in the US were all making strong demands for increased protection, chiefly in the form of negotiated import quotas, and were having some success. Other industries, such as chemicals, have continued to benefit from strong protection throughout the post-war period.

The government does not always seize the role of protector and promoter with enthusiasm. Sometimes it has been obliged to succour a private industry that has failed in an activity that the government thinks is essential; it has become a legatee in bankruptcy. The Federal government, for example, has been obliged to guarantee the operation of some significant parts of the nation's railroad system. In 1973 it set up the United States Railway Association, a government agency, to finance a 'private' corporation called Consolidated Rail Corporation (ConRail) which in turn took over and operated the bankrupt properties of Penn Central and several other railroads in the north-east quadrant of the United States. ConRail was to operate 'for profit' and sell securities to the government and to the public. It has received over $3 billion in Federal funds to acquire, modernise and operate railroad properties. In 1977 its deficit was still running at about $500 million per year, matching earlier deficits under private ownership.

Amtrak was set up in 1970 as a government corporation to take over operation of most US rail passenger service, which was then in an advanced state of dilapidation. Amtrak is a direct government service, but it operates in conjunction with privately owned railroads. It has had some success in reviving self-sustaining rail passenger service in the North-East Corridor between Boston and Washington, but little elsewhere. Amtrak too is incurring very large deficits (nearly $500 million in 1977)—in effect the government is heavily subsidising rail passenger service.

In view of the experience of other countries, it is not surprising that rail transportation in the United States is passing under government control and operation. The remaining private railroads in the United States are almost the last survivors in the world. Evidently governments everywhere are willing to operate rail transportation, typically at a financial loss, for the sake of the large external benefits that they think it brings to the nation. In the United States, rail transport may be an example of creeping socialism by default of the private sector. It is not clear how much the government itself may have contributed to the demise of the privately owned rail system by ill-co-ordinated policies toward transportation and ill-considered regulation after the need for it had largely passed. The process seems irreversible.

The Government as Proprietor or Operator

Now we come to the government ownership and operation of the means of production—socialism in the classic sense. It must be clear by now that most government intervention in the economic system of the United States is not of this nature.

We leave out of account governmentally-provided goods and services having large external benefits, such as national parks which could conceivably be operated by private enterprise if those benefits were forgone. Government operates the post office, which could also run in some sense as a private business, but the nature of the service would be greatly different from what it has been. We only briefly mention government housing (mostly municipal) which provides the poor with services they

cannot buy in the market and hence is in a class with welfare expenditures, even though local governments are gradually becoming the unwilling heirs to the entire growing problem of inner-city housing. Our
present interest is in those government activities which could be, or
perhaps still are in part, owned and operated by private business.

There are not many of them. Most are public utilities. Municipalities
in the United States often own and operate water systems, gas utilities,
public transportation systems such as the New York subway and bus
network. Less often, they own and operate electric utilities. In the early
1970s, about 10 per cent of the power produced in the United States
was generated in state and local government enterprise. State governments are most frequently involved in rural electric co-operatives.

Another 15 per cent or so of US electric power was produced by the
Federal government. It entered this activity first as a by-product of its
programmes of improving navigable waterways and controlling floods.
Power generated at the dams erected for these purposes was at first
always sold to private distributors. This policy changed in 1933, with
the advent of the Tennessee Valley Authority.

The TVA was a multiple-purpose programme of river basin development, including flood control, recreation, community infrastructure,
afforestation and agriculture as well as power generation. Electric power
quickly became its primary focus. In 1977, some 90 per cent of its
total investment of $9.1 billion was allocated to power production and
transmission, while 94 per cent of its operating costs of $1.7 billion
was incurred for that purpose.[20] Moreover, its power production now
came primarily from thermal and nuclear plants, not from the hydro-
electric installations. TVA has consistently sold this power, to municipal and other publicly-owned systems only, at wholesale rates that
were about half the national average per kilowatt hour. It required distributors to pass the low rates along to the public. In recent years, TVA
rates have risen sharply with fuel costs, but so have electric costs across
the nation. The result of its low rates was that electric power use per
capita in the Tennessee Valley, once among the lowest in the country,
has become one of the highest − rivalled only by that in the area of the
public power systems of the Pacific North-West.

Is the TVA a Model?

The TVA is famous throughout the world. Distinguished foreign visitors,
especially from less developed countries, usually pay it a visit. It has
been held up as a model of enlightened government intervention both
within and without the United States. Few questions can be raised about

its success in achieving its missions. However, its achievements do not necessarily offer a compelling argument for undertaking similar programmes of government enterprise elsewhere in the United States.

Conditions in the Tennessee Valley were highly favourable for a multiple-purpose project. It was one of the least developed parts of the country economically, and topographic conditions favoured river basin development. In the normal course of events the various Federal agencies responsible for flood control, navigation and agricultural development would probably have taken up the opportunities in the Tennessee Valley; the TVA did it faster and better, benefiting from economies of integration. It forced the pace of electrification much faster than the market would have done.

But were TVA power prices lower than the full economic cost of electric power? Anything can be subsidised, of course. The TVA has achieved low costs in thermal generation and transmission because of its large scale and use of the latest technology – advantages which would also be available to private firms of comparable size. TVA also gained an advantage from its position as the largest buyer of coal, by far, in the southern coal fields. It was able to keep the price of its coal needs at rock-bottom levels for some thirty years until the energy crisis broke over the nation after 1970. These too would have been private advantages for a private power company in its place.

The 'subsidy' issue concerns two types of cost: interest and taxes. In the early years, TVA got its capital funds from the Federal Treasury at very low interest rates. However, since 1953 it has had to raise its own new capital by selling its securities in the open market and has been obliged since 1959 to repay the US Treasury's investment over time. (Funds raised from investments by the public in TVA securities now account for over 20 per cent of its total capital.) Since then the only interest subsidy – a small one – has arisen from government guarantee of its obligations. As for taxes, TVA does make payments in lieu of taxes, but private utilities do not have to repay a major part of their capital investment as TVA does. Probably there remains some tax subsidy, but not a large one.

We have dwelt on these details because of the belief in some quarters that the TVA is the wave of the future, demonstrating the superiority of government-owned production not only in electric power but in complex and extensive enterprises of all types. Actually its conditions were very special though other river-basin projects have offered similar opportunities that by now have been almost fully realised. TVA demonstrates that government can produce electric power efficiently, and that it can manage large-scale multi-purpose public projects for the public benefit. TVA does not demonstrate that government can produce and distribute electric power more efficiently than private power companies can, under ordinary conditions, if the same rules apply to both. Nor does it presage inevitable conversion of electric power to government ownership.

When the government does operate electric power systems, divorced from multiple-purpose projects, it is likely to run them in much the same way. A comparative study of municipal and private systems recently found that government-operated power systems are likely to have somewhat simpler rate structures (with less discrimination) and slightly lower rates of return than private ones;[21] otherwise they seem to react similarly to the same circumstances. In fact, demands are frequently heard from the customers of publicly owned systems for better controls on them.

The Shadowland Industries

Some sectors of the American economy by now have become so pervaded by government intervention, so dependent on government, so greatly affected by public policy, that they are quasi-public while still maintaining the institutional forms of private enterprise. One of these sectors has already been described: public utilities and transportation, or the directly regulated industries. Not only do regulatory agencies get involved in management decisions on price, output, quality of service, investment and innovation; government is increasingly setting the environment and basis for such enterprises, providing the infrastructure, subsidising, channelling capital flows to them, dictating their rates and direction of expansion, and moving in to some degree as actual proprietor. Government intervenes, permanently, in their micro-structure, as it has not done for most other activities in the private sector. We shall consider two other sectors in the overlapping shadow of direct government control.

The Armaments and Aerospace Industry

Until World War I, governments produced a considerable part of their weapons in their own arsenals. The proliferation of weapons technology and its increased dependence on advanced chemistry, metallurgy, automotive and aerospace engineering, and electric and electronic systems has made self-production of arms and munitions increasingly impractical for governments in the western world where such resources are to be found principally in private industry. Instead, governments have turned to partnership and participation arrangements.

In the United States, there has developed since 1940 a whole sector of industry devoted to weapons and to the governmental needs of the space programme, which is civilian but similar to the military. The total is huge. The government spent over $40 billion on weapons and other military and aerospace procurement, research and development in Fiscal Year 1977. In addition to some old-line suppliers of equipment to the armed services, such as builders of naval vessels, there are seven full-line suppliers of aircraft (such as Lockheed, McDonnell-Douglas, General Dynamics) and a number of specialised manufacturers of aircraft and aerospace systems, major diversified firms (such as General Electric Company) that are heavily involved in defence as well as in civilian business, and many suppliers of electronic and aerospace subsystems that are almost wholly committed to defence procurement.

For a major weapons system such as the F-16 fighter plane, the government negotiates with a prime contractor—an aerospace manufacturer, or perhaps two or three. It discloses the performance characteristics it has in mind, and signs one or more research and development contracts for development of a suitable design and perhaps a prototype. Until this R & D contract has been completed, the product does not even exist. At that point, the government is 'locked in' to the developer of the design it chooses. This prime contractor almost always has to be chosen for the production contract. The prime contractor then subcontracts for components and subsystems with other suppliers, except that the government may do so directly for certain major components such as jet engines.

The significant things about this procurement process are: first, the buyer participates intimately in the definition and creation of what it is seeking to buy, and pays for much of the research cost and production facilities. Second, the major systems come along infrequently and in large 'lumps'. Third, the buyer and the seller negotiate with each other under such conditions that their alternatives are likely to be severely curtailed, at least for major systems. The prime contractor also may find itself as a buyer under similar conditions of bilateral monopoly when dealing with subcontractors. But these are not arm's length transactions; they require participation of the buyer in the seller's decisions and underwriting of much of the seller's risk by the buyer.

The foregoing observations do not apply to all procurement actions. The government continually tries to develop competitive options for 'reprocurement' of spare parts and components at arm's length, and sometimes it succeeds. Some of the components that it or its prime contractors buy, such as electronic communications devices, may be minor variations of civilian products sold 'off the shelf' and can be bought in a conventional market relationship. But the major systems and unique design equipment require an intertwined relationship of dependence, almost of symbiosis. The major defence and aerospace contractors and their satellites are not a 'private' sector in any meaningful sense of the word. The government is to a large extent the custodian of their fate and fortunes. On the other hand, they have a strong influence upon the defence sectors of the government. Some observers have expressed fears that the combination of defence industry and the military establishment can exercise too much influence on national policy, and that the civilian 'government' cannot easily control that combination. President Eisenhower himself, in his Farewell Address, warned of the power of the 'Military-Industrial Complex'.

Energy

As in many other countries, energy in the United States has become a leading economic problem in the 1970s. Government has responded with massive intervention in the energy sector. Some parts of the energy economy, such as electric power generation and natural gas transmission, had already long been regulated as public utilities, and other elements had been affected by various *ad hoc* policies. What is new in the 1970s is the elevation of energy policy, as a general approach, to a paramount problem for the national government.

Why should the government have rather suddenly perceived a general market failure in the energy sector? Needless to say, energy is fundamentally important to an advanced industrial economy, but that fact alone would not disqualify it from governance by markets and prices. The new approach resulted from two converging influences. One was the shift from surplus to scarcity in energy, both in the United States and the world at large, which caused the prices of all forms of energy to begin climbing steeply after 1969 and which led some circles in the government to perceive a pressing need for strict conservation of depleting energy resources over the long term. By itself, the shift from cheap to costly energy might not have called for a general mobilisation of policy, but it was accompanied by a second force: a growing perception of a problem of national security, which was suddenly thrown into high relief by the Arab oil embargo of 1973-74 and the subsequent four-fold increase in world oil prices. A market system cannot easily assimilate abrupt changes of large magnitude in fundamental economic parameters, and it is an unsuitable instrument for achieving national security. Hence the call for government intervention on a broad front.

It would be comforting to be able to report that energy policy in the US has made substantial progress toward solving these problems. It has not. For years the government has attempted to define the issues, to identify the means for achieving various ends, and to broker the many conflicting claims on the process from powerful interest groups. The first overall policy statement was 'Project Independence'[22] which at least began to define the objectives of policy after the weltering confusion of the embargo. Its overriding objective was to lessen US dependence on insecure oil imports by promoting domestic production of energy and converting from oil to other fuels. It was far too optimistic, but in any event there was no serious attempt to translate Project Independence into effective action.

Meanwhile the actual energy policy had become preoccupied with distributive questions. Even before the embargo, price ceilings were imposed on oil (they had long existed for natural gas moving in interstate commerce). All restrictions on oil imports were removed in April 1973, in the hope of keeping oil prices stable while domestic output continued to decline. Unfortunately, the huge increase in prices mandated by OPEC in December 1973 frustrated that hope. Government policy prevented domestic prices from rising in proportion. Instead, it administered a two-price and then (after 1975) a three-price system — a low price for 'old' oil produced from previously developed reserves; a higher price for 'new' domestic oil, newly discovered; and a still higher world price for imports. Obviously the resulting blended price did not restrain growth of domestic consumption as much as a uniform price floating on the world price would have done.

But the world price is a monopoly price, set by OPEC. Large numbers of the public, and some government offices, are convinced that the US oil industry is also a monopoly, and that the primary object of energy policy should be to allocate petroleum supplies directly and prevent any producer from making 'windfall' profits. Some elements of that approach could be discerned in the National Energy Plan announced by President Carter in April 1977.[23] The policy seemed to be predicated on the assumption that the US had developed most of its oil and gas supplies, and that government should see to it that they were equitably distributed and properly conserved, meanwhile offering strong tax incentives to convert to alternative fuels. Little consideration was given to increasing supplies of petroleum. For example, price ceilings were imposed on gas produced and consumed within a single state — over half of the total US output — which had previously been exempt. The government intended to substitute direct end-use allocation for allocation by price under conditions of shortage perpetuated by the ceiling.

Energy policy is concerned with more than petroleum, of course. Its scope has become vast. We cannot go into details. The Federal government in 1977 elevated energy policy and administration to Cabinet status in a new Department of Energy, recognising its emergence as a dominant economic problem. The government for several years has been rapidly substituting its judgment and vision of national needs, in large part, for the results of the market process. Its policy pervades the energy price system now at all points. The futures of coal development, nuclear energy, shale oil, offshore oil and gas development, imports, hydrogeneration and gasification of coal and other exotic technologies, as well as solar energy, are largely in its hands. The government has been repeatedly urged to enter the production of oil and gas from Federal lands itself. It has intervened massively in the exceedingly complex system of energy inputs and outputs in the industrial sector, and has begun to take over the job of distributing scarce supplies of fossil fuels.

We cannot say what solutions the government will find to the many conflicts that still remain; as yet the policy is not consistent. The point is, however, that the solutions and results, even the chaos if that is the outcome, will be largely imposed by the government. The private sector in energy is becoming but a means to those ends.

Regional Equity

Both military spending and energy have recently become involved in another rising issue for economic policy in the United States regional equity. The older economies of the north-east and middle west are declining. The 'Sunbelt' — the south-east, south-west, and far western regions — are booming. Population, capital investment, industry and employment are moving south and west, leaving the older regions to struggle with obsolescent industrial plant, decaying cities and a heavy burden of local public expenditures. As it happens, most military spending, both for bases and for procurement, is in the Sunbelt. Older regions have been demanding major compensatory shifts in Federal spending to benefit activities in those areas and to offset emigration.

Energy also generates controversy among regions. Most oil and gas is produced in the south-west. Government price control and allocations are likely to deprive these states not only of fuel supplies for industry but of some of the economic rents that they would otherwise have collected — a policy that the north-eastern states consider entirely just. Yet the north-eastern states have strongly resisted development of their offshore oil resources, the building of refinery capacity, construction of nuclear plants, etc. – at least as long as the Federal government will transfer supplies to them from elsewhere. Similar questions are in the offing regarding development and allocation of new coal supplies from the western states. Protection of the environment greatly complicates the issue. So far the government has not articulated a policy on regional equity for energy, but its intervention is producing results different from those of a market price system.

The Federal government has actually never had a consistent 'regional' policy. It has intervened with policies to help economically retarded areas such as Appalachia, which for a time in the 1960s benefited from industrial development subsidies and public works under an ambitious plan for rehabilitation. It has attempted to improve the economic environment in the rural areas of South Texas inhabited by impoverished Spanish-speaking migrant families. It has promoted river-basin development in the South, the Plains states and the Pacific North-West, as noted. It used to have a policy of subsidising frontier settlements through such devices as the Homestead Act (free land) and grants to railroads. The New Deal of the 1930s proclaimed the South (i.e. the South-East) as 'The Nation's Number One Economic Problem'; it attempted to narrow the income gap between that region and the rest of the country with such policies as price supports for cotton and aid for the bituminous coal industry. Government policy toward the Sunbelt, as well as toward other regional claimants on its country, will doubtless continue to be shaped piecemeal by the crosshauling of a myriad of special interests and a patchwork of political influences in all parts of the country.

Slouching Toward New Jerusalem

There is no apparent 'goal' in the spasmodic growth of government intervention in the US economy. Its aims are not Utopian. In so far as government intervenes to remedy some specific failure of the private system, however, it must perceive some norms by which to judge economic performance. Policy needs such norms by which to rationalise its acts, if for no better purpose.

The criteria for government intervention in the micro-structure of the economy really falls into two groups, suitably labelled 'efficiency' and 'equity'. No policy, perhaps, is entirely one or the other; but the norm of economic efficiency was the primary rationale for the older forms of government intervention. Anti-trust policy, regulation of public utilities, insurance of bank deposits, patent policy, even operation of multi-purpose river-basin projects, were designed to improve efficiency in allocation of resources and to maximise output of goods and services. They did not always succeed in those aims, of course. And even in the early days there were some regulations primarily for the purpose of protecting vested interests or raising the incomes of favoured groups—a type of policy which under some conditions can be loosely called the promotion of equity, though greater equality has not always been its aim.

Efficiency and equity may conflict. Economic efficiency is capable of a reasonably precise and objective definition. It is possible to determine in large measure where and how private markets have failed to produce efficiency, though (as pointed out earlier) it is not always possible to devise effective government remedies for such market failure. But everyone has his own definition of equity. It may range from proclamation of the paramount interests of the economic group to which one happens to belong, all the way to a crude egalitarianism which decrees that anything that reduces inequality in income distribution is good regardless of what it does to efficiency, i.e. to the size of what is to be distributed. Unfortunately, some specific policies and controls designed to improve equity have adverse effects on efficiency. The most familiar example, frequently encountered, is cartellisation: restriction on entry, minimum price regulation to protect and bolster the income of beneficiaries. Another is ceiling price control (as in oil markets) ostensibly to protect the poor from the adverse income-effects of market prices. Economists have often pointed out that tinkering with the prices of goods and services is a poor (inefficient) way to change the distribution of income, but policy increasingly is choosing that means to attain loosely defined ends of equity.

The ends of equity are increasingly pushing to the fore in the United States, superseding efficiency. Much of the new regulation, in fact, has ceased to take serious account of economic efficiency as a norm of policy. There is another side to this preoccupation with equity: some advocates of new-type regulation seem to regard the price system as a mere artifact, which can be manipulated at will for any social purpose. For them, the cause of equity is furthered by promoting the interests of all disadvantaged persons and groups, eroding the power of the 'establishment', protecting the individual against the 'system', and guaranteeing various kinds of 'rights' for people. Such equity, writ large, means fundamental institutional reform.

Galbraith's 'Socialist Imperative'

In the opinion of John Kenneth Galbraith, the American economy is

drifting inexorably toward a kind of socialist system which will still
leave some role for private enterprise but in which the government will
have taken over a large part of what is left of the private sector. It will
do this in two ways: first, by enlargement of the production of public
goods and services, traditionally the role of government. (Galbraith has
long thought that the public sector is too small and that private production of goods and services is wastefully large, because of an inherent
market bias against optimum funding of public services.) Second, the
government will be obliged to envelop those activities now in the private
sector that suffer from 'retarded development' in the market system —
for example, housing, medical services, local and rail transportation; he
advocates socialisation of the arts and enlarged intervention 'on behalf'
of agriculture — all of the 'weakest parts' of the economic system. (Writing in 1973, he did not mention the energy sector, but he probably
would now.)

Galbraith thinks that 'the new socialism is not ideological; it is
compelled by circumstance.'[24] The government will have to intervene
to sustain the weaker sectors, as the residual claimant. He does not
really answer the question whether economic performance would be
improved in those sectors if the government took them over. If he is
right, of course, we need only wait for the inexorable operation of
'historical circumstance', reserving a sense of uncertainty as to whether
the process will stop before the government has assimilated the whole
economy. It is of course true, however disagreeably so, that the US
government has already become an unwilling operator, in part, of
such things as housing and rail and local transportation.

National Economic Planning

In the United States, this phrase now refers not to a blueprint for comprehensive government operation of the economy but to a particular
approach to economic policy that is gaining popularity in governmental
circles. It was embodied in the Full Employment and Balanced Growth
Act of 1976 (the Humphrey-Hawkins Bill), which has not yet become
law.[25] That Bill advanced National Economic Planning as a supplement
to the Employment Act of 1946, which had committed the government
to planning of the macro-economic factors of the economy on a short-
run basis — money, interest, compensatory spending, and all of the familiar apparatus of fiscal and monetary policy.

The main emphasis of the National Economic Plan would be on full
employment. Its orientation would be to long-run planning; it would
seek 'balanced growth' to achieve long-run economic goals that the

administration would periodically determine. Its instruments would be not only the macro-economic tools of monetary policy and Federal budgeting but specific incentives. It would use taxes, subsidies, public works, grants-in-aid to state and local agencies, allocation of Federal funds, regulations, possibly selective price controls to influence capital allocation to particular industries and regions, promote labour mobility, training and employment, influence income distribution, etc. The national plan would extend into the micro-economic structure. No plan is contained in the proposed legislation — only provisions for the planning process.

The Current Drift: Countervailing Pressures

The current drift toward extension of government intervention is not unopposed. In recent years several national administrations have taken an official position in favour of deregulation of some sectors such as transportation and reducing the scope and burden of regulation in others.[26] President Carter was elected in 1976 on a platform that included a strong attack on red tape and mountainous paper work inflicted on the public by regulation. Moreover, many of the experts on regulation — academic economists and political scientists, and dedicated public servants who have practised regulation — are highly sceptical of its claims to perfect or even to improve the economic process.

The benefits of government intervention defy measurement, especially when they consist of promotion of such intangibles as 'equity'. We should not overlook the costs. Federal regulatory agencies alone spent almost $4 billion in fiscal 1977 on regulatory activities. Table 3.2 gives current figures for the leading Federal regulatory agencies. Table 3.3 shows the budgeted outlays for support and intervention by the Federal government in one major economic sector: agriculture.

Table 3.2:   Direct Costs of Principal Federal Regulatory Agencies Fiscal Year 1977

Agency	Regulatory Budget ($ million)
Banking and Finance	
Commodity Futures Trading Commission	14
Comptroller of the Currency	89[a]
Federal Deposit Insurance Corporation	83[a]
Federal Home Loan Bank Board	105[a]
Federal Reserve Board	700[a]
Securities and Exchange Commission	56

Agency	Regulatory Budget ($ million)
Competition and Trade	
Anti-trust Division	27
Civil Aeronautics Board	22
Federal Communications Commission	60
Federal Maritime Commission	9
Federal Trade Commission	55
Interstate Commerce Commission	57
Employment and Discrimination	
Equal Employment Opportunity Commission	70
National Labor Relations Board	83
Pension & Benefit Welfare Programs	21
Office of Federal Contract Compliance	15
Energy and Environment[b]	
Corps of Engineers[c]	35
Environmental Protection Agency[c]	865
Federal Energy Administration[c]	156
Federal Power Commission	42
Nuclear Regulatory Commission	256
Safety and Health	
Consumer Product Safety Commission	39
Federal Aviation Administration[c]	228
Food & Drug Administration	240
Occupational Safety & Health Administration	128
Mining Enforcement & Safety Administration	95
National Highway Traffic Safety Administration	100
	3,650

Notes:
[a] Financed by fees from regulated industry.
[b] In August 1977, several of these agencies were combined into a new Department of Energy.
[c] Regulatory expenditures only.

Source: Business Week, 4 April 1977, pp. 52-6.

Table 3.3: Budgeted Funds of Agricultural Control and Support Agencies, Fiscal Year 1977

	($ millions)
Agricultural Stabilisation and Conservation Service[a]	157.9
Animal and Plant Health Inspection Service	394.3
Farmers Home Administration	161.4
Federal Crop Insurance Corporation	16.4
Soil Conservation Service	215.3
Rural Electrification Administration	21.3

	($ millions)
Agricultural Marketing Service	57.1
Commodity Credit Corporation	943.9
Total for above agencies	1,967.6

ªNet of transfers from other Federal agencies.

Source: The Budget of the United States Government, Fiscal Year 1977. Support services primarily for the foreign market not shown.

To the Federal costs are added the considerable costs of compliance that regulation places on the economy. The indirect costs consist not only of business expenses of paperwork, higher product costs, costs of effluent control, etc., but also of the distortions in resource allocation that may result when the government supports prices or limits entry to markets. That some government intervention has generated much public benefit can hardly be doubted; but the overall ratio of benefit to cost is a mystery.

The public temper in the United States is uncertain. Doctrinaire socialism has practically no role in public opinion. Yet the public has lost much of the faith that it once had in the free market and private enterprise. While expressing antagonism to government regulation in general, it is prone to demand governmental intervention to deal with any specific problem that comes up, whether or not the government is likely to have a solution. The government is likely to become further enmeshed in the structure of the economy as new and more complex problems arise and elicit new demands for intervention.

The foregoing description indicates how far that process has already gone, even in an economic system which is still considered to be largely privately controlled. Moreover, this intervention is over and above the huge presence of government in providing public services, taxing and exercising control of the macro-economic factors of the economic system. It is supplementary to and mainly beyond the scope of the 'welfare state' in the usual meaning of that phrase. It has become so pervasive that we would now have great difficulty in finding definite boundaries between the public sector and the private sector in the economy of the United States.

Notes

1. Figures compiled by US Department of Commerce and reported in the *Federal Reserve Bulletin*. In addition, governments (mostly the Federal government)

affected income transfers of over $200 billion.

2. *Standard Oil Co. of New Jersey v. US*, 221 U.S. 1 (1911). Several other 'trusts' were broken up at about this time.

3. This principle was laid down in several anti-trust decisions, notably in *US v. United Shoe Machinery Corp.*, 110 F. Supp. 295 (1953).

4. The case against the eight oil companies was actually initiated by the Federal Trade Commission (see below). For an excellent comprehensive survey of the US anti-trust law, cases, and economic principles applying to them, see Phillip Areeda, *Antitrust Analysis: Problems, Text, Cases*, 2nd Edition (Little, Brown & Company, Boston, 1974).

5. This statute, passed in 1936, is actually an amendment of Section 2 of the Clayton Antitrust Act of 1914.

6. See, for instance, M.A. Adelman, *A & P: A Study in Price-Cost Behavior and Public Policy* (Harvard University Press, Cambridge, Mass., 1959).

7. Data from US Bureau of the Census, organised and presented by James V. Koch, *Industrial Organization and Prices* (Prentice-Hall, Inc., Englewood Cliffs, New Jersey, 1974), pp. 155, 158. Some industries still showing high concentration in 1972 for the largest four sellers were cellulosic fibres (96 per cent), flat glass (92 per cent), primary lead (93 per cent), turbine generators (90 per cent), electric lamps (90 per cent) and motor vehicles (93 per cent – not including imported automobiles).

8. The first regulation of industries as public utilities actually was regulation by the State of Illinois of railroads and grain elevators, sanctioned by the Supreme Court in *Munn v. Illinois*, 94 US 113 (1877).

9. For example, George J. Stigler and Claire Friedland, 'What Can Regulators Regulate? The Case of Electricity', *Journal of Law and Economics*, Vol. 5, No. 2 (October 1962), pp. 1-16; Thomas G. Moore, 'The Effectiveness of Regulation of Electric Utility Prices', *Southern Economic Journal*, Vol. 36, No. 4 (April 1970), pp. 365-75.

10. For a survey of this question see William J. Baumol and Alvin K. Klevorick, 'Input Choices and Rate-of-Return Regulation: An Overview of the Discussion', *The Bell Journal of Economics and Management Science*, Vol. 1, No. 2 (Autumn 1970), pp. 162-90. The viewpoint in question is frequently identified as the Averch-Johnson Thesis.

11. George J. Stigler, 'The Theory of Economic Regulation', *The Bell Journal of Economics and Management Science*, Vol. 2, No. 2 (April 1971), pp. 3-21; Sam Peltzman, 'Toward a More General Theory of Regulation', *Journal of Law and Economics*, Vol. 19, No. 2 (August 1976), pp. 211-40.

12. See Merton J. Peck, 'A Competitive Policy for Transportation?' in Almarin Phillips (ed.), *Perspectives on Antitrust Policy* (Princeton University Press, Princeton, NJ, 1965).

13. For an interesting example see E.W. Kitch, M. Isaacson, and D. Kasper, 'The Regulation of Taxicabs in Chicago', *Journal of Law and Economics*, Vol. 14, No. 2 (October 1971), pp. 285-350.

14. See Harvey J. Levin, 'Spectrum Allocation Without Market', *American Economic Review*, Vol. 60, No. 2 (May 1970), pp. 209-218, and discussion papers, pp. 219-224.

15. Roger G. Noll, Merton J. Peck, and John J. McGowan, *Economic Aspects of Television Regulation* (The Brookings Institution, Washington, 1973), Chapter 7. VHF (Very High Frequency) is assigned to commercial television between 54 and 216 MHz; UHF (Ultra High Frequency) between 470 and 890 MHz.

16. Further discussion is offered by William Lilley III and James C. Miller III, 'The New "Social Regulation"', *The Public Interest*, No. 47 (Spring 1977), pp. 49-61.

100   *The United States*

17. Little has been said recently about strengthening regulation to prevent consumer fraud, shoplifting, damage to rental housing, etc. – those activities in which the consumer appears as villain rather than as hero. See Martin Bronfenbrenner, 'The Consumer', in J.W. McKie (ed.), *Social Responsibility and the Business Predicament* (The Brookings Institution, Washington, 1974), pp. 178-82.

18. The agencies performing these functions are, respectively, the Federal Deposit Insurance Corporation (FDIC) and the Federal Savings and Loan Insurance Corporation (FSLIC).

19. FNMA was a Federal agency from 1938 to 1968; it still is subject to some forms of government control, but is substantially independent. Federal housing subsidies are now handled through an agency created in 1968, the Government National Mortgage Association (GNMA). Most Federal agencies conducting lending and insurance operations to support the private sector obtain their funds by borrowing from the Federal Financing Bank, created in 1973 to co-ordinate Federal and Federally-assisted borrowings from the public. The Federal Financing Bank has become the vehicle through which most Federal agencies finance credit market instruments, agency securities, guaranteed obligations, etc.

20. Figures from *The Budget of the United States Government*, Fiscal Year 1977 (US Government Printing Office, Washington, 1976).

21. Sam Peltzman, 'Pricing in Public and Private Enterprises: Electric Utilities in the United States', *Journal of Law and Economics*, Vol. 14, No. 1 (April 1971), pp. 109-47.

22. See Federal Energy Administration, *Project Independence Report* (US Government Printing Office, Washington, November 1974).

23. 'The National Energy Plan' was published by the Executive Office of the President on 29 April 1977.

24. J.K. Galbraith, *Economics and the Public Purpose* (Houghton Mifflin, Boston, 1973), p. 277.

25. The text of the 1976 Bill is given in *Challenge*, Vol. 19, No. 2 (May/June 1976), pp. 56-69, which also includes an explanation and defence by Senator Hubert H. Humphrey, 'The New Humphrey-Hawkins Bill', pp. 21-29. A watered-down version of the Bill, merely declaring a commitment to 'goals' of full employment rather than setting mandatory standards and establishing systematic controls for that purpose, received favourable action in Congress in 1978.

26. For example, several Bills have been introduced in Congress to remove some of the Federal regulations on scheduled inter-state airlines, beginning with the Aviation Act of 1975. The latest version, the so-called Cannon-Kennedy Bill, would permit the airlines to compete in price within a range from 10 per cent above to 35 per cent below the July 1977 levels, and would allow airlines to enter new domestic markets (already served by other lines) at a limited rate. The proposals have been vehemently opposed by most regulated airlines, though not by all. Other Bills would have permitted more freedom of pricing and easier entry in freight transportation. The established firms in the motor freight industry, as well as the interested trade unions, have fought the proposals to a standstill. These Federal initiatives to reduce regulation have been supported by both Republican and Democratic administrations.

4 GOVERNMENT INTERVENTION IN THE ECONOMY OF SWEDEN

H.G. Jones

Political Background

With a population of only eight million, Sweden has a small economy
with natural resources restricted to iron ore, timber and water power,
yet in the twentieth century it has created a gross domestic product
per capita amongst the highest in the world.[1] At the same time, Sweden
has pioneered a number of progressive legislative measures that in the
main have arguably reacted favourably on the growth of the economy.

To appreciate the significance of the legislation, it is necessary to
examine, at any rate cursorily, the political system in Sweden.
Proportional representation is the method of electing the members
of the house of parliament, known as the Riksdag. Since 1971 there
has been only one chamber which now has 349 members. One of the
features of PR is that major changes in party representation leading to
frequent changes in government are less likely than in a two main party
system working with a simple majority result in individual constituencies.
Continuity of government and of policy are therefore possible. One of
the main universal criticisms of PR is that whenever it is applied often
no single party can command a clear majority in parliament so that
government is by coalition, also often with a small majority: legislation
that is intensely partisan can then be difficult but not impossible to pass.
A dialogue between the shades of opinion in different political parties
can occur in order to establish common ground: bitter polarisation can
be avoided and given the will the system can work well.

Sweden has exhibited all the characteristics of PR. The Social Democrats were in office continuously (apart from 100 days) from 1932 to
1976, sometimes with the support of the few Communists in the Riksdag and sometimes in coalition with the Centre Party. The majority
has never been large and for the four elections (at three yearly intervals)
ending in 1976, the Socialist share of the vote has been slowly declining.
Table 4.1 shows that the Centre Party requires the support of the Lib-
erals and Conservatives to govern. Many of the policies of the Socialists
have been seen to be successful and in fact there is now a measure of
general support both in the Riksdag and in the country for many of the
established lines of development. A major change in direction seems un-

likely, but a slowing down in the rate of change is almost certain to occur.

Table 4.1:   Distribution of Seats in the Riksdag

	1973		1976	
Communists	19	} 175	17	} 169
Social Democrats	156		152	
Centre Party	90	} 175	86	} 180
Liberals	34		39	
Conservatives	51		55	
Totals	350		349	

In the 1973 election, there was an equal number of representatives of the right and of the left so the number of seats was reduced by one for future elections. Minority groups are not represented because to win a seat, a party must win at least 12 per cent of the vote in a particular constituency or 4 per cent of the national vote (by which 39 members of the Riksdag are elected).

Stability of economic purpose is also aided by the method adopted to administer the laws in Sweden. Cabinet ministers are responsible for the formulation of policy but decision is a collective responsibility of the cabinet as a whole; nor are the ministers responsible for the day to day administration which is in the care of a number of bureaucracies each of which is vested with considerable authority within its own sphere of interest. The bureaucracy is headed by a director general, appointed by the cabinet for a fixed, renewable term. As well as having sufficient staff to discharge the function, the director general receives advice from a board of usually about a dozen people representing the various parties concerned. For example, in the Labour Market Board, which is one of the most effective as well as one of the most influential of the bureaucracies, the governing board is made up from representatives of the employers (3), the blue collar unions (3), salaried staff unions (2), the professional unions (1), together with two other representatives for particular interests. Government control is through the annual budget.

This system has the advantage that the central administration is largely in the hands of professionals who can carry out their duties without undue heed to the vagaries of ministers who in their climb to political fame may change office at frequent intervals. The present generation of top bureaucrats has arguably behaved responsibly and with considerable competence. A bureaucratic system, however, always possesses the inherent danger arising from the concentration of State power in the hands of a few unelected individuals. Recognising this factor, the Swedes invented the office of ombudsman in 1809; a few countries in recent years have followed suit.

In Sweden, there are now seven ombudsmen, three of whom operate in special areas such as consumer protection. In the case of the press an ombudsman is sponsored by the press organisations themselves. The four general ombudsmen are concerned with the administration of the law at all levels. They are usually prominent judges appointed by the Riksdag to the office of ombudsman for renewable terms of four years. Their chief duty is to see that the courts and administrators do not infringe the law particularly in so far as the freedom and security of the individual are concerned.

The ombudsman, or some of their legally trained staff, will investigate *every* complaint made against the abuse of power. They can also initiate investigations and can make visits of inspection anywhere in the country. Prosecutions in a court or a tribunal can be instituted by the ombudsmen, but more usually an offender is reported to a superior for appropriate action to be taken. A detailed annual report is also presented to the Riksdag. The independence of the ombudsmen is acknowledged on all sides as being a major contributory factor in the build up of public confidence in the administrative machine; the existence of this confidence no doubt in turn helps the typical Swede to be remarkably law-abiding.

The office of Attorney General also exists in Sweden. The appointee is again a judge who has duties and powers similar to the ombudsmen but is responsible for overseeing the interests of the State.

In addition to the national administration, there is a network of services provided by 23 county councils and 278 municipal or district councils, all financed from central income tax and all elected on the same day as the Riksdag. Each county has a governor appointed by the cabinet. The activities of all these bodies come within the surveillance of the ombudsmen.

Formulation of Legislation

Anyone in Sweden can initiate action leading to new legislation. In practice, the action is most likely to be initiated by a body with sufficient resources to present a reasoned and well documented case in favour of the suggested new law. The blue collar unions have been prominent in this area, especially in the 1970s, when there has been pressure for considerable legislation in industrial relations. The employers' organisations have been more defensive but can clearly press the case for legislation if they so wished—in fact, the employers believe negotiation is preferable to externally imposed legislation. The ombudsmen can make recommendation but the usual source is the government or the opposition with individual members of the Riksdag rarely promoting private members' Bills.

If a proposal is acceptable in principle to the government, it is usually examined in detail through the appointment of a Royal Commission of Inquiry with specific terms of reference and a reporting back date quoted in months rather than years. Membership of a commission is made up of representatives of bodies likely to be affected together with a sprinkling of politicians from both sides of the house. The commission produces a report for general publication assessing both the advantages and disadvantages of the proposal and concludes with recommendations; in controversial matters, the report will probably contain a substantial amount of expert evidence and a lengthy debate before reaching a conclusion. There have been suggestions that with major issues, particularly those affecting the economy or those of an irreversible nature, there should be financial support and, if need be, official backing for a parallel 'lightweight' inquiry charged with the task of examining a range of alternative strategies in considerably less detail than the 'heavyweight' official commission which in general is only concerned with one approach: so far, the parallel exercises, when they have been mounted, can only submit evidence to the royal commission.

A draft Bill is next prepared by the legal department of an appropriate ministry in the light of the Report of the Commission of Inquiry but it must be admitted that the government will sometimes omit recommendations that are not in tune with its general philosophy. The draft Bill is then submitted for informed comment under the so-called 'remiss systems' to a number of official and quasi-official bodies—SACO, the union for professional workers, regarded its first inclusion in this list as a recognition of its growing power in the market place, but at the same time views its responsibilities seriously and comments each year on about 200 new measures. If a Bill is concerned with criminal or civil law, the government can also seek a statement of opinion from the Law Council. All the comments and opinions are examined carefully before the Bill is finalised by the appropriate ministry for presentation to a committee of the Riksdag where, of course, further amendment might be made before finally being approved by the Riksdag.

Although the system sounds complicated, it works smoothly and unexpectedly quickly. It has the merit of providing a filter for the elimination or improvement of unsatisfactory legislation and moreover so many people have been involved that the law when passed has a good chance of being generally accepted and therefore more readily obeyed. One point of criticism is heard: because of the flood of legislation, a new tendency has been for much of the consultative process to take place within one or other of the ministries with a corresponding reduction in the interplay of public opinion, a move that is deplored in certain quarters.

Swedish law is based essentially on the Germanic system but extensive codification is largely avoided. While written laws form the basis of the legal code, the clauses of the law are often expressed in broad terms of intent: interpretation of a clause is then made by the courts in order to establish precedents upon which later judgements are founded. The interpretation is greatly influenced by the preamble to the statutes and by the reported investigations of the royal commission.

It is not proposed to dwell upon the Swedish Court system which is in many respects similar to that in other countries of the Western world. However, two points are worthy of mention. There are a number of courts which discharge specialised functions and have their own procedures; the Labour Court and the Market Court are examples that will be discussed later. Secondly, the dividing line between the judiciary and the administration is much less firmly defined in Sweden than in other countries both in respect of the duties they perform and in the movement of personnel between them.

The Labour Market Board and the Economy

The Social Democratic party in Sweden has been fortunate in having within its ranks a succession of competent economists: it has been equally fortunate for Sweden that their advice has been heeded. They have maintained that the best way of achieving rising standards for the workers is through the creation of a prosperous economy, and in this policy they have had the co-operation of the unions. As a generalisation, this policy would be acceptable in many countries but the Swedes have paid it more than lip service by also accepting its corollaries. Strikes are regarded as an injurious method of settling disputes. Industrial investment to obtain modern levels of productivity is an essential factor and is more forthcoming in profitable situations that encourage a measure of self financing. Flexibility on the part of both management and the labour force to meet changing conditions is equally as important as the

investment. Full employment is a desirable end but jobs must be productive: full employment within a buoyant economy is less than 100 per cent
because jobs will change and there will always be some people in the
state of moving into more productive jobs.

The previous paragraph expresses in compressed form the principles
that have governed the Swedish economy for half a century. The success
of the policy can be seen from the growth in Gross Domestic Product
that has risen to a value in 1973 of $5910 per capita, and was only
exceeded in Western Europe by Switzerland. (See Table 4.2.) Sweden
having created a prosperous economy, can afford to increase the
workers' share as can be seen from the labour costs which over the
last twenty years have increased by nearly 300 per cent during which
period the GDP rose by about 40 per cent. The social conditions of
employment have also improved in a distinctive fashion over the same
period.

Suitable legislation to facilitate the operation of the principles has
been passed by the Riksdag. A main instrument to influence the economy has been the Investment Funds for which the first legislation was
passed in 1938, with subsequent modification in 1947, 1955, 1963 and
1974. The current position is that every Swedish company can allocate
for capital investment up to 40 per cent of its pretax profits in any year
(tax free). The main condition attached to the tax concession is that
the timing, the nature and location of the investment must be approved
by the Labour Market Board.[2] As a possible sanction against firms that
might be tempted to proceed without the Board's approval, 46 per cent
of the investment allocation must be deposited in an interest free account
in the Swedish Central Bank: infringement leads to the loss of the tax
concession (but after five years no approval is required).

1974 was a boom year in Sweden with many companies recording
higher than usual profits (which in fact to the shareholders are relatively
low in Sweden): the Riksdag passed a decree that 15 per cent of all pretax profits for that year in excess of £100,000 *had* to be allocated to
the Investment Funds for eventual use in the provision of buildings and
equipment. A further 20 per cent of pretax profits in excess of £10,000
had to be set aside in a special fund in each company for improvement
to the working environment (up to a maximum of £7m).

Depreciation allowances to be set against tax are generous in order
to encourage investment. Any capital investment, including buildings,
financed out of tax-free monies must be depreciated fully in the first
twelve months; a further 10 per cent of the capital released from the
Investment Funds can be set against the tax returns for the following

financial year – this concession also applies to stocks which in recent years can be financed out of the Investment Funds. Stock making in lean years is encouraged by legislation enabling inventory, of either in-process or finished goods form, to be written down to 40 per cent of value or cost, whichever is the lesser, and the other 60 per cent shown as an untaxed reserve. All other investments must for tax purposes be depreciated fully over the first five years, either uniformly or on a sliding scale which allows 45 per cent depreciation in the first year.

Most Swedish companies utilise the facilities offered by the Investment Funds although there are instances of firms after a period of heavy investment being content to use the depreciation allowances to the full in order to obtain working capital. The net effect is that the Labour Market Board controls about one eighth of the total investment of the country: in some industries, such as mining and general manufacturing, the figures in which the Labour Market Board has a voice is of the order of 25 per cent. In addition, the biggest single investor is the National Pension Fund, controlled by another government agency which, without sacrificing its own interests, works closely with the Labour Market Board.

Socialists generally believe in the virtues of the concept of planned control, and in particular in the control of the economy in order to maintain full employment in times of recession as well as in boom periods. The simplest version of the control is to grant release of the Investment Funds in times of slump and to withhold approval for a firm to spend its own money in boom periods. Sweden has experienced a cycle of boom and slump of roughly four years periodicity starting with the slump of 1958. To meet these conditions, the Labour Market Board has acted predictably even if at times the response has been a little late to be fully effective. It is not easy to control an economy and it is not easy to recognise the early signs of an approaching recession; however in 1971-73, the timing seems to have been better which suggests

Table 4.2: Gross Domestic Product per capita of Seven Developed
Countries in 1973

United States	$6,200
Sweden	$5,910
W. Germany	$5,320
France	$4,540
Australia	$4,350
Japan	$3,630
United Kingdom	$3,060

Source: World Tables 1976, World Bank

the Board is benefiting from experience. As part of the warning system firms must advise the Board six months in advance of intended layoffs.

During recent recessions, the Riksdag has been prepared to make money available for relief work on an increasing scale. The responsible agency is again the Labour Market Board: great care is devoted to ensure that the relief work results in a meaningful output. Civic amenities such as sport complexes or hospitals are sometimes created and in other places a modern road system is being constructed to replace miles of unsurfaced tracks.

To be effective either in relief work or in the utilisation of Investment Funds, it is necessary for detailed plans to be in a state of preparedness at all times. It is a feature both of the Labour Market Board and of Swedish industry that short-term forward planning and longer-term strategic planning receive substantial commitment because of their own merits and also in order to meet recession problems. In industry, a strong control element, usually through the budget, is associated with the planning function.

An indication of the effectiveness of the national policy can be obtained from the unemployment figures. The typical level of unemployment in Sweden is about 1.5 per cent of the working population.[3] For single quarters only in 1972, 1973 and 1974, unemployment rose to just over 3 per cent while throughout 1975 and 1976 — which was a difficult year for most of the developed world — unemployment in Sweden was never higher than 1.7 per cent. Moreover, during the years 1973 to 1976, the numbers in employment actually rose by 6 per cent.

About 5 per cent of the working population consists of immigrants, a figure that has been more or less static since 1970; many of the immigrant workers are from other Scandinavian countries (with Finland predominating) with whom Sweden has reciprocal agreements for unrestricted access for employment and for educational facilities. The rising number in employment is largely accounted for by the number of women entering the labour market which now consists of about 40 per cent women. To some extent the trend has been favoured by the growth of the service industries which have traditionally been a female preserve but many women are also employed in a productive capacity, on the shop floor of industry, for instance as fitters or welders, under conditions of equality with men. Equality of the sexes in the eyes of the law has existed in Sweden since 1960 but it must be admitted that the proportion of women in the higher posts is still relatively few — estimated on some bases as about 1 in 15 — although higher than, say, in the UK.

In spite of determined efforts both by the National Board of Education and also by the schools to eliminate inequality through sex education, and through the teaching of wood and metal working to girls, and the teaching of domestic science and home nursing to boys, the bias to the traditional occupations still persists in school leavers. For example, in 1973, 63 per cent of the new students in the arts faculties at universities were women but in the mathematical and scientific faculties there were only 29 per cent women. Similarly, a lower proportion of women work in forestry, mining or heavy manufacturing. Job opportunities for women may thus vary greatly from one geographical area to another. The presence of child-care facilities to support working mothers is also variable being almost non-existent in the remoter and possibly more conservative areas. The government has tried on an experimental basis to compensate for these inequalities by insisting that grant aided industries (a few in the northern deprived areas) must employ 40 per cent men in typical female occupations: thus males can be seen operating sewing machines in some textile firms. This is consistent with the philosophy that the man should be equally involved in the responsibility of running the home—the time off for the birth of a child or for looking after a sick child can, for example, be divided between the man and the woman if both are in work. Such is the theory—the practice, however, seems more frequent among the better educated than with shop floor personnel.

Another aspect of the socialist philosophy of equality is found in the desire to integrate the handicapped into society, and particularly into gainful employment. It is believed that the description 'handicapped' is a relative term that covers a wide range of skills that should be tapped for the good of the community. As the agency responsible, the Labour Market Board runs special training courses and then offers grants of up to £3,500 per person if it is necessary to modify an industrial work place and to provide special tools to meet the capabilities of a particular individual. While there are a few sheltered workshops, the aim is for the handicapped person to work in competitive situations for which the State is prepared to pay 40 per cent of the salary. A considerable effort is spent in breaking down the mental barrier to successful integration that often exists in the minds of the handicapped themselves—who are usually described officially as 'the hard to place in employment'. During a recession, these people are often hard hit, so the Board will mount special relief work for them—7,400 people so benefited in 1972.

Restructuring and Redeployment

In addition to the well defined processes of consultation already discussed,

Swedish governments have been assisted in their choice of action by another Swedish characteristic, namely the existence within the confederation of blue collar unions (LO) of a capable economic research section. These economists are commissioned by the quinquennial congress of LO to undertake studies into specific questions, the research culminating in a substantial report to a later congress. One such investigation, headed by Dr Rudolf Meidner, on 'Economic Expansion and Structural Change', reported in 1961, was a remarkable statement of policy that found wide acceptance and was adopted for action by LO and by successive governments.

The report recognised that rising living standards for the workers could only be achieved through rises in productivity, and that steady gains in productivity would surely require the restructuring of some parts of industry. Weak and unprofitable firms could not afford to pay high wages, and should be allowed to perish: the workers would have to be absorbed in other firms which could afford high wages. To obtain economies of scale, some works would have to close in order to concentrate production elsewhere. Other firms would have to reorganise their product mix quite dramatically to be able to pay the high wages demanded for the workers. In other companies, more work might be accomplished with less manpower because of new methods. The way forward was for the workers to accept change and to adapt to change. Job mobility and geographical mobility might be required from the workers as an essential part of the modernisation process.

Employers in many countries would reason in this vein, as indeed did the employers' confederation, SAF, in Sweden. But it is unusual to find *unions* expressing the issues so clearly and accepting the consequences as far as their members are concerned. The unions were prepared to collaborate with the employers to attain these ends but insisted that redeployment must be as palatable as possible. The Labour Market Board was empowered by the government to provide substantial practical retraining courses with adequate maintenance for the participants. Mobility allowances were also payable by the Board both to attend interviews and to examine the facilities of the infrastructure before moving, and also to assist in the actual removal to new living places—which very probably would be in newly constructed flats. Redeployment and its associated factors have accounted for more than half of the budget of the Labour Market Board.

The result has been that redeployment has been exceptionally successful. The increased efficiency, largely brought about by some form of restructuring, has enabled rising labour costs to be contained without loss of competitiveness. The number of companies involved in mergers or takeovers has been rising steadily since 1950 and in 1976, 480 companies were so involved. Government action has been minimal with little suggestion of anti-trust feeling; the philosophy has been similar to that of management and unions. An unforeseen effect has been the disadvantages of migration to the larger conurbations. Forestry and agriculture through major mechanisation over twenty years have increased their output but halved the labour force. Small town companies have ceased to exist. The work has been concentrated in a few big units, and the population of necessity has followed the work. Remote parts of the country were rapidly depopulated with little prospect of work for the few who remained.

For many years, this trend was regarded as an acceptable price to be paid for the generally improved living standards enjoyed by the bulk of the populace, more than 25 per cent of whom were concentrated on the three main conurbations of Stockholm, Gothenberg and Malmö, with about eight other urban areas accounting for a further high proportion of the population.

By the mid 1960s there were misgivings that the trend towards increased urbanisation had gone too far and the Labour Market Board tried to stop further movement in this direction. In the 1970s, there has been a positive reaction in the form of a 'green movement' demanding a marked reversal in the pattern of the migration. Opposition is also developing to restructuring. The average cost of employing a person in manufacturing industry has been rising rapidly, 22 per cent in 1975 alone, but there is likely to be strong 'grass roots' opposition to restructuring just to meet rising costs on the grounds that the social costs to the workers have been too high in the past. It may be the only acceptable restructuring in the future will be that associated with creating employment in the depopulated areas.

Government action has been through the Labour Market Board. Investment Funds for use in the 'deprived areas' have been released at all times provided the project appeared viable. Pressure has been applied through the Investment Funds to firms wishing to expand in the main conurbations, for them to consider other regions. Substantial grants have been available to firms creating new jobs in these areas, and special training allowances have also been payable. Some success has been obtained by directing industry in this fashion, but extra costs can be thrown on the firms so involved and one or two of the ventures have collapsed.

Depopulation of the North of Sweden was an election issue in 1973 because of a socialist proposal to establish in the county of Norrbotten a major steel complex known as Steelworks 80, at a cost of around £100m. A small state-owned steel making unit already existed on the site of Lulea and had not been over profitable: the proposal was to make substantial increases in steel making capacity and to install a range of rolling equipment to make Sweden self-sufficient in mild steel with a considerable capacity available for export markets. This ambitious proposal has met strong opposition and has been subject to a series of reductions in its scope. Part of the criticism is that this major invest-ment could more usefully be made elsewhere. The opposition has not been directed against State activity in the commercial field but against the economics of this particular proposal. One of the arguments is that although private enterprise has been very successful in the manufacture and sale of products in the special steels area, the home market is not big enough to sustain the economies of scale necessary for mild steel to be successful, and since all the coke (or coking coal) would need to be imported, why build a plant nearly in the Arctic Circle? The unanswered question is whether Sweden can sustain a mild steel industry and if so, should it be structured with a mix of State and private ownership and expertise?

The socialists in Sweden have rarely advocated an extension of State ownership as a main instrument for preserving jobs. Only about 6 per cent of industry is owned by the State, and it is expected to be efficient and profitable. The responsible government agency, *Statsföretag*, oper-ates in the same way as a public company with a number of subsidiaries, the only difference being that it may take over a declining company while a search is made for profitability through rationalisation or integ-ration with other production units, or sometimes for the injection of new and possibly risky capital.[4] Continued unprofitability is not accepted. At times, the governing board of Statsföretag has taken an independent line against government pressure to extend this kind of activity. Overheads are kept to a minimum — as a holding headquarters Statsföretag is manned by only 50 people in an organisation employing a total of 46,000: this is possible because of a policy of decentralised decision making. There is also considerable emphasis in Statsföretag on worker involvement but in practice the degree of involvement can be equalled by many private companies. The state and municipalities together own 95 per cent of the country's railroad system, 25 per cent of the area under forestry but 42 per cent of the electrical supply is undertaken by private companies.

For a number of years Statsföretag has had within its control several shipyards which have operated successfully. A new tendency occurred in

1976 when, because of the recession in world shipbuilding, two major shipyards in Sweden approached the government for financial support; the effect of this has been to give the State a controlling interest in all the major yards except one, Kockums at Malmö in the southern tip of the country. Sweden is second only to Japan in the tonnage launched each year so the new development is of significance.

The state-owned Swedish Investment Bank was established in 1967 with £100m credit and no other resources. Its objectives exclude participation in conventional banking activities except that of supplying finance to industrial companies; the bank's particular remit is to finance new and possibly risky ventures, preferably those containing an innovatory element which might cause difficulty in raising capital on the market. Making a profit was a secondary consideration but none the less only those enterprises showing a viable prospect would be supported. By 1975, the bank was showing a return on total assets of 1 per cent, with outstanding loans amounting to £600m. Throughout this period there has been no intervention by any member of the government.

From the nature of its activities, some of the companies financed by the Investment Bank can be expected to run into financial and maybe practical difficulties; the Bank is prepared to protect its interests by taking over an ailing company, either reorganising the management and production methods into profitable channels ready for sale to new owners, or arranging for liquidation. At any one time, the Bank can be running half a dozen industrial companies with a rescue rate of about 1 in 5. Before a loan is granted, the Bank insists on adequate market research, and if necessary will itself undertake this task.

The activities of the Investment Bank in encouraging new industrial ventures or major expansion of existing facilities can be interpreted as action to slow down the migration of workers from productive industry to service functions. In the early 1960s, 26 per cent of the working population were employed in the service industries but by the mid 1970s, the number so employed had increased to 33 per cent of a working population that had itself increased by about 12 per cent. The quality of life in developed countries is to a certain extent determined by the relative size of the service function, so there are obvious reasons for its growth in a socially conscious country such as Sweden but these services are largely the responsibility of national or local government and can only be supported by the output of industry, including in this term the agricultural, forestry and mining industries of the country. Fortunately the productive output has been increasing at a faster rate (4.9 per cent p.a. in 1972-75) than the services industries (4.0 per cent p.a. in the same period), but unless this differential can be preserved, there is clearly a limit to further migration of this kind.

National Pension Funds and Welfare Services

Another factor influencing the acceptability of redeployment has been the existence of fully transferable pension rights. The basic pension payable to all Swedish citizens and to certain foreigners resident in the country has been available since 1914. Prior to 1976, the pension was payable at the age of sixty-seven or at a reduced rate at sixty-three, or it could be deferred until the age of seventy with increased benefits. In 1976, the normal pensionable age was reduced by two years, and if so desired at the age of sixty a worker could take a reduced pension and continue to work for a reduced number of hours.

Sixty per cent of the costs of the basic pension are borne by the government. The remainder is derived from contributions levied at a current rate of 6.2 per cent of the taxable income up to a maximum contribution *per capita* of £150 a year. Prior to 1975, the contributions (at 5 per cent) were paid by the workers but from that year, in exchange for a measure of wage restraint, the contributions have been paid by the employers.

All pensions in Sweden are paid as multiples of a base rate which is tied to the consumer price index. In 1960, the base amount was £420 but this had risen to £1250 by 1976. The single person's basic pension is 90 per cent of the base amount while a married couple receive 50 per cent more.

An earnings related supplementary pension scheme was introduced in 1960 by an Act passed by the Riksdag in the previous year after political controversy. The pension is founded on a points system, each point being equal to the base amount. The pension is calculated on the average of the number of points earned in the fifteen best years. Points are obtained for that part of the income between the base amount and 7.5 times the base amount, the maximum in any year being 6.5 points. The supplementary pension is then 60 per cent of the qualifying points with proportional reduction for less than thirty years at work. Interim arrangements are made for people retiring at present since no-one could qualify for full pension until 1990.

The full costs for this generous supplementary pension are paid by the employers at a rate of 3 per cent of pensionable salary in 1960 rising to 11 per cent by 1976. Administration is through the income tax system with the National Pensions Funds agency being responsible for the investment of the very considerable capital accruing. Without going into detail on the Funds, a feature is that every company can borrow back 50 per cent of its contributions to the Pension Funds, thus helping to keep capital in the productive sector of the economy.

Unemployment benefits in Sweden have largely been an insurance responsibility carried out by the unions under the supervision in principle of the Labour Market Board; benefits can be 91 per cent of earned income to a maximum of £19 per day but are restricted to 300 days or 450 days for those over 45 years of age. For people not in benefit from an insurance scheme, the Labour Market Board can pay up to £6.50 per day but to qualify recipients must have worked or been on a training scheme for five of the previous six months. With all unemployed, the Board is usually effective in finding job opportunities – a suitable post cannot be turned down without loss of unemployment benefits, including redundancy make-up pay.

Sickness benefits and other welfare services of a similar nature are provided on a massive scale. Briefly, pay during sickness is 90 per cent of earned income (to a maximum of £7,000 p.a.) and is both taxable and pension qualifying, while 'stay at home spouses' of either sex are paid over £1 per day untaxed when sick. At childbirth, seven months' sick leave can be paid at the same rate to either parent in work, or split between the parents. A charge of £2 is paid for each visit to a doctor or hospital, while a patient pays at most half the cost of dental treatment, but travel costs in excess of £1 per visit are paid by the local welfare bodies who also pay the balance of the costs to doctors and so on. Children receive free treatment. No charges are made for drugs to cure serious illness or for the supply of contraceptives to those attending welfare counselling, but charges are made for other pharmaceutical products.

The government pays 25 per cent of the total bill for the health services: the remainder is paid by the employers by means of a levy which in 1976 amounted to 8 per cent of each employee's wage or salary up to 7.5 times the base amount. The general administration of the health services and pension schemes is governed by the National Insurance Act and its frequent amendments and as usual in Sweden there is an adequate complaints procedure which in the last resort can lead to the National Social Insurance Court.

Industrial Relations

The quality of industrial relations has for many years received the admiration of the Western world. When performing as a backup function to the negotiating machinery, legislation has contributed to the smooth working of industry. Since 1973, a new tendency has been for the Riksdag to take an initiative by passing laws in sensitive areas where the process of negotiation has failed to yield agreement; it is too early to judge whether the change in emphasis will lead to still greater harmony or whether it will generate strains that industry will be unable to accommodate without losing its competitive ability.

Viewing the situation today (see for instance Table 4.3), it is difficult to realise that industrial relations in Sweden have in fact not always been good. Indeed during the early decades of the twentieth century, the strike record was devastatingly high and was accompanied by considerable bitterness. In spite of this, until about 1970, the employers confederation (SAF) and the confederation of blue collar unions (LO) were both of the opinion that industrial affairs were better settled between the conflicting parties with the minimum intervention from outside bodies such as the government.

Table 4.3:   Comparative Figures for Days Lost through Disputes per 1000 Workers

Year	1967	1968	1969	1970	1971	1972	1973	1974	1975	1976
Sweden	—	—	30	40	240	10	10	30	20	10
Germany	30	—	20	10	340	10	40	60	10	40
Japan	100	160	200	200	310	270	210	450	390	150
UK	220	370	520	740	1190	2160	570	1270	540	300
USA	1430	1590	1390	2210	1600	860	750	1480	990	1190
France	430	n.a.	200	180	440	300	330	250	390	420
Australia	320	460	860	1040	1300	880	1080	2670	1390	1490

Note: The statistics for Sweden before 1972 are not truly comparable with those for subsequent years, as only since 1972 have separate figures been available for the industry groups to which the table relates. Where no figure is given the number of days lost per 1,000 employed is less than five.

Source: Department of Employment Gazette, December 1977, p. 1342.

Unions in Sweden are organised on an industry basis which makes it possible for a few unions, such as in agriculture, for instance, to be outside of LO: the employers match this structure with corresponding groups. There are also separate unions for foremen (SALF), salaried staff (TCO) and professional people (SACO). SAF and LO dominate the position so the issues will mainly be discussed in terms of these bodies only. With the distinctions between shop floor and staff disappearing rapidly, it would be no surprise to see LO and TCO amalgamating.

The government attempted to intervene in 1928 by passing legislation requiring the maintenance of industrial peace as long as a collective agreement was in force and introduced a Labour Court to deal with offenders. However the Court was ineffective until 1938, when wise counsel from both sides of industry, recognising that conflict was harmful, signed a collective agreement known as the Basic or Saltsjöbaden Agreement broadly in line with the 1928 law. This agreement has been one of the main cornerstones of industrial relations in Sweden.

In accordance with the concept of 'the third man's rights', the Saltsjöbaden Agreement stated that no dispute should be allowed to harm the interests of anyone not directly involved in the dispute. Two kinds of problems are recognised; those in which resources can be pooled to find the best solution as for example in safety, or in devising better production methods, and those in which the interests of SAF and LO are poles apart, as for instance in the allocation of the fruits of increased profitability. The spirit of the agreement is that negotiation should be the method of solution in both cases with the use of the strike weapon or the lockout seen as an admission of failure, only to be exercised after the disputes procedure has been exhausted. In the so called 'conflicts of rights' which can arise from the interpretation of an agreement, the Labour Court has become the ultimate arbitrator, but the Court has no jurisdiction in 'conflicts of interests' which might arise during negotiations before a collective agreement is signed.

Collective agreements between LO and SAF have been the principal means of establishing industrial procedures in Sweden. That signed in 1906 was of particular importance because it recognised the right of the unions to organise and to negotiate on behalf of the workers, and it gave the employers the right to hire and fire, and to organise the work place. In later years, collective agreements on work study and rationalisation (1946, 1966 and 1973), works councils (1946) and occupational health services (1967), for example, have been important factors in the creation of an efficient economy.

Collective agreements are not legally binding documents. The agreements function because both LO and SAF are powerful central organisations well able to control their constituent members. SAF has been prepared to impose fines on offending firms and to withhold compensation if a firm undertook a lockout or action precipitating a strike without central authorisation. LO has ruled its 25 constituent unions, making up most of the labour force in Sweden, in an authoritarian manner: no union can call a strike affecting more than 3 per cent of its members without central approval, and approval will be withheld if the strike would hurt other unions, the labour movement or the nation as a whole. There is a considerable emphasis on negotiation and reconciliation by LO and by SAF.

The Labour Court and the state mediators have the backing of the law. Sweden is divided into eight mediation areas. Some days before a stoppage of work, the state mediator must be informed; the parties will be called together to state their case and must be prepared to advance positive proposals for the solution of the dispute. If a solution is not found, the mediator can suggest arbitration, which is not compulsory, but if arbitration is agreed then the decisions must be accepted—failure to do so can result in summons to the Labour Court and the payment of compensation to injured parties.

The Labour Court is made up of seven members nominated by the Crown. The chairman and one member must have legal experience and are usually judges. Another member must be independent of employers or unions and have legal experience in industrial relations. The remaining members are split equally between employers and unions. All are sitting in a judicial capacity having taken a judicial oath in a spirit of impartiality. About 40 cases a year are heard by the Court which relies heavily on precedents in reaching a verdict so that many cases are settled out of court by reference to the precedents. It is believed in some quarters that this system tends to favour the organisation at the expense of the individual. The government rarely interferes in this area, the exception being in 1971 when legislation was passed ordering striking civil servants (mostly SACO members) back to work.

Pay negotiations are conducted centrally at annual or triennial intervals and are consolidated in collective agreements which are regarded as binding for an agreed time. After the principles of the settlement have been established, the details are worked out by a small delegation of three from each side: individual industries then negotiate within the terms of the general agreement and finally all the agreements are signed simultaneously. A logical structure for pay negotiations has thus been defined.

The policy of SAF has been based on equal pay for equal work regardless of the industry. The policy of LO was not very different—it was based on solidarity, or equal pay. Of the two, LO has had the greater success in achieving its aims, the percentage differential between higher and lower paid having roughly halved over two decades.

The equal pay policy has had two effects. Firstly, it has made it difficult for Sweden to compete even in the home market in trades, such as textiles, which are traditionally low-paid areas in the rest of the world:

as a result, many textile and shoe making firms have ceased to exist, or sometimes have opened factories overseas. Secondly, it has made the highly skilled dissatisfied with the differential. The central agreements have for several years been subject to 'wage drift', that is a certain amount of modification to meet local conditions. In the 1970s, local groups of skilled workers in particular industries have become militant in pressing demands for local differentials, by a few wild cat strikes and by threats of strikes in nearly 30 per cent of firms. SAF, too, has been less energetic in imposing fines on firms breaking a central agreement—Volvo Torslanda in 1970 is a case in point.

The resulting increase in annual wage drift from 3.5 per cent in 1965-68, to 6.4 per cent in 1973-75, has also had two effects. Firstly, the current rate with wage drift tends to become the base for the next round of pay negotiations leading to a general rise in wage levels. (Over the ten years preceding 1974, hourly wages rose at annual rate of just under 10 per cent but in 1974 and 1975, increases greater than 14 per cent p.a. occurred. The consumer price index has risen throughout at an annual rate of about 4 per cent less than wages so there have been substantial increases in real wages). Secondly, the visible success of local action has diminished the central authority of LO. Over the three years ending in 1977, the cost of employing labour increased by 50 per cent to make Swedish labour costs the highest in the world.[5]

The dominance of LO as the central figure on the labour front received a further blow in 1971. Over the preceding ten years, salaries had suffered a cumulative fall relative to wages amounting to 17 per cent. In that year SACO succeeded in halting the decline and in 1975 secured an increase that to some extent restored the position of the salaried worker. With less ability to absorb rising employment costs, and faced by a central union organisation with declining authority (but still very powerful), the employers may elect to adopt a tougher policy in future pay negotiations.

A departure from the traditional pattern appeared in the 1970s. Failure by LO to achieve any point of substance through negotiation was followed almost immediately by a request to the Socialist government for legislation to determine this point in their favour: usually the Socialist government was eager to mount the legislation, so there has been a spate of new laws on industrial relations.

The Security of Employment Act of 1974 laid down conditions for dismissal, right of appeal and redundancy payment. The unusual features are that the period of redundancy pay is linked to age as well as length of service, and that when an ex-worker is in receipt of redundancy pay he cannot refuse the offer of a job and when in the new job, the redundancy pay is reduced to a make-up-to-previous earnings value. The Act also offers additional safeguards for the handicapped as well as defining re-employment policies for the company.

One of these laws, relating to the appointment of worker representatives to the Board of operating companies, became effective in April 1973. Prior to that date, a few companies had appointed workers of known integrity to their single-tier Boards, but under the new law all companies employing 100 (later reduced to 50, and then 25) or more must have two workers' representatives on the Board if the workers so wish. By 1977, the option had been exercised in about 70 per cent of Swedish companies. To support these representatives, the unions pressed for the compulsory appointment of external 'consultants' (paid by the employers) and a draft Bill was prepared in 1974: after strong opposition from the employers who feared commercial security would be at risk, the Bill was replaced by a collective agreement that the consultants would only be appointed if the information could not be obtained and explained through internal mechanisms. So far, very few consultants have been appointed but there has been a growing emphasis on economic committees within the companies to interpret company economics through the balance sheet.

A third step towards involvement at an official level has been expressed in the 'Co-determination' Act which came into effect in January 1977. Under this Act, the workers must be kept fully informed on all aspects of company policy and decisions must be approved by the workers. The precise mechanism, and to some extent the areas involved, have still to be worked out through collective agreements but there is general concern among employers, particularly in small companies, that this Act may adversely affect efficiency. In 1977, a merger between Volvo and Saab was proposed in order to improve the competitiveness of the car divisions. The proposal was accepted at Board level but because of the 'Co-determination' Act, the proposal was submitted to the unions for discussion and after two months, was agreed by them. But during this period, the Saab management organised strong technical opposition to the merger which was then dropped.[6] So the effect of the Co-determination Act in this instance was to enable the voice of management to be heard! Incidentally at no time during the discussions were the shareholders consulted. A common element in this trilogy of laws is that the unions recognise there is a considerable educational problem to be solved before the Acts can be fully effective: a major training programme has accordingly been mounted. SAF, too, acknowledge that junior and often senior production management as well will have problems in adjusting to changed situations and have their own rather less formal educational programme. Such programmes may be the key to future success.

To many, the official level of industrial democracy is of less relevance than the worker involvement at shopfloor level in the determination of the layout of the work place, in discussion on the working methods and in the local division of functions between operatives. Experiments in this direction have been taking place for several years through group working, and through works councils and the committees of the works councils. By these means, job satisfaction has been materially increased.

Important changes have been embodied in a series of Acts becoming effective at varying times between January 1974 and January 1977. The status and rights of safety officers nominated by the work force have been defined, as indeed have those for shop stewards. A change in principle was incorporated in the Shop Stewards Act to the effect that in the event of a dispute, in future, the view of the union will prevail pending a solution through arbitration or agreement—in the past, the *status quo* has prevailed, and in practice this generally meant the view of the employers. Previously, the right to strike was reserved for certain situations; all restrictions have been removed and a duty imposed on the employers to negotiate even with wild cat strikes. The amount of compensation a worker can be required to pay has also been limited, but compensation is still payable by workers causing damage deliberately or through negligence. A simplified legal procedure has been introduced for small claims in order to help individual workers.

The 1976 quinquennial congress of LO adopted the proposals made by the economic research section of LO for 'economic democracy'. Because workers are greatly affected by the economic decisions made by industry, it was believed to be essential for the workers to be able to influence and even to determine the decisions. The method proposed was for a percentage of the 'excess profits' of all companies to be allocated in the form of shares to central funds controlled by the workers—a figure of 20 per cent has been discussed so the build up for the 'Meidner Funds' could be rapid to the extent that economic control rested with the workers.

A committee appointed by SAF to consider the implications of the Meidner Funds regards the proposals as an unwarranted confiscation of assets belonging to the shareholders; this, it is claimed, would have an adverse effect on share prices and make the raising of new share capital virtually impossible. The committee recognised the benefits of employee involvement in the economic performance of the company but would prefer this to be through the voluntary purchase of shares held in groups associated with individual companies. Savings of 1 per cent of wages would raise roughly the same amount of money as the Meidner Funds, and, if frozen for five or ten years before becoming available to individual workers, might be subject to income tax relief.

LO approached the Social Democratic Government to support the Meidner Funds but the Socialists were at pains to play down the issue during the 1976 elections, although a commission of inquiry was appointed. With a new moderate government in office, LO will presumably find it less easy to secure legislation but there can be little doubt that the unions will continue to press for the Meidner Funds or something similar.

Consumer Protection

In the consumer area, the Social Democratic government has been committed in principle to passing legislation designed to take care of the interests of the community in preference to the interests of the individual. Operating through various bureaucracies, the State has tended in most instances to take a 'big brother' attitude to citizens by deciding what is best for them. The conspicuous exception is in pornography for which the government has opted to leave the decision to the individual with the result that pornography is openly on sale – and largely ignored; this approach has the benefit that the problem of underground organisations and the possibility of corruption of officials are avoided.

Similarly smoking and the consumption of spirits have not been legislated against, but prices are kept very high by the shops owned by the State monopoly in order to discourage over indulgence. However, the State has decided that seat belts must be worn in cars (operative January 1975) and that it is unwise to drink and drive; breaches of either of these laws receive penalties sufficiently heavy to represent a real discouragement. Legislation and the quality of life seem unlikely bed-fellows but a satisfactory compromise is evolving in Sweden. A series of measures have been pioneered to improve the protection of the consumer or to maintain environmental standards with the 1970s in particular seeing a marked increase of legislation in these areas. Mail order selling is big business in Sweden and this no doubt accounts for the activity of the Consumer Ombudsman, Sven Heurgren, and his secretariat of thirty-five. Advertisements are regularly screened and samples of goods tested under rigorous conditions for compliance with description. In the last resort, a supplier can be taken by the Ombudsman to the Market Court; usually an approach to the supplier is sufficient to secure redress because, apart from business ethics, the possibility of adverse publicity through appearance in the Market Court is a powerful disincentive.

Services advertised in the press and elsewhere are also under scrutiny by the Ombudsman. There is a school of thought advocating that plumbers and the like should not be allowed to sell their services without a certificate of competence granted by a public body: however there is opposition to this concept on the grounds that it would be an infringement of personal liberty by denying an individual the right to earn his living in the way he wished. An alternative approach has been made by the Ombudsman with some success to the association of motor repairers for the association to guarantee on a national basis the quality of workmanship undertaken by its members.

Unlike the Consumer Ombudsman who, after judicial experience, is appointed by the government, the Press Ombudsman is appointed voluntarily by the press; the main concern of this office is to ensure fair reporting and the right of reply.

Food laws have been tightened and at the same time there has been a campaign (not wholly successful) to raise the expectations of the public. All packages, including even milk, must exhibit an analysis of contents as well as showing quantity, while it is an offence to offer goods for sale after the expiry of the shelf life which also must be clearly marked. Maximum storage temperatures are defined for perishable goods. Standards of hygiene are laid down and every food establishment must appoint a person responsible for maintaining the standards.

Complaints can be made through the National Complaints Board, which has a staff of thirty, to the Consumer Ombudsman who in addition carries out independent checks. The emphasis in the complaints procedure is on informality, most of the complaints being registered by telephone. As a result, about 30,000 complaints a year are examined, by far the most of which are dealt with by the secretariat or the Consumer Ombudsman, leaving only about 50 cases a year to go before the Market Court. This Court consists of three legal judges and is mainly concerned to set precedents, although it can impose fines.[7]

A discordant note is that the passing of so many laws containing vague general clauses is placing too much power in the hands of the administrators: there is consequently a danger that the real interests of the consumer may be obscured. In addition to the bodies quoted here is for instance a National Food Administration, a National Price and Control Office, a National Debt Inspectorate and an Anti-trust Ombudsman.

Environmental Protection

The car has encountered a certain amount of legislation concerned
mostly with protecting the public as opposed to the individual. From
1976, new models must be equipped with headlight wipers and exhaust
emissions (for heavy vehicles as well as cars) must be reduced drastically
to about a quarter of previous levels. Seat belts must be worn by all
front seat occupants; 'drinking and driving' is discouraged by heavy fines
and automatic loss of licence for relatively small amounts of alcohol in
the blood stream.

Right of access to non-cultivated land, and especially to the forests
and lakes, has long been part of the common law in Sweden. In recent
years, there has been an increasing awareness that Sweden has a beautiful
countryside and the legislator has stepped in to plan the use of land.
Industry can only expand in certain areas and pollution control is receiving much attention. No new building can be erected within 100 metres
of natural water and in areas of outstanding beauty, this distance can be
increased to 300 metres. It must be said, however, that so far, planning
ideals have been tempered by economic reality.

Historically the disposal of solid waste has been the responsibility of
industry which has developed some profitable reclamation processes. By
1981 the municipalities will have the monopoly of waste disposal thrust
upon them, with a pressure to develop methods of re-cycling usable
material. By the same date, households will have a legal responsibility
to separate paper from other domestic waste.

A halt to the nuclear power programme of the Socialists was made
one of the election issues by the Centre party in 1976 on environmental grounds. This party won the election but since Sweden has no
fossil fuels, many doubt if the new prime minister, Thorbjörn Fälldin,
will be able to do more in this direction than delay the planning of new
stations for a few years.

Having obtained an admirable material standard of living through
the second highest GDP in the world, the Swedes are concerned that
the quality of life should be equally high. This concern is demonstrated
by the actions described here and in the magnificent swimming pools
and sports complexes that have been constructed in many urban areas,
often to provide employment in times of recession. The working combination of social objectives and pragmatic realism offers a useful
example to the rest of the world.

The Future

Developments in Sweden continue to be of absorbing interest. Many issues are assuming patterns predictable from experience of recent years. During the world recession in trade of 1975-78, both the outgoing Socialist Government and the new Centre Coalition Government maintained a low level of unemployment of less than 2 per cent, by encouraging firms to invest in stock, by financing retraining schemes, by undertaking public works and, in certain cases, by granting subsidies regarded hopefully as a temporary expedient calculated to place Swedish industry in a strong position to profit from the upsurge in world economy when it came. For most of this period, investment in Swedish industry continued when it was falling in the remainder of the developed world.

When the limited increase of 12 per cent in world trade came in late 1977, in spite of the state of preparedness, Swedish exports failed to capture a proportionate share of the market and rose by only 3½ per cent.[8] It is believed that three main reasons lie behind this relative failure. The first is the high labour costs (which by 1977 were well in excess of the rest of the world). As long as Sweden had high productivity and technical supremacy, high labour costs could be met and yet leave Swedish goods competitive. However, progress in both of these areas has, in general, been less rapid in recent years (although certain engineering companies still maintain their technical lead). The third factor – of the Swedish kroner being linked through the 'snake' to the German mark without at the same time having the internal discipline to combat inflation – also made Swedish goods expensive; three devaluations of the kroner have helped but not sufficiently to offset the other trends.

Ironically, it is the Centre Government that has been saddled with subsidies and State involvement in industry on an unprecedented scale for Sweden.[9] Although it has been agreed that the shipbuilding industry will be streamlined to about a third of its present capacity, massive subsidies amounting to over £720m are being paid to the state-owned yards, Svenska Varv, which have estimated losses in the three years to 1980 of £460m. The privately-owned yard of Kockums has received a credit guarantee of £40m towards the cost of £60m for building a third gigantic tanker for liquefied gas for 'own account', i.e. as a speculative venture. The state steel making unit of LKAB in the North will not be expanded. Instead, the State is taking a third share in a company formed to support the mild steel industries of Sweden in a loss making situation until the 1980s; the labour force is expected to fall from 18,000 to 14,000. The problems in mild steel were to be expected. Less so is the position in the special steels industry. Over the years, the Swedish special steels companies had developed technology and skills that enabled their products to be sold on quality throughout the world: but several countries have caught up on technology and, with lower labour costs, cause the Swedish products to be uncompetitive. In 1977, the special steels industry in Sweden lost £125m and as a result, drastic restructuring involving the loss of 12,000 jobs over the next few years is proposed, under a government sponsored merger of the main producers. A further State move has been made in taking a 50 per cent share in Datasaab in order to preserve another industry of high technology.[10]

However, the position is not entirely one of gloom. The seriousness of the situation has been recognised. The unions are adopting a responsible attitude in refraining from excessive wage demands (12 per cent was generally agreed for 1978, a figure below the rate of inflation for the first time for many years) and in not using the new industrial legislation obstructively. (The government in fact tried to intervene for the first time in wage negotiations to secure a lower figure.) The Coalition Government is redeeming one of its election pledges by easing the burden of taxation on small firms to the tune of nearly £60m in 1978. A similar grant is being made to local authorities to build advance factories for letting and to provide advice. These are more than political gestures because it is believed that small firms have an important part to play in the generation of new ideas and new products. The Government is also helping to revitalise the technology by sponsoring mainly basic research (£655m) to supplement the £356m spent each year on research and development by the larger companies.

Sweden has been a pioneer in legislation directed towards improving the environment. Many technical problems have been solved. It is now believed Swedish companies should be in a strong position to supply the world with complete systems for controlling pollution and conserving energy. So far there has only been a limited realisation of this potential.

It is very typical of the commercial enterprise of Sweden that two of the major shipyards, faced with a declining world market, are seeking other advanced technical outlets for their skills and equipment. The Swedish yards were late in entering the bidding for contracts to build platforms for North Sea Oil and have had limited success in that direction. Kockums (already diversified into heavy forestry equipment, chemical plant and special purpose computers, for instance) has proposed a package in which it supplies 20 super tankers for carrying liquefied gas from the Middle East or North African oilfields to Sweden where it would be utilised in a number of gas fired power stations also supplied by Kockums. Part of the work would go to the state-owned yards. The Gotaverken yard has developed modules for turnkey chemical (and oil) plants built on barges which will be towed to locations lacking the infrastructure to construct complex plant; the barges could be towed to a new location, if the initial demand ceased, and then linked to provide a different combination of facilities. Neither of these imaginative schemes is airborne yet. It seems as if the Swedish Government will opt for a cheaper system than Kockums by piping gas from Germany but the spirit of commercial technology is far from dead in a country which can still produce such advanced ideas. The concept of providing complete systems is developing rapidly. Trelleborg for instance have for some years supplied not only conveyor belts but also mechanical handling systems.

Still in the energy field, one of the issues on which the Centre party fought the 1976 election was the abandonment of nuclear power projects. Already this policy has been relaxed by the commissioning of a previously built nuclear power station, albeit with more stringent regulations on safety. Although substantial research is taking place into the utilisation of renewable sources of energy (including the combustion of low grade forestry products!), the nuclear policy of the Fälldin administration is under heavy criticism; this criticism could lead to more changes in government policy or even to a change in government.

There has been a gradual but dramatic change in housing policy. Up to and including the 1960s, the demand was for greatly increased accommodation of better quality which was usually provided by the municipally planned block of flats constructed away from the city centre for letting. Now that demand has been met, and with increasing affluence, many wish to own their own homes; building effort is now directed to individual houses and to the refurbishing of older premises, sometimes in the city centres. There has at the same time been a carefully cultivated swing from bureaucratic planning to community involvement.

The impression is of an economy that has just taken some hard knocks but is by no means down and out. A few cherished ideas of the industrial philosophy have been severely challenged. Government intervention has been unexpectedly widespread; whether this will remain as a long term policy remains to be seen. The Swedes will fight to retain their high living standards and their quality of life. They have readily adapted to change in the past and will no doubt react to the need for change in the future.

In Conclusion

The Swedish economy in the twentieth century has maintained a record of outstanding growth, a conspicuous element in the success being the preparedness of management and unions to co-operate in widespread change in the structure of industry. Government intervention has been minimal even when mergers or takeovers could lead to near monopolistic situations. Similarly, state ownership of industry is at an extremely low level for a state which has had a socialistic government in office for four decades.

Government has taken constructive measures to foster the growth of the economy by encouraging investment and by developing a progressive policy in the labour market. Stability of economic purpose is also enhanced by the method of government — election by proportional representation and administration by autonomous bureaucracies — provided safeguards are incorporated to avoid abuse of power.

The Swedes have been pragmatists, good at accommodating change. These virtues could serve them well in dealing with the new problems of the 1980s.

Notes

1. For more particulars of the Swedish economy see the author's book *Planning and Productivity in Sweden* (Croom Helm, London, 1976), pp. 3-13. This book includes a bibliography. See also 'Sweden' A Survey (six pages) in *The Times*, 17 November 1976, pp. 21-6; 'Sweden' A survey (eight pages) in *The Financial Times*, 25 May 1977, pp. 19-26.

2. The role of the Labour Market Board is discussed in Chapter 2 of H.G. Jones, op.cit. The counter-cyclical Investment Funds approach was admired in Britain in 1976. The Chancellor of the Exchequer, Mr Denis Healey, actually referred to it in his Budget speech. However, the government appeared to lose its enthusiasm later in the year.

3. See 'Sweden's absentee workers', *The Economist*, 28 August 1976, pp. 63-4.

4. See J. Poole, 'The NEB of the North', *Sunday Times Business News*, 21 March 1976; 'Sweden's state companies', *The Economist*, 28 August 1976, p. 64; 'NEB-Swedish style', *CBI Review* (*Confederation of British Industry*), Spring 1976; A. Hamilton, 'Problems of a state-owned conglomerate', *The Financial Times*, 25 August 1976.

5. 'Sweden: the model loses her glamour', Business Brief in *The Economist*, 27 August 1977, pp. 66-7.

6. 'Bigger than General Motors — in a way', *The Economist*, 14 May 1977, p. 113; C. Webb, 'Volvo and Saab-Scania: what made marriage so appealing', *The Times*, 9 May 1977; T. Dodsworth and G. Owen, 'A surprise Swedish marriage', *The Financial Times*, 7 May 1977; W. Dullforce, 'The merger that backfired', *The Financial Times*, 23 September 1977; 'Volvo and Saab-Scania: saved in time', *The Economist*, 3 September 1977, p. 78.

7. The Swedish approach to competition policy has recently attracted increased attention in the UK. D. Harris, 'Fair trading: is there anything we can import from Sweden?', *The Times*, 13 April 1978.

8. P.M. Wijkman, 'The Swedish economic situation: growing balance of payments deficit', *EFTA Bulletin*, September-October 1977, discusses the deteriorating trade position.

9. See 'Sweden joins the hand-out club', *The Economist*, 23 April 1977, p. 89; M. Hallvarsson, 'Gloomy prospects for Sweden's high cost industries', *EFTA Bulletin*, January-February 1978.

10. See 'Swedish profits: vanishing', *The Economist*, 26 November 1977, p. 93. 'Swedish Engineering and Shipbuilding', Survey (4 pages) in *The Financial Times*, 14 December 1977; 'Swedish Steel: time to merge', *The Economist*, 11 March 1978, p. 81; 'Swedish shipbuilding: more money than sense', *The Economist*, 1 April 1978, p. 74, are sources of further details on these industries.

5 GOVERNMENT INTERVENTION IN THE ECONOMY OF THE UNITED KINGDOM

Peter Maunder*

> 'Believe me, my young friend,' the minister said with a dreamy
> smile, 'there is nothing—absolutely nothing—half so much
> worth doing as simply messing about with industry'. Moreover,
> he might have added (and probably did), it is both necessary
> and logical to do so, as well as fun; . . . It is, in fact, eminently
> logical to intervene in industry, but the trouble is that there is
> no logical end to the process—short of a complete takeover.
> Unfortunately, too, as the example of Britain's nationalised
> industries shows, however rational and logical detailed inter-
> vention in industry appears to be, it does not work. *The Econ-*
> *omist*, 11 January 1975, p. 88, reviewing R. Vernon (ed.), *Big*
> *Business and the State: Changing Relations in Western Europe*
> (Macmillan, London, 1974).

The extent to which the state ought to intervene and influence private
industry at the micro level continues to be an active political issue in
the United Kingdom. The most obvious recent illustration of this fact
has been the debate on whether the commercial banks and certain other
key financial institutions should now be absorbed into the public sector.
But there are plenty of other examples concerning manufacturing industry
during the past two decades of major issues that have involved political
controversy: for example, the creation in 1966—and its later abolition—
of the Industrial Reorganisation Corporation (discussed below but for a
further analysis see Young and Lowe[1]), the rescue of Rolls-Royce in
1971 and the setting up four years later of the National Enterprise Board.
Concern has been expressed in several quarters within (and indeed outside) the UK over the size of the British public sector. The reasons for
this worry have varied. Some feel the relatively large-sized public sector
involves fundamental problems in macro-economic management. Others
have concerned themselves with the issues of efficiency and productivity given the muting of competitive pressures within mammoth state-
owned organisations. The actual measurement of the public sector inevitably causes problems. It is not difficult to have either a majority or

*I am indebted to Eric Owen Smith and Michael Fleming of the Department of
Economics, Loughborough University for helpful comments on an earlier draft.

minority public sector share figure i.e. over or below 50 per cent depending on the treatment of transfer payments, spending by the nationalised
industries, interest on the national debt and definition of what constit-
utes a publicly-owned company. Since the rise in total public expenditure in the early 1970s attracted much attention one can cite its ratio
to gross national product increasing from 38 per cent in 1971-72 to a
peak of 46 per cent in 1975-76. A narrower definition of the public
sector – general government expenditure on goods and services – produces figures of 22.5 per cent and 27 per cent for these same years.
Whatever the choice of measure it is important for the reader to appreciate
that there has been growing concern, implicit or explicit, about the other
side of the coin – the size of the private sector and, more specifically, the
state of manufacturing industry. Two Oxford economists, Bacon and
Eltis, feel that Britain has 'too few producers'.[2] 'De-industrialisation'
has indeed become an addition to the economics literature and is supposed to reflect concern over the (irreversible?) decline in the number of
jobs being offered in British manufacturing industry.[3] Since we are refer-
ring to the country that pioneered the Industrial Revolution the significance
of this subject should not be lost on the reader. However, to give an
indication of the public/private sector split we can without contention
use a measure on an employment basis. About one quarter of Britain's
25 million workers are employed by the public sector. Of these 6½
million, one third are employed by corporations involved essentially in
the market economy through the sale of their goods and services: the
bulk of the public sector labour force, however, is employed by central
and local government providing mainly services without the operation
of market prices.

Table 5.1 shows the extent of individual programmes of public
expenditures and Table 5.2 a subdivision of the fourth listed such
programme – relating to trade, industry and employment. It is in respect
of that part of the economy that the following discussion essentially
relates.

As regards the outlook of the main political parties to industrial
policy the Labour party has generally aspired to an extension of the
public sector and greater intervention in the pursuit of socialist ideals.
Given the party's title this is perhaps hardly a surprising statement but
those not familiar with British politics should be aware that the party
includes those whose views are of the far left as well as those who, in a
wider European perspective, would be described as having a more centrist, social democratic outlook. The Conservative party broadly supports
the cause of private enterprise and opposes an extension of the public

Table 5.1:   Public Expenditure by Programme and in Total (£ million at 1977 survey prices)

		1976-77	% of Final Total
1	Defence	6,361	11.0
2	Overseas aid and other overseas services	1,188	2.0
3	Agriculture, fisheries, food and forestry	1,133	1.9
4	Trade, industry and employment; refinance of home shipbuilding and fixed rate export credit	636	5.5
	other	2,542	
5	Government lending to nationalised industries	330	0.5
6	Roads and transport	2,784	4.8
7	Housing	4,870	8.4
8	Other environmental services	2,682	4.6
9	Law, order and protective services	1,895	3.2
10	Education and libraries, science and arts	8,293	14.3
11	Health and personal social services	7,287	12.6
12	Social security	12,717	22.0
13	Other public services	848	1.4
14	Common services	896	1.5
15	Northern Ireland	1,737	3.0
	Total programmes	56,201	
	Contingency reserve	—	
	Total	56,201	
	Debt interest	1,662	2.8
	Total	57,863	
	Total programmes, contingency reserve and foreign and market borrowing of nationalised industries	57,635	100

Source: The Government's Expenditure Plans, 1978-79 to 1981-82, Vol. 1, Table 9, Cmnd 7049 – I, (HMSO, January 1978).

Table 5.2:   Public Expenditure on Trade, Industry and Employment

	1976-77	% of Grand Total
Regional support and regeneration		
Regional development grants	392	
Provision of land and buildings	21	
Selective assistance to industry in assisted areas	27	
Other regional support	13	
Regional employment premium	238	
Residual expenditure under repealed sections of the Local Employment Act, 1972	−14	
Scottish and Welsh Development Agencies	28	
Total	706	22.2

	1976-77	% of Grand Total
Industrial innovation		
General industrial R and D	43	
Technological and industrial sponsorship	7	
Aircraft and aeroengine general R and D programme	20	
Concorde—development	20	
—production	20	
RB 211	10	
Other aircraft and aeroengine projects and assistance	—	
Space	34	
Nuclear	138	
Total	301	9.4
General support for industry		
National Enterprise Board[a]	158	
Selective assistance to individual industries, firms and undertakings	90	
Promotion of tourism	18	
Refinancing of home shipbuilding lending	71	
Interest support costs	50	
Assistance to the shipbuilding industry	14	
Future industrial support	—	
Other support services	1	
Investment grants	26	
Total	428	13.4
Support for nationalised industries (other than the transport industries)		
Compensation for price restraint	—	
Assistance to the coal industry		
Coal Industry Acts	71	
Pneumoconiosis scheme	—	
Other compensation	70	
Total	140	4.4
International trade		
Export promotion and trade co-operation	16	
Refinancing of fixed rate export credits	565	
Interest support costs	224	
Cost escalation guarantees	−1	
Total	804	25.3
Functioning of the labour market		
Employment services and employment rehabilitation	140	
Industrial training	257	
Redundancy and maternity fund payments	103	
Industrial relations and other labour market services	152	
Total	652	20.5

	1976-77	% of Grand Total
Health and safety at work	38	
Regulation of domestic trade and industry and consumer protection	−5	
Central and miscellaneous services		
Employment	47	
Other	68	
Transactions in British Petroleum Company shares	—	
Total	148	4.6
Grand Total	3,178	100

aFigures are in money terms and not at constant prices.

Source: The Government's Expenditure Plans 1978-79 to 1981-82, Volume II, Table 2.4. Cmnd. 7049−II, (HMSO, January 1978).

sector but in the 1970s made many decisions which rather strained this traditional standpoint. These decisions included, within a short space of time, the rescue of 'lame ducks', the nationalisation of Rolls-Royce and a statutory incomes policy. The broadly centrist Liberal party in the UK has much less strong Parliamentary support than either of the other two parties and has not been elected to power for over fifty years. It lacks crucial financial support from either organised labour or companies as is accorded to both its rivals.

The following indicates the nature of post-war British governments and Prime Ministers:

1945-1951	Labour	Atlee
1951-1964	Conservative	Churchill; Eden; Macmillan; Douglas-Home
1964-1970	Labour	Wilson
1970-1974	Conservative	Heath
1974-	Labour	Wilson; Callaghan.

In the case of the United Kingdom interventionist measures at the micro level have been, as the opening sentence implied, very conspicuous by their number. The various twists in strategic approach and turns in policy detail are such that in the following overview it has not been easy to structure a sequence of topics in complete isolation from one another. The opening section examines the state-owned part of the private-public sector divide.

Nationalisation

The fundamental extension of the public sector in the UK took place

within the space of five years after the end of World War II in 1945. Mr
Attlee's newly-elected Labour government proceeded to take into full
public ownership the Bank of England, the coal mines, railways, steel,
civil aviation, cables and wireless, gas and electricity. Waterways and
some road transport also became state-owned. The overwhelming reasons
for this remarkable interventionist activity were political. The party's
commitment to managing the capitalist system and to injecting a socialist
philosophy was paramount. Clause Four of the Labour party's constitution called (and still does) for 'the public ownership of the means of
production, distribution and exchange'. In practice the party both in
1945-51 and since was content to take over what the late Aneurin Bevan
called 'the commanding heights' of the economy. From the list of new
state industries above, it can be seen that these commanding heights
included at its core the fuel, power and transport industries. The
influence these state-owned industries could have over the remainder
of the economy in private hands is obvious enough. The proponents of
nationalisation in the early 1950s argued that only the co-ordination
resulting from unified (geographical) ownership could produce really
efficient industries as in the case of the railways. In this case, however,
it was not too clear whether it was intended that they should be run on
a commercial basis: the social service argument was never far in the background. They also held that in the case of the 'natural monopolies' these
must be state-managed to ensure the realisation of scale economies in
large scale units and to prevent abuse of monopoly power i.e. gas and
electricity. To such general arguments specific reasons, applicable to
certain of the industries, were advanced. In the case of the coal mines
there was a strong belief in the need for state ownership as a means of
both improving technical methods and industrial relations since it was
judged that industry's record up to 1939 was particularly deficient in
these respects. But the steel industry was very much at the heart of the
political divide. The incoming Conservative government denationalised
the industry in 1953 but retained a measure of central control concerning pricing and investment policies over the industry through the Iron
and Steel Board. The Wilson government nationalised the leading 14
firms in 1967 at a time when the industry was facing strong international
competition and making very low profits. The ailing state of the industry
and the need for drastic measures to improve efficiency in fact tempered
the political debate in 1967.[4]

Verdicts on the economic record of the nationalised industries have,
inevitably, been many and varied. Given the fact that together they now
account for about 11 per cent of UK net output, employ some 8 per

cent of the nation's workforce, and are responsible for 24 per cent of all industrial investment, the relevance of assessments of their performance is at least obvious. It is not difficult to point to problems of overmanning, labour relations, low productivity and low (or even negative) returns on capital invested.[5] But political interference has bedevilled the operations of these industries. The public corporations that manage these large industries were supposed to have considerable day autonomy in the interest of efficiency, within a measure of ministerial direction. Mr Herbert Morrison, who oversaw Labour's nationalisation programme after 1945, had argued that the public corporation would try to get the best of both possible worlds – 'the worlds of vigorous industrial enterprise without the restrictions imposed by civil service methods and Treasury control, and the world of public service and accountability'.[6] The 'arm's length' relationship between government and state corporation envisaged by Morrison in practice has been very difficult to discern. White Papers in 1961 and 1967 offered clearer political direction for the nationalised industries on the crucial matters of financial targets and investment appraisal.[7] But although these measures offered a more effective business framework within which to operate, the new objectives were overridden by government decisions concerned with macroeconomic policy. Both the Heath government, between 1972-74, and the subsequent Wilson administration deliberately froze prices of nationalised industries as part of other anti-inflation measures. The government later insisted that the nationalised industries still meet their financial targets. These industries then lost the special subsidies that they had been receiving to offset the losses arising from price restraint. Inevitably they had to effect massive price rises to meet their required rates of return. Thus there occurred the distortions of artificially low prices during the period that the public sector observed price restraint followed by rapid rises to correct the situation.

The long record of the predisposition of government Ministers to 'meddle and muddle' in the affairs of these industries has inevitably led to a call for new arrangements under which decisions would be made. As yet no solution seems in sight.

Samuel Brittan has argued that 'nationalisation transforms the most humdrum commercial decisions into major political issues'.[8] A good example of how strong political pressures manifest themselves was the decision in November 1958 over the siting of a new steel strip mill. After much delay due to resolving local and government department pressures the decision was announced by no less than Prime Minister Macmillan himself. He declared that there would be government support for *two* new steel mills. One was to be built in Wales, one in Scotland. The Welsh steel mill was to be sited at the then remaining nationalised firm of Richard Thomas and Baldwins. The Scottish mill was to be built at the privately-owned firm of Colvilles' Ltd. The government lent sums to both concerns. This itself is an interesting comment on the nature of intervention by a Conservative administration. The decision neatly solved the problem of disappointing one country but at the price of saddling the Scottish plant at Ravenscraig not only with a sub-optimal plant but also no local ready market for its output. Justifying his decision in the House of Commons the Prime Minister referred to it as 'a matter of judgement, perhaps a little like that of King Solomon'.[9]

A more recent example of intervention in the steel industry, where political pressures were again to the fore, was the decision to delay the closure of certain high-cost plants in order not to exacerbate the existing problem of high local unemployment. A similar policy was applied in the case of the coal industry in the 1960s and the electricity industry's choice of primary fuel being deliberately biased in favour of coal rather than atomic energy. On the political dimension one can also cite the doubts as to whether Parliament feels it has adequate accountability of the public corporations. Even with the assistance of its own bi-partisan Select Committee which can call for papers and summon witnesses, the House of Commons has had difficulty in making an effective check on the government-nationalised industry interface.[10]

Planning

Many direct controls of business activity which had come into existence during the Second World War disappeared during the early 1950s despite the inevitable delays caused by the Korean War. Such controls included the allocation of and restriction on the use of materials, price controls, licensing of various kinds and government purchasing of imports. Rationing of consumer foodstuffs finally ended in 1954 and this also marks the virtual disbandment of the cumbersome regulations which had necessarily been introduced for a war-time economy. On the other hand restrictions on public borrowing by companies were still controlled by the Capital Issues Committee until 1959. The process of abolishing such controls was essentially carried out by successive Conservative administrations after 1951. In so far as these governments represented a party broadly sympathetic to the interests of private enterprise these policies are thus not surprising. But the change in government in 1951 and the Conservative party success in two subsequent elections made less difference than might be supposed.[11]

What is certain is that after a decade in power the Conservative party's traditional hostility to any notion of planning weakened given the weak performance of the UK economy at least as compared with her European rivals. It was dissatisfaction with the generally slow pace of economic growth and also the 'stop-go' character of demand management that provides the background to the creation of the National Economic Development Council (Neddy) in 1963. Its tripartite membership — representatives of government, industry and trade unions — discussed the industrial implications of a 4 per cent economic growth target. Following the end of 13 years of Conservative governments, 1965 witnessed the publication of the much heralded National Plan produced by the Labour government's newly-established Department of Economic Affairs. But any intention on the part of Mr Wilson's new government to make the Plan a lasting centrepiece of its legislative programme, and indeed a statement of its broad industrial policy, disappeared with the passage of emergency deflationary measures just ten months later. Both the NEDC Office and its 'little Neddies' for various industries have produced since 1963 a lengthy list of various reports and plans. But clear evidence that they have had a major, continuing influence on government or industrialists in their first ten years is very difficult to discern.[12] On the other hand in November 1975 the NEDC moved again rather nearer to the forefront of policy-making with its creation of 37 working parties set up to report on supply constraints in their own particular sectors. This was the inauguration of the Labour government's 'new industrial strategy'. In a sense it was a planning exercise beginning at the micro level — from the bottom — rather than, as in the case of the abortive National Plan, from the top. The reports of the various Sector Working Parties, involving over 300 recommendations for action (mainly by government), were considered by the NEDC in July 1976. The practical effect of this planning approach is to be seen in government financial measures to improve efficiency in the private sector and it is therefore appropriate at this point to turn to the issue of industrial investment.

Investment

Incentives to businessmen to invest greater sums in plant and equipment have existed in various forms throughout the post-war period.[13] Various governments have tinkered with their form and availability: whether they should be as grants or loans, for manufacturing industry only or also for the service trades, available only in specific regions or throughout the country. At the heart of the matter has been the belief that

Britain's record of slow economic growth is fundamentally a problem
of a lack of investment. The alleged reluctance by businessmen in Britain
to invest compared with their European counterparts has led to claims
that the answer lies in the fact they are constrained by a lack of finance.
In other words financial sources were failing to support worthwhile investment opportunities. It was against this background that it was proposed
by Mr Tony Benn, the then Secretary for Industry, that financial institutions should be compelled to channel up to £1.5b per year into manufacturing investment. The National Executive Committee of the Labour
Party indeed proposed in 1976 taking the banks and insurance companies into public ownership for their alleged failure to support manufacturing industry.[14] The City of London has thus been on the defensive. The Bank of England in 1974 had already persuaded the financial
institutions into offering up to £1b for Finance for Industry, a new
holding company incorporating two bodies which had aided both small
and large companies ever since 1945. These bodies, the Finance Corporation for Industry (FCI) and the Industrial and Commercial Finance
Corporation (ICFC) had been set up by the Bank of England together
with the London and Scottish clearing banks to assist respectively large
and small firms in the return to peacetime business activity. By 1974
their combined investments stood at £270m, a sum clearly felt to be
inadequate given the escalation of support announced in that year.

In October 1974 ex-Prime Minister Wilson was appointed head of a
committee to establish how effectively financial institutions were
operating in the UK with particular reference to the provision of
funds for industry and state. To understand the rationale of this Committee to Review the Functioning of Financial Institutions the reader
needs to appreciate that many in the Labour party during the past decade have sought nationalisation of the banks and insurance companies.
But the new body was set up at a time of growing doubts concerning
the ability or willingness, given their traditional functions in this respect
unlike some of their European counterparts, of the banks to support
industry. The insurance companies and pension funds responded rather
unwillingly to pressure from the Bank of England to channel equity
capital into industry by setting up Equity Capital for Industry in mid-
1976. But its resources of some £40m were small, particularly if one
believed firms could not for example generate funds through rights
issues. The first chairman of the National Enterprise Board (a body discussed later), Lord Ryder, not untypically asserted that 'substantial
sections of British industry are having to hold back essential programmes
of modernisation, expansion or reequipment because of inability to raise

the right kind of finance and that this is particularly true of medium-sized, unquoted and family-controlled companies'.[15] This is a bold claim that is less easy to substantiate, but the preliminary report of Mr Wilson's committee seemed to argue that if there is a finance problem in industry, it is more a demand than a supply one.

The continuing concern about the level of investment in manufacturing industry has involved a strong regional influence. It is therefore necessary at this point to show interventionism has had this geographic dimension.

Regional Policy

Government policy towards the location of new industrial enterprises has become progressively more active involving concern with the problem of localised unemployment. Powers existed under the 1945 Distribution of Industry Act for the government to undertake a variety of measures to make such problem areas more attractive for the siting of new plants. There was also the need for an industrialist to secure an Industrial Development Certificate if he wished to erect any building over 5000 square feet. But not until the 1958 recession in the economy was the latter power really used to steer plants into areas of relatively high unemployment. The announcements in early 1960 by the five leading British car firms that they each intended to site new car plants in either Merseyside or Scotland heralded a more active phase of government policy towards location. The previous section of investment indicated a certain bias built into the incentives concerning capital expenditure. The 1966 Industrial Development Act allowed grants of 40 per cent in the development areas (20 per cent elsewhere) towards the cost of new plant and machinery in manufacturing industry. Services were excluded. Only in development areas was there 25 per cent or 30 per cent grants for buildings. From 1967 till 1977 manufacturing enterprises in the areas of high unemployment also received a regional employment premium. This wage subsidy (which partially offset the labour-saving bias of the capital grants) was justified as an effective export subsidy as well as on the grounds of promoting greater regional equality. But both the REP and the selective employment tax (see below) which operated from 1966 till 1973, were strongly criticised for their bias against the service sector. What becomes evident from the above is the attempt by the Labour government to use strongly discriminatory taxation and subsidy policies in pursuit of the aims of alleviating localised unemployment and generally assisting industrial expansion. In 1970 the Heath government favoured tax incentives on the grounds that investment grants favoured inefficient firms as much as efficient ones. It therefore moved to a system of investment allowances and free depreciation (100 per cent allowances in first year) on plant and machinery in the development areas. But grants with a regional bias were brought back again in 1972 for the development areas. It should now be obvious that British governments have certainly not been unwilling to offer inducements or 'carrots' to employers to effect what is believed to be a more optimal location of industry. There has also been an accompanying policy of 'penalties' and bans through the need for an Industrial Development Certificate outside the Development Areas and, since 1965, an Office Development Permit in the south-east of England. The latter measure had been introduced as a result of the 1965 Control of Office and Industrial Development Act but since 1975 such permits have only been needed for very large office developments in London and the southeast of England. The 1965 Act reflected the then concern with the physical growth of London and the wish to contain its expansion in the interests of national efficiency. It is a measure of the capital's changing fortunes that by 1977 the Location of Offices Bureau was now asked to steer firms to the metropolis rather than fulfil its original purpose of trying to assist firms to shift their head offices outside London. In 1969 the Labour government had introduced special help for the so-called Intermediate Areas, a definition for those parts of the country which, although they were not as depressed as the Development Areas, were certainly not visibly prosperous. This assistance was offered following the recommendations by the Hunt Report and indicated that Britain had now evolved a basic four-part sliding scale of regional aid (Special Development Areas/Development Areas/Intermediate Areas/Rest of Country).

The dispersal of government departments from London to the provinces and the publication of various regional strategic plans also bear testimony to the activist nature of British regional policies. Both the measures outlined above and the political effort they involved indicate that British governments have been much concerned with regional disparities in prosperity whether the latter is measured by income, unemployment rates or some more explicit social indicator like housing or health. The evidence as is available suggests that regional policies have had some impact in diverting investment to the development areas.[16] In assessing their effectiveness in hard economic terms we have, of course, to realise also the social and political motivations for regional policies.

Micro Repercussions of Macro Policies

This account does not attempt to review the rationale and nature of economic policies since the war concerned with the stabilisation of the British economy. But it is necessary to point out the impact on certain industries of the fiscal, monetary and incomes policies that have been pursued. It became conventional wisdom by the mid-1960s to state that fiscal and monetary policies had failed during the 13 years of Conservative government. 'Stop-go' was the term to indicate successive swings in policy. Certainly the changes in demand management strategy caused many industrialists to lament the absence of a stable environment in which to operate and it is not surprising that there developed enthusiasm for French-style economic planning. The motor car industry in particular argued that the operation of hire purchase regulations and purchase tax had the effect of weakening the export drive. The argument was that in the periods when deflationary measures were being applied car firms faced higher unit costs as their market contracted.[17] They did not enjoy the full benefits of scale economies in mass car production and were thus penalised in world markets. The motor manufacturers therefore argued for a stable car market at home as being supportive of a good export market and not, as might be supposed, in competition with it in the sense that there would be minimal efforts to export cars if the home market was buoyant. Similar claims were made by manufacturers of other consumer durable goods. Between 1950 and 1975 there were no less than 47 changes in consumer credit restrictions, rental deposits and tax levels.[18]

The replacement of purchase tax by a value added tax in 1973 is explained essentially by copying EEC practice but is in part by the wish to have a fiscally more neutral instrument in the field of indirect taxation. The various rates of purchase tax had attracted much criticism on the grounds of anomalies that inevitably arose in a system attempting a fine gradation of goods from necessities to luxuries. But VAT itself became a two-tier tax in 1975 and the new 25 per cent rate on certain 'luxury' items had the effect of worsening the already depressed firms making products like colour television sets, domestic appliances, caravans and boats. It was not surprising that firms in these industries witnessed falling sales and redundancies and felt that they had quickly returned to that part of the economy subject to short-term macro-economic regulation In November 1976 the then second permanent secretary of the Treasury, Mr Alan Lord, claimed that a more consistent approach in government policies towards industry was badly needed. Citing the fact that there had been 14 changes in the rates of tax on domestic electric appliances over the last two decades, Mr Lord argued that:

> The effect of these changes has in the long run been highly debilitat-
> ing, not least in the case of some of the changes which were meant to
> be expansionary because these often tended to ignore the fact that
> manufacturing industry in Britain has a relatively low rate of response
> to increases in demand for its products so that any rapid expansion
> of demand risks at least a temporary increase in imports and at worst
> a permanent diminution of the home products' market share.[19]

He was reported as saying that a major policy defect of the past 20
years had been 'the failure to provide any effective link between analysis,
prescription and action as they relate to those economic problems which
have their root in our inadequate manufacturing performance'.[20] The
fiscal measure affecting industry that caused most political controversy
in the 1960s was undoubtedly selective employment tax (SET) introduced in 1966. Its creator, Professor Nicholas Kaldor, was a year later
to argue in his inaugural lecture that it was needed to rectify the problems
caused by Britain's 'premature maturity'.[21] The expanding service sector
where allegedly productivity was low was seen by those who supported
SET as a drag on Britain's economic prospects, and needed to carry a
fiscal penalty. As *The Economist* at the time put it, SET was 'a huge
payroll tax, amounting to some £375 million a year, deliberately imposed
on the service industries, who are at the same time kept deprived of any
investment incentives, so that they cannot replace with machines the
surplus labour that they should now be shedding; plus an actual payroll
subsidy, amounting to some £135 million a year, to manufacturing
firms, who are thus encouraged to use their labour even more wastefully,
at the same time as they are the only people who are given an incentive
to put in new machines to replace it.'[22] Whatever the case for raising
more taxation from the service sector or its productivity performance
compared with manufacturing industry, one can make the following
uncontentious comments. Firstly, that in practice the Standard Industrial
Classification used as the basis for the tax's operation was at the outset
inevitably going to result in serious anomalies. The allocation of industries
as between the favoured manufacturing sector and the penalised services
sector was bound to be arbitrary at the margin. At the level of the individual firm the impact of SET of course depended on the industry to
which one was classified. For multi-product firms the tax inevitably gave
rise to anomalies. A second comment on SET, concerning the claim that
productivity in retailing had been enhanced by the imposition of SET, is

suspect given the pressure of other factors at work notably the ending of resale price maintenance arising from Mr Heath's 1964 Resale Prices Act.[23]

British industry was much affected by the Labour government's prices and incomes policies after 1965. The National Board for Prices and Incomes, established in April 1965, issued no less than 170 reports before its demise five years later. The NBPI saw itself as stimulating improvements in efficiency and productivity but for both trade unions and employers a reference to the Board usually meant a frustrated wage and/or price increase. The Board's importance lay not only in the range of its references concerning the private sector but also from its 'efficiency audit' of the nationalised industries after 1967 and its continuing concern (as standing references) with three cases including the pay of the armed forces. Its impact in certain cases was clearly crucial. Within the private sector the baking industry was the subject of six reports and there were three concerning engineering. Bus transport was reported on no less than nine times, coal on five occasions and gas six times. Some of the effects of the NBPI's work is difficult to assess because of the long-term nature of the proposals made but in the case of the public sector its pricing recommendations—involving the application of the marginal cost principle—appear to have been particularly successful.[24]

The Heath government's 'U-turn' on the desirability of a statutory prices and incomes policy in 1972 led to the creation of the Price Commission to administer the Prices Code. The Commission continued to influence industry by making individual industry reports for government consideration.[25]

The final issue on a macro plane to be referred to is the profitability of British industry. For industrial and commercial enterprises the rate of return, on a replacement cost basis, fell from 12 per cent in 1964 to below 4 per cent ten years later. It was against this background that in November 1974 the government announced measures to ease the burden on companies of corporation tax and also a relaxation of price controls. The low level of profitability in recent years has been acknowledged as deterring companies from undertaking investment in new plant. The provision of state finance under such schemes as 'accelerated projects', 'selective investments', and 'sectoral industry schemes' at least enables industry to survive under such an unhealthy environment. It is inappropriate here to dilate on the merits of state funds as a suitable alternative source but it should be noted that government aid is selective and implies no role for the capital market. In an earlier section it was shown how British governments have willingly offered investment incentives such that they, in effect, pay about half the cost of investment. The rider to this situation is that funds are liable to be deployed in many strictly unprofitable investments.[26] With this appreciation of certain macro dimensions, it is now time to trace the course of British industrial policy in the past decade.

Industrial Policy

1966 really marks the beginning of a more comprehensive and continuous policy towards British industry than had been the case hitherto. Before this date intervention had been essentially *ad hoc* and specific to one industry, except for regional policy which was in our sense here of general nature.

Perhaps the most dramatic selective example of intervention in manufacturing industry before 1966 that can be cited is the 1959 Cotton Industry Act which both subsidised the removal of old cotton spindles and looms (two-thirds of the cost being state-financed) and encouraged existing firms to replace them with more modern equipment. In this case the government's wish to help eliminate excess capacity had seemed to be based on the belief that it was appropriate for the nation to assist in the rescue of a former great industry that had played so important a role during the Industrial Revolution in prompting the rise of British capitalism. No doubt too the then highly marginal nature of many Parliamentary constituencies in Lancashire, the home of the cotton industry, was a pressing factor in explaining the special attention of Mr Macmillan's Conservative administration! Having ruled out the possibility of tariff and quota protection for the cotton industry to stave off the import competition problem, government intervention in this case effected the only remaining alternative — a reallocation of existing resources. It is important to note that under the Act the generous compensation offered for scrapping old plant was conditional on firms receiving it paying adequate redundancy compensation to displaced employees. Thus this interventionist measure had both labour as well as product market dimensions.[27] But we must revert to our present point — the lack of a systematic approach to an industrial policy until the mid-1960s. The activities of the Industrial Reorganisation Corporation (IRC) inevitably received considerable public attention and criticism: its rationale was indeed an arguable one but at least there was a White Paper that spelt out what it was supposed to do.[28] The IRC was set up in 1966 with large funds to actively foster mergers and was notably involved in the bid by the General Electric Company (GEC) for AEI in 1967. Its prescription for acting as a catalyst in Britain's industrial reconstruction seemed to rest as one distinguished American industrial economist drily put it, on finding the most efficient firm and merging the rest of them into it.[29] It was not surprising that critics argued that British policy on monopolies and mergers was ambivalent: the Monopolies Commission existed to act as a restraint on them while the IRC encouraged them.[30] The IRC, and indeed the government, was active in encouraging a merger between the British Motor Corporation and Leyland Motors in 1968 and the problems of the newly-created car giant were to prove a severe test for the Labour government in its next period of office.[31] One of the directors of the IRC has argued that it was perhaps 'the most novel, most high-powered, most entrepreneurial, most publicised, most controversial, but ultimately the most significant and successful, of the innovations in economic management introduced by the Labour Government of 1964-70'.[32] Whether true or not, the IRC was wound up by the incoming Conservative administration in May 1971.

If the creation of the IRC is taken as the beginning of British industrial strategy it was further developed two years later by the terms of the 1968 Industrial Expansion Act. Now with the aim of 'modernisation and technological advance of industry and in the expansion of its capacity' in mind the government had powers to give aid to 'desirable' projects otherwise lacking financial support and in so doing, have the benefit of the views of the Industrial Development Advisory Board. From the government's viewpoint the Act had the great merit of economising on scarce Parliamentary time since it eliminated the need for new specific legislation on each case deemed deserving of support. Mr Wilson's state support for the development of the British aluminium smelting industry is worthy of comment since it was one project justified in terms of its beneficial import-saving effect for Britain's weak balance of payments position.[33] Given the general weakness of the pound sterling in the mid-1960s the Labour government was attracted by the hope of making foreign exchange savings of some £40m a year by importing alumina rather than dearer aluminium ingots. Thus in July 1968 the government announced its support for the building of three smelters one each for England, Scotland and Wales and every one in a development area. Not only were loans made under the terms of the 1966 Industrial Development Act and the 1968 Industrial Expansion Act but two of the new plants were favoured by special low-cost electricity charges. Norway, the largest aluminium ingot producer in Europe, had made a formal protest to Britain in 1968 concerning the expansion of the British smelting industry on the grounds that the government had breached the agreed European Free Trade Area rules on unfair competition. Norway alleged

that the loans and grants given to the aluminium smelting companies
constituted an illegal subsidy but had to be satisfied with a British government denial and a trimming of the planned capacity on two of the
smelters.

Mr Heath's administration avowed its belief in 1970 in disengage-
ment from industry. It sold off the Carlisle and Scottish public houses
which were in public ownership and also the two travel agents, Lunn-Poly
and the world-famous Thomas Cook & Sons. But its disinclination to
put public money into failing firms—so-called 'lame ducks'—was however severely tested by the Rolls-Royce crisis in early 1971. The un-
characteristic outcome was the nationalisation of the company's aero-
engine division by a party of the Right. The Heath government, like
its predecessor, also became embroiled in the troubles of the shipbuilding
industry and in particular the fate of the Upper Clyde Shipbuilders con-
sortium.[34] UCS collapsed in June 1971 after less than three years of life
as a forced fusion of hitherto rival companies. UCS was not an example
of concentration arising from voluntary merger as proposed by the
Geddes committee of inquiry but one effected by government pressure
with the financial backing of the then Shipbuilding Industry Board. In
a later comment (in 1976) on the industry *The Economist* argued

> For 10 years, British shipbuilding has been in a perpetual Chrysler-
> type crisis; panic rescues have bought time, but nearly all failed to
> cure low productivity, late deliveries, bad design, bad labour relations,
> inept management, and Victorian marketing. Today, £329m of public
> money later, the same diseases afflict the industry, and the beneficiar-
> ies of these past rescues are, by and large, still the weakest firms.[35]

In 1977 the ailing industry passed into public ownership as British Shipbuilders. What the Upper Clyde Shipbuilders and Rolls-Royce crisis had
done in 1971 was to fray the tight rein of the Conservative government's
purse strings. In 1972 there was a change in direction.

In its 1972 White Paper *Industrial and Regional Development* the Conservative government had also argued that to achieve faster economic
growth Britain's industrial base had to be strengthened by encouragement of investment. Its 1972 Industry Act enabled financial assistance
(up to £5m without Parliamentary approval) to be given to firms if the
government considered this to be in the national interest when the sums
needed could not be obtained elsewhere. Thus the main political parties
in Britain had each within a space of five years now accepted the case
for selective short-run intervention. (The reader will recall the Labour

government's introduction in 1967 of REP.) But the greater enthusiasm for interventionism, not surprisingly, was to be found in the Labour party which proposed in 1973 the creation of a National Enterprise Board 'to introduce public ownership into the strongholds of private industry'.[36] This proposal was not a new one since a state holding company had first been discussed five years previously. The Labour Party Study Group that argued the case for the NEB argued that similar agencies existed in Europe and elsewhere. The Industrial Development Institute in France, the West German VIAG and the IRI in Italy were all held up as parallel bodies acting as sources of finance, managerial expertise and advice. The Study Group hoped that the proposed NEB would likewise make British industry more responsive to public need rather than to private profit. Their hopes were able to come to fruition with the Labour party's return to power in 1974 and the subsequent passage of the 1975 Industry Act. The NEB was indeed to have the function of acting as a holding company for existing government equity shareholdings and also restructuring British industry. But its role was to be less free-ranging than the Study Group had proposed. Government approval was necessary before acquiring either any shareholding of 30 per cent or more or one that involved over £10m. Moreover the NEB was to be subject to ministerial direction as part of the government's industrial strategy and it was intended that as part of its normal activity it would have a particularly important role in creating employment in the assisted areas. The NEB's resources were not unlimited (£1b total limit and funds also restricted per year) and overall an 'adequate' return on the capital employed was required from the investments made by the NEB. This reality contrasts strongly with the 1973 Study Group's report where controlling interests in twenty-five of the largest British firms had been regarded as crucial for the success of the whole exercise. The NEB's teeth had been as one commentator put it 'well and truly drawn'[37] and as another observed the NEB was likely to belie the second word in its name. Rather than be enterprising it was in danger of becoming 'the emergency department of the national lame-duck and job-preservation clinic'.[38]

This second comment no doubt had in mind the fact that the NEB had become responsible for managing Britain's sickly motor manufacturer, British Leyland. The first chairman of the NEB, Lord Ryder, had in December 1974 become involved in the troubles of the company having been asked to report to government on British Leyland's problems and prospects. The Ryder Report of April 1975 was a severe indictment of British Leyland's management structure and market performance. No triumph here for the 'big is best is British' thinking as represented by the work of the Industrial Reorganisation Corporation, a body discussed above. The Labour government accepted the report's proposal that the government acquire the company for a nominal consideration and the need for a reorganisation of its corporate structure. Political considerations ruled out harsh surgery: Prime Minister Harold Wilson himself argued that a rescue of British Leyland was called for since a million jobs were at stake. A similar overriding concern with job-preservation was clear in the £162m aid for Chrysler (UK) announced in December 1975. This crisis clearly revealed conflicting views within the Cabinet as to the appropriate response the British government should make to an American car manufacturer that wished to close its ailing British subsidiary. The timing of the Chrysler rescue is particularly worthy of comment since it came but a month after the inauguration of the highly publicised long-term 'industrial strategy'. The British government had within a year propped up two unprofitable motor car firms: it was now proposing, in concert with industry and the trade unions, through the machinery of the NEDC, to pick on growth sectors which would be stimulated by government. For some observers it was difficult to resist the feeling that the (now familiar) calls for more investment in manufacturing industry and higher labour productivity to improve Britain's industrial performance were but the shadow of a new policy. Its substance would remain as before in the preservation of firms which had experienced falling sales. Large sums of public money would continue to be forthcoming to shore up concerns over whose future the government would indulge in optimistic thinking about their profitability.

To stimulate investment during the recession in the economy the government announced in April 1975 a scheme for assistance to bring forward major projects which had been postponed, using the provisions of the 1972 Industry Act. This accelerated projects scheme was followed by the selective investment scheme which enabled the present government to assist major projects which would not be undertaken in the absence of state aid. Under Section 8 of the 1972 Industry Act over £240m has been allocated for spending on 'industry schemes'. In these cases the NEDC industrial working parties have been invariably involved in drawing up a modernisation scheme for all firms within a given sector. The industries receiving such aid include ferrous foundries, machine tools, wool textiles and clothing. As is clear from the above the Conservative government's 1972 Act has been extensively used by their Labour successors to an extent the former could hardly have foreseen.

The Labour government's 1975 Industry Act in fact facilitated intervention since the need for the state to establish a lack of existing private sector support (as required in the 1972 Act) was removed. This Act was the measure also formally creating the NEB and the scheme of Planning Agreements with leading firms. The need for a dialogue between large firms and government was argued for in a 1974 White Paper with its own telling title — *The Regeneration of British Industry*. That document argued for a less distant and refereeing approach by the state to industry and its replacement by 'a closer, clearer and more positive relationship between government and industry'.[39] But as yet in the summer of 1978 it is difficult to evaluate the substance of this new relationship as expressed in planning agreements.

A second comment is needed on the 1972 Industry Act concerning its use by a Labour government. The scale of financial support given to certain worker co-operatives — below £5m — was such as to not involve immediate Parliamentary approval. The sum of £4.95m for the Meriden Motorcycle co-operative was hardly coincidence! On this case, and indeed other examples of selective assistance, it should be noted that the House of Commons Public Accounts Committee strongly criticised the Industry Minister in 1976 for his use of public funds.

A more long-standing area of intervention by government has been in the field of research and development. The state has directed aid to the National Research Development Corporation (NRDC) since its foundation in 1948, with the aim of encouraging inventions and their exploitation. Jointly-funded ventures with industry now number over one thousand. The technical record of the NRDC appears to have worldwide acclaim though some feel government support for it needs to be enhanced.

Some State-Dependent Industries

British government support for the aircraft industry since 1945 has been given on grounds of defence and the balance of payments as well as with consideration of national prestige. As an expert economist on this industry has put it:

British government support for advanced technology projects such as Concorde and the RB211 jet engine is more appropriately explained by an economic theory of politics. With such projects there exists a readily identifiable producer interest group with employment, relatively favourable earnings, technology and other vote-winning attributes supported by a Ministry with a major budgetary involvement.[40]

It has been estimated that for the period 1950-70 state support for the British aircraft industry amounted to £1200m in terms of what could have been saved by purchasing aeroplanes from a lower cost source of supply i.e. the United States. The size and state of the industry has obviously been fundamentally affected by government decisions. In the 1950s the captive nature of the industry's market enabled the government to effect a drastic structural reorganisation of the industry in a short space of time. Moreover the hasty concentration of the industry into just five concerns—two each for aircraft manufacture and aero-engines and one for helicopters—was achieved with hardly any explicit ministerial explanation of its rationale. The computer industry is also an industry that has been critically affected by government policy. The bulk of the government's needs since 1968 have been bought under one tender from International Computers Ltd, in which the state has a large holding. ICL was formed in 1968 from ICT and the newly-merged English-Electric Computers—Elliott Automation to shore up British industry in the face of IBM domination. Since 1968 the micro-electronics industry has received nearly £10m state assistance principally through the NRDC quite apart from the hidden protection arising from ICL's captive market.

Government policy towards British agriculture reverted from a *laissez-faire* approach to one of active interventionism during the depressed 1930s. It involved the imposition of certain tariffs and quotas and encouraged the creation of monopolistic producer marketing boards. But it was the 1947 Agricultural Act which was the foundation of post-war agricultural policy, since it provided for an Annual Review at which the government and the National Farmers' Union negotiated guaranteed prices for most products for each year ahead. The Review system thus created a unique arrangement by which one small section of the community had the clear opportunity of influencing the government's determination of its prosperity. The political importance of the farmers' vote may have declined but agriculture continued to enjoy state support on the contentious grounds of farming's contribution in assisting Britain's invariably indifferent balance of payments position. Not until 1965 was there any real effort made to tackle structural problems as a means of meeting the low income farm problem. Since Britain's accession to the European Economic Community in 1973 agricultural policy has, in much more marked contrast than with manufacturing industry, been evolved in a European framework.

Competition and Consumer Protection Policy

Both Labour and Conservative governments have passed legislation concerned with monopolies, mergers and restrictive practices. The Labour
government's 1948 Monopolies and Restrictive Practices (Inquiry and
Control) Act, which created the Monopolies and Restrictive Practices
Commission, did not emulate the American anti-trust *per se* approach
but embodied a case by case approach. But the series of reports produced by the Commission (and in particular its 1955 special report on
Collective Discrimination) suggested a widespread and deeply entrenched
nature of restraints within many sections of British industry. Both main
parties were persuaded by the evidence available to take action and in
1956 the Conservative administration passed the Restrictive Trade
Practices Act. Its requirement that the various parties to restrictive
arrangements must publicly register them provided confirmation of the
belief that trade associations had been operating price-fixing and other
arrangements in virtually every sector of manufacturing activity. The
Act's judicial approach to restrictive trade practices is widely considered
to have been highly successful but it made more acute the need for a
policy on mergers.[41] Not until 1965 was any government able to prevent
the creation of undesirable monopolies. This was an early piece of legislation by the new Wilson administration and followed a year after legislation ending individual resale price maintenance passed by the Tory
government in its last months of office. But the government's powers,
under the 1965 Monopolies and Mergers Act, to refer merger cases to
the Monopolies Commission were not actively used in the following
decade and the permissive attitude that developed to mergers assisted
the rapid movement towards a more concentrated industrial structure in
British industry. Whereas the 100 largest UK firms accounted for about
one-third of net output in 1958 the figure now is probably over one-
half.[42] The scepticism about the social gains from this concentration
process has grown in the late 1970s and is likely to result in a tougher
policy on mergers. The generally sympathetic attitude to company
mergers particularly during the period of the 1964-70 Labour government was reflected in the work of a body already discussed — the
Industrial Reorganisation Corporation.

The past decade has seen an escalation of British interest in matters
concerning consumer protection and this has been reflected in an increase
in legislative and other measures to assist consumers. Long established
laws on Weights and Measures (since 1878), Sale of Goods (1893) and
Food and Drugs (1955) have been supplemented by various Acts concerning such matters as hire purchase (1965), medicines (1968) and the

receipt of unsolicited goods (1971). There have also been more general pieces of legislation passed since 1961 i.e. the Consumer Protection Act (1961), the Misrepresentation Act (1967) and the Trade Descriptions Act (1968). More spectacular from a political standpoint was the Heath government's about turn on consumer matters. After abolishing the Consumer Council, an advisory body, its 1973 Fair Trading Act provided for the appointment of a Director-General of Fair Trading whose task was to act as a public watchdog on all matters of relevance to consumers. The Director-General has certain powers concerning monopoly and mergers policy but for our purpose here it is necessary to indicate his work with the new Consumer Protection Advisory Committee in introducing measures for Parliamentary approval. It is clear that, competition policy apart, the Director-General has not been short of consumer complaints to keep him busy. Whether since 1975 the newly-established Consumers' Council has the same public standing and political punch is more doubtful. All the activity implied above (and much more besides) is however an indication of the soaring extent to which much British parliamentary time has switched to consumer matters. Food-stuffs are the striking example of this fact. As part of Labour's anti-inflationary policies since 1973 subsidies on certain foodstuffs were introduced and also maximum prices laid down. Unit pricing orders were introduced in 1974 for meat, fish and many vegetables. In the same year the government persuaded large retailers to voluntarily concentrate their promotional price cuts on staple foodstuffs. The Price Check Scheme in early 1976 was a scheme to restrain price rises below 5 per cent over a six-month period for a range of goods. This voluntary scheme may cynically be seen as a public relations exercise by a government anxious to be seen to be 'doing something' and that something that few would disagree with! Whatever the conclusion on this the consumer legislation cited above is evidence that Britain has clearly not been aloof from the call for more laws, as part of the consumer revolution.

Labour Market Policy

There has been a considerable increase in interventionist policies concerning the labour market in Britain in the past decade. It was in the period of a Conservative government that the 1964 Industrial Training Act provided for the establishment of Training Boards to improve the supply of skilled manpower. Even the party sympathetic to free market principles felt that existing training schemes in private industry were deficient and a state-imposed levy-grant system was now necessary to rectify the serious shortages that were believed to be a bottleneck on industrial expansion. The Manpower Services Commission was set up as a result of the 1973 Employment and Training Act to improve the operation of the labour market. The MSC co-ordinates the working of two subsidiary agencies. Firstly there is the Employment Services Agency which is responsible for the state employment service as reflected in the Job Centres. The professional and executive register is operated to find situations for white-collar workers. This agency also runs an occupational guidance service and effects financial assistance to those whose job change involves geographic mobility. The second agency, the Training Services Agency, is responsible for the work of the Government Training Centres and the Industrial Training Boards. The number of re-training places in Government Skill Centres has doubled in the 1970s though admittedly from the low level of around 17,000. But if the above measures indicate some bi-partisan thinking on improving the working of the labour market it needs to be contrasted with the fierce political debate on the subject of industrial relations and the role of the law concerning trade unions. The Conservative government's 1971 Industrial Relations Act followed the North American legal approach to collective agreements. It was followed by a reversal of its concept of unfair industrial practices to curb the incidence of strikes. The National Industrial Relations Court proved short-lived and was repealed by the 1974 Trade Union and Labour Relations Act.

Trade union opposition culminating in Mr Wilson facing lack of support from his own Cabinet, especially Mr Callaghan, had previously ended the proposals for reform expressed in the 1969 document 'In Place of Strife'. There was inevitably keen debate over the passage of the 1976 Trade Union and Labour Relations (Amendment) Act which was concerned with the emotive issue of the closed shop. The 1975 Employment Protection Act strengthened employees' rights in several ways and indicates that a pattern of legal intervention concerning industrial relations has now been established. This Act put the independent Advisory, Conciliation and Arbitration Service (ACAS) on a statutory footing. ACAS has been at work trying to improve the collective bargaining process.

Other recent measures affecting the labour market include the 1965 Redundancy Payments Act, the 1968 Race Relations Act, 1970 Equal Pay Act, the 1974 Health and Safety at Work Act and finally the 1975 Sex Discrimination Act. This together amounted to a formidable addition to the statute book.

The main political parties also have quite different viewpoints on the issue of industrial democracy. Lord Bullock's Committee's proposals

issued in 1977 indeed seem to have found a singular lack of strong support for its proposals from either organised labour or industrial
employers.[43]

Assessment

Irrespective of their political complexion governments have intervened
to an increasing extent in British industry. Just on the financial dimension
the degree of financial support is now large. The subsidies to privately
owned firms between 1974-75 and 1977-78 at 1977 survey prices is
estimated at £1,849m.[44] Interventionist measures have crucially affected
the shape of Britain's mixed economy and the concentration of production in the private enterprise portion of it. One theme running through
the series of interventions is the belief in the need to boost investment
to secure faster economic growth in Britain. Given the failing of macro-
economic policies to achieve higher living standards, detailed micro
measures have been felt required to fulfil the task. But there has also
been the concern to save jobs. As another observer has said, certain firms
receiving assistance 'were self-selected, that is they were problems which
presented themselves to governments'.[45] Solutions were needed with a
close eye on electoral consequences.

Writing of the Chrysler rescue one political commentator has written
that a principle of Sherlock Holmes is as relevant in politics as in crimin-
ology. David Watt, citing Conan Doyle – 'When you have eliminated the
impossible, whatever remains, however improbable, must be the right
answer'–said 'it is by this rule of thumb that most politicians survive'.[46]

The general effectiveness of the regional industrial and job-saving policies is open to doubt.[47] As has been cynically pointed out 'subsidies are
one of Britain's few growth industries these days'.[48] Peter Wilsher went
on to say that 'no one, in government or outside, has the faintest idea,
most of the time, of how these vast injections of subsidy-cash are
supposed to work, what they are intended to achieve, or whether, after
they have been withdrawn or amended, they can be held to have had any
effect'.[49] *The Economist* has said that 'The present government has
never had an answer to the Morton's fork of private enterprise theor-
eticians: healthy ducks don't need intervention, lame ones should not
get it'.[50]

One important dimension of British intervention is that it has
involved a nationalistic sentiment resulting in protection for British firms.
To take just one example, the £10m loan to British Leyland in 1970 on
condition that it bought British machine tools. The British motor industry
is one indeed that offers several illustrations of interventions with the

domestic concern being uppermost.

Max Corden has suggested that if there is a logic to intervention it is 'the principle of sectional income maintenance'.[51] He sees the aim of a 'conservative social welfare function' as preventing 'severe falls in incomes of any significant section of the community even if this intervention prevents incomes of other sections from rising'.[52] Let Samuel Brittan have the last word: 'One danger of this corporatist new world is that business success will come to depend on keeping in the good books of politicians and officialdom and in understanding how they operate, rather than in profitable low-cost service to the consumer. Some philosophers make a distinction between "knowing how" and "knowing that". They now need a third category "knowing whom".'[53]

Notes

1. A detailed examination of the IRC is to be found in S. Young & A. Lowe, *Intervention in the Mixed Economy* (Croom Helm, London, 1974).

2. R. Bacon & W. Eltis, *Britain's Economic Problem: Too Few Producers* (Macmillan, London, 1976).

3. The then Secretary of State for Industry, Mr Tony Benn, began the concern in an article in *Trade and Industry*, 4 April 1975, p. 2.

4. A detailed examination of the process of improving competitiveness in the steel industry is to be found in E. Owen Smith, *Productivity Bargaining: A Case Study in the Steel Industry* (Pan Books, London, 1971).

5. See 'The State and its Monopolies' in *The Uncommon Market, 15 Briefs on Markets, Money and Microeconomics* (The Economist, London, 1977), pp. 27-9. R. Pryke in 'Are nationalised industries becoming more efficient?' *Moorgate and Wall Street*, Spring 1970, and *Public Enterprise in Practice* (MacGibbon & Kee, London, 1971) argued that the productivity record of these industries was comparable to that in private manufacturing industry. This data was criticised in G. Polanyi and P. Polanyi 'The efficiency of nationalised industries', *Moorgate and Wall Street*, Spring 1972, and in *The Economist*, 30 October 1971, pp. 59-60. More recently Pryke seems to have become more critical of one nationalised industry at least. With J. Dodgson he wrote *The Rail Problem* (Martin Robertson, London, 1975) which was a strong condemnation of British Rail management and its use of manpower on the railways.

6. H. Morrison, *Government and Parliament: A Survey from the inside* (2nd edition) (Oxford University Press, London, 1959), p. 251.

7. White Paper 'The financial and economic obligations of the nationalised industries', Cmnd. 1337 April 1961, White Paper 'A review of financial and economic objectives' Cmnd 3437, November 1967.

8. S. Brittan, 'Nationalisation—an old controversy is back', *Financial Times*, 27 April 1972.

9. *Weekly Hansard*, Vol. 595, No. 437, 18 November 1958, Col. 1020.

10. In the case of the British Steel Corporation, its chairman and the Minister for Industry were strongly criticised in early 1978 for withholding critical information. See 'Committee on its metal', *The Economist*, 21 January 1978, pp. 15-16.

11. This is certainly the view of P.D. Henderson in 'Government and Industry' in G.D.N. Worswick and P. Ady (eds.), *The British Economy in the Nineteen-Fifties* (Clarendon Press, Oxford, 1972), p. 334.

12. For a recent review of planning see H. Shanks, *Planning and Politics: the British experience 1960-76* (Political and Economic Planning, London, 1977). A caustic comment on government intervention in British industry, and the NEDC in particular, has been made by the first managing director of the IRC, Mr Ronald Grierson.

Competition, with the accompanying penalties for failure, is not man's natural habitat. He accepts its discipline only if, and to the extent which, the rewards for success are correspondingly enticing. When these rewards cease to attract him the average businessman either opts out or seeks the safe anchorage of the corporate state and the cosy get-togetherness of the world of Neddy and public patronage.

Whenever a particular industry comes under Neddy scrutiny, the predictable discovery is that if only there were more collaboration and less competition and if only the Government would support – a convenient euphemism for subsidies – certain unprofitable activities, that industry would improve its compliance with the national interest.

If the national interest is deemed to lie in increased exports, Whitehall stimulates them by selective subsidies or guarantees; if the national interest is deemed to lie in shrinking an industry down to a single UK firm, incentives are offered to induce several firms to merge.

'The mirage of the state's entrepreneurial role', *Journal of Royal Society of Arts, Manufacturers and Commerce*, June 1978, p. 403.

13. A valuable survey is to be found in the issue of *The Economist*, 12 November 1977, 'Investment in Britain: A Survey'.

14. National Executive Committee of the Labour Party, *Banking and Finance Statement presented to 1976 Conference*, August 1976.

15. Cited in *Financial Times*, 11 November 1976.

16. B. Moore & J. Rhodes, 'Regional economic policy and the movement of manufacturing firms to development areas', *Economica*, Vol. 43, February 1976, pp. 17-31.

17. The industry had support from the National Economic Development Office as evidenced by reports in 1968 (*The Effects of Government Economic Policy on the Motor Industry*) and in 1970.

18. M. Parr & J. Day, 'Value added tax in the United Kingdom', *Westminster Bank Review*, May 1977, pp. 9-10.

19. 1976 Sir Ellis Hunter Memorial Lecture, *A Strategy for Industry* (University of York), p. 6.

20. Ibid., p. 7.

21. N. Kaldor, *Causes of the Slow Rate of Economic Growth of the United Kingdom*, An Inaugural Lecture (Cambridge University Press, 1966).

22. 'The Extraordinary Budget', *The Economist*, 7 May 1966, p. 559.

23. This problem was one that the report by W.B. Reddaway on the effects of SET could not overcome and caused considerable debate in the retail trade. *Effects of the Selective Employment Tax – First Report. The Distributive Trades*, HMSO January 1970.

24. See A. Fels, *The British Prices and Incomes Board* (Cambridge University Press, London, 1972).

25. See D.C. Hague, 'The Price Commission' in D. Lethbridge (ed.), *Govern-*

ment and Industry Relationships (Pergamon Press, Oxford, 1976). I. Lightman, 'Price controls in the United Kingdom 1973-78: natural development or radical change?' *Journal of Agricultural Economics*, Vol. 29, No. 3, September 1978.

26. *The Economist*, in comment on investment incentives said in its issue of 4 March 1978 (p. 10):

> Britain serves as an awful example of the country which for 30 years, has subsidised its stagnation in yesterday's industries, both by its crutches for lame ducks and by 'incentives' like its investment allowances. These latter mean that, for existing firms, the government pays about half the cost of investment, so that (to quote Mr Tony Harris of the Financial Times) 'investment attracting this treatment need only show half the return of any investment not so treated'. The British then wonder why their industry has made so many unprofitable investments, and why profits are such a low proportion of gnp but cannot easily be boosted by a cut in corporation tax since (after receiving those investment allowances, etc.) many corporations are not paying any net corporation tax at all.

27. See C. Miles, 'Protection of the British textile industry' in W.M. Corden & G. Fels, *Public Assistance to Industry: Protection and Subsidies in Britain and Germany* (Macmillan, London, 1976).

28. Cmnd. 2889, January 1966.

29. R. Caves, 'Market Organisation, Performance and Public Policy' in R. Caves (ed.), *Britain's Economic Prospects* (Allen and Unwin, London, 1968), p. 321.

30. The title of C.K. Rowley's article seemed not unfair: 'Monopoly in Britain: private vice but public virtue?', *Moorgate & Wall Street*, Autumn 1968, pp. 37-68.

31. The political machinations are vividly revealed in G. Turner, *The Leyland Papers* (Pan Books, London, 1973).

32. W.G. McClelland, 'The Industrial Reorganisation Corporation 1966/71: An Experimental Prod', *Three Banks Review*, June 1972. A more lengthy survey of the IRC is in S. Young & A. Lowe, *Intervention in the Mixed Economy* (Croom Helm, London, 1974).

33. This episode is discussed in G. Denton, 'Financial assistance to British industry' in W.M. Corden & G. Fels (eds.), *Public Assistance to Industry: Protection and Subsidies in Britain and Germany* (Macmillan, London, 1976), pp. 143-5.

34. See F. Broadway, *Upper Clyde Shipbuilders* (Centre for Policy Studies, London, 1976).

35. 'The deck's burning', *The Economist*, 14 February 1976, p. 85.

36. Opposition Green Paper, *The National Enterprise Board: Labour's State Holding Company*, Report of a Labour Party Study Group (Labour Party, 1973), p. 12.

37. K. Richardson, 'How they roped and tied Lord Ryder', *The Sunday Times*, 7 March 1976.

38. 'Curate's NEB', *The Economist*, 6 March 1976, p. 71.

39. Cmnd. 5710, para. 4, p. 1.

40. K. Hartley, 'Industry, labour and public policy' in R.M. Grant & G.K. Shaw (eds.), *Current Issues in Economic Policy* (Philip Allan Publishers, Oxford, 1975), p. 40.

41. D. Swann, D.P. O'Brien, W.P.J. Maunder & W.S. Howe, *Competition in British Industry: Restrictive Practices Legislation in Theory and Practice* (Allen and Unwin, London, 1974), pp. 195-7. S. Young in *Intervention in the Mixed Economy* sees the 1956 Act as an example of how the Conservative government 'set the rules' but did not become involved as a positive player in the game. Op.cit., p. 12.

As regards rules it also should be noted that legislation on company disclosure was passed by the Labour government in 1967 – the Companies Act – and at the present time it is proposed to demand still more information.

42. S.J. Prais, *The Evolution of Giant Firms in Britain* (Cambridge University Press, 1976).

43. *Report of the Committee on Industrial Democracy*, Cmnd 6706, HMSO, January 1977.

44. *Hansard*, Vol. 947, 10 April 1978, No. 92, Col. 954.

45. J. Mitchell, 'Government intervention and industrial policy' in R.T. Griffiths (ed.), *Government, Business and Labour in European Capitalism* (Europotentials Press, London, 1977), p. 69.

46. 'When you eliminate the impossible . . .' *Financial Times*, 19 December 1975.

47. Moves to instigate an appraisal are at last being made. For example C. Jones, 'Time to review industry aid', *Financial Times*, 11 January 1978.

48. P. Wilsher, 'Thank you for your support: I shall always wear it', *Sunday Times Business News*, 15 February 1976. This article was in comment on A. Whiting (ed.), *The Economics of Industrial Subsidies* (HMSO, February 1976).

49. Ibid.

50. 'Curate's N.E.B.', *The Economist*, 6 March 1976, p. 71.

51. M. Corden, 'Conclusions on the logic of government intervention' in M. Corden & G. Fels, op.cit., p. 215.

52. Ibid., p. 216.

53. S. Brittan, 'The new industrial strategy: Putting British companies on the dole', *Financial Times*, 19 August 1976. Relevant in this context is the £5m loan to Lonrho in June 1977 for purchasing most of the assets of Brentford Nylons from the receiver in bankruptcy. This loan coincided with publication of a critical government report on the firm that had been criticised earlier as showing 'the unacceptable face of capitalism'. *The Economist* at the time referred to the loan in discussing 'politically-motivated industrial patronage'. See 'Intervention without tears?', 25 June 1977, p. 83.

6 GOVERNMENT INTERVENTION IN THE ECONOMY OF THE FEDERAL REPUBLIC OF GERMANY

Eric Owen-Smith*

Introduction

Before the analysis can concentrate on the actual extent of government intervention in the Federal Republic, three introductory points should be made. First, the received theory of intervention in West Germany does not to a certain extent accord to the facts. In the first main section, therefore, the history and current philosophy of state intervention are examined. Secondly, the subject matter of this book is concerned with micro intervention, and the macro aspects are therefore generally not analysed. Some facets of social policy are the most notable omissions in this context, even though they may have important micro-economic ramifications such as hospital costs and labour market intervention. Thirdly, West Germany has a federal structure of government. The Federal Government accounts for only about half of total government spending. It follows that the Federal (*Bund*) and state (*Länder*) Governments share responsibilities for interventionist policies. The Länder Governments, and for that matter hundreds of local authorities, have on occasions opposed Federal Government intervention by displaying fiscal conservatism if faced with the possibility that their expenditure would rise more rapidly than their tax revenue.[1] Possibly as a result of this, the control over the Länder by the Bund has tended to increase for reasons of economic stabilisation.[2] The degrees of co-operation and conflict in this respect cannot be examined here.

The History and Current Philosophy of Government Intervention

History

The extent of government intervention in the economy of the Federal Republic is not only of economic significance. Many authors have attributed the ostensible post-second world war apprehension of government intervention in the Federal Republic to the experience of the country

*Dr Owen-Smith gratefully acknowledges two useful conversations with Federal Government officials but emphasises that any errors of facts, judgement or in translation are his own responsibility.

during the Hitlerite era. During this epoch the influence of the state was all pervasive; ultimately in the economic sphere a multiplicity of bodies, increasingly under central direction, 'interfered daily in the war economy'.[3]

The balance of opinion seems to favour the hypothesis that the extent of Nazi interventionism was the culmination of a trend discernible since the dramatic take-off of the German economy in the last quarter of the nineteenth century. Bowen has questioned this hypothesis in the sense that he stresses the economic aspects of the Hohenzollern Reich which approximated to the 'classical model of private capitalism'.[4]

But most authors, including the present one, would dissent from this view. One example is Barker – although perhaps his sixth edition would fall into Bowen's 'pro-Allied war propaganda' category. Nevertheless, Barker convincingly claimed that events vindicated Bismarck's 'far-seeing policy' of almost compelling German shipping lines to place orders with German ship yards by means of subsidies. On the other hand, Barker maintained that although all other German industries were fostered by the 'most skilfully framed protective tariff', the German chemical industry achieved its success practically without fiscal aid. Even here, however, the role of the government in promoting education and research was of crucial significance.[5] Further evidence of intervention over a long period, in the form of state ownership of potash and coal mines as well as cartel policy, is given by Gordon.[6] Moreover, the notion that the state has traditionally played a large role in German economic life is pursued in two classics of the literature. Stolper and Dahrendorf have no doubts on this score. Stolper sees the Bismarck era as responsible for pioneering the organisations and attitudes necessary for the first world war economy, the Weimar experiments and finally the Nazi period. This process, as both Stolper and Dahrendorf show, continued in the interwar period until the state controlled 'the circulation of the body economic'.[7]

The Social Market Economy

It is necessary to briefly examine the social market economy philosophy, because its chief academic proponent, Professor Eucken, saw this system as one of free price level adjustments in the market as opposed to an authoritarian economy with state control. Professor Erhard, who is credited with the political implementation of the social market economy, saw competition as the most promising means of securing prosperity. A national economic policy of neutrality was, however, a thing of the past: the state would find it necessary to obviate poverty and business collusion. But social policy must not run counter to the basic principles of the market economic order, as that would undermine industrial enterprise.[8]

After the second world war, the ostensible mistrust of state economic intervention did not immediately crystallise. The nationalisation of basic industries was generally advocated by both the Christian (CDU) and Social (SPD) Democrats.[9] Their rationale was to permanently arrest economic power from the industrialists who had condoned the rise of National Socialism. But then there was a metamorphosis. According to Adenauer, the CDU in 1949 fought the election campaign on the economic principles of the social market economy. Indeed, Adenauer associated nationalisation with the SPD, but the CDU narrowly emerged as the strongest party and he was selected (to his 'surprise') to become the first Federal Chancellor of the social market era.[10] The CDU then formed a coalition with the liberal FDP. However, Marxism was abandoned by the SPD in 1959 and, in effect, the social market economy has been adopted by all the major political forces in the Federal Republic.[11]

The economic 'miracle' of the 1950s, and the general continued economic expansion during the 1960s which resulted in the West German economy becoming one of the most important in the world, have been attributed to the social market economic philosophy. Some commentators maintain that the recession of the mid-70s has not been sufficient to shake the faith of the Federal Government, although suggestions for reform have been made by some academics.[12] Moreover, Professor Biedenkopf, a prominent CDU member, has gone as far as to regret the threat to the social market economy emanating from the 'acquisitive society'.[13] For the purpose of this analysis, the merits of such arguments can be ignored. It is only necessary to point out that there has been an increasing amount of state intervention, especially over the last fifteen years. This intervention has taken the form of legislation, the creation of specialist institutions, subsidies and government involvement in business and commerce. These areas are analysed below.

Legislation

There are three principal areas of legislation with respect to government economic intervention in the Federal Republic. The first is legislation against what is known in Germany as the restriction of competition. The second concerns the Promotion of Stabilisation and Economic Growth Act of 1967. The third area is that of regional policy, including agriculture

Legislation against the restriction of competition

In 1897 German law affirmed the legality of cartel agreements as equal to that of any other private contract. The first cartel law was introduced at the end of the hyper-inflation in 1923. It was not intended that the state should control the general pricing and production policy of cartels, but rather that the abuse of monopoly power should be prevented. Cartel agreements were not outlawed although a cartel court was established. Both the Court and the Minister of Economics were given powers of intervention to protect the public interest.[14] This did not prevent further concentration. German heavy industry, which prior to 1914 had already been concentrated in fewer hands than anywhere else in the world, was reduced to a few empires. In a wider context, the official estimate of the number of cartels in the mid-twenties was 2,500. By 1929/30 the number had grown to between 3,000 and 4,000.[15] In 1930 a further attempt at state control of the general behaviour of cartels was undertaken, including a general reduction in their agreed prices as part of a deflationary package.

At the end of the second world war, each of the Allied Powers in their separate geographic areas attempted to reduce business concentration. Chemicals, steel, coal and banking were the principal sectors involved. But it was in the American sector where the anti-trust philosophy was most evident.[16] (In the British zone more reliance was placed on involving the trade unions in the processes of re-democratisation and putting an end to cartels and monopoly power. Indeed, the re-introduction of co-determination, which has been significantly extended of late, was seen as one method of achieving this end.)[17] Hence, the initial attempts to draft legislation were modelled on American anti-trust policy.[18] The business community was active in lobbying against these proposals, arguing that a conflict existed between tough competition policy and speedy recovery.[19] Although Erhard and his officials in the Economics Ministry argued in favour of general prohibition of cartels, the majority of his Party held out for basic acceptance of the cartel principle with legal curbs on the exploitation of monopoly power.

A draft law first appeared in 1951, but it required the introduction of a number of highly important exceptions before the Act against the Restriction of Competition (*Gesetz gegen Wettbewerbsbeschränkungen*– GWB) eventually became law in 1957, by which time much of the pre-war concentration was again evident. A relaxation of Allied control, together with the encouragement of the ECSC in the case of steel, contributed to this process.[20] The chemical industry was an exception in the sense that IG Farben, which had been formed in the twenties but divided into three companies (Bayer, Hoechst and BASF) by the Allies, was never re-formed, although as Mann lucidly shows 'each of the three new companies achieved a bigger turnover than the parent body had ever reached and the heads of these concerns had considerable power'.[21]

The 1957 Act, amended in 1965 and 1973, all seem to have some loopholes, although the 1973 Act, introduced by a SPD/FDP coalition, went much further in its definitions of mergers than anything previously known in Germany. The absolute number of cartels has fallen from the inter-war period peak, probably due to recent activity on the resale price maintenance side. A Cartel Office was established by the 1957 Act and it has been responsible for a number of important investigations. If it rules against a restrictive agreement, however, affected companies can appeal through the courts, including the Supreme Constitutional Court. Ultimately, the Minister of Economic Affairs may overrule any judgement if he feels that a merger is in the public's interest. The introduction of the 1973 Act coincided, of course, with a dramatic increase in the level of unemployment and Ministers of Economics have often modified Cartel Office decisions where a merger would maintain or increase employment levels. The Cartel Office was for over 18 years led by a former member of the unsuccessful campaign for the prohibition of cartels. The whole ethos of the Office became one of relentlessly pursuing active public campaigns against business restrictive practices. It was the government which softened its attitude. The Office itself now has a more pragmatic president who since taking office in 1977 has introduced a re-organisation.[22] An independent Monopolies Commission was also established in 1973. Its first biennial report was published in 1976. It has also published special reports, including one on the partially state-owned VEBA corporation which will be examined below. The Commission's terms of reference require it to examine the position and development of business concentration.

Legislation against business restrictive practices in the Federal Republic remains, in effect, relatively weak. On the whole the German law was, for example, less tough than the British.[23] German law traditionally regarded combination as legitimate, whereas in English law a contract in restraint of trade was unenforceable in this context.[24] On the other hand, the recent German legislation marks something of a change in the traditional German attitude to cartels. However, if the total picture of the extent of government influence over business concentration has tended to be desultory, the importance of the German commercial banks, and later to a lesser extent the trade unions, receive almost universal acceptance as being key issues in this respect. Indeed, because of the influence they can exert over businesses by means of controlling voting rights, the big three commercial banks have been seen as almost a substitute for state economic planning, particularly when taken together with the concentration in heavy industry.[25] The proxy and direct voting powers of the banks on company boards are considerable. The role of trade union enterprise has been analysed by Hesselbach who shows how the trade unions today own extremely large enterprises.[26] One final point must also be emphasised. The Federal and Länder Governments have made grants and tax concessions worth hundreds of millions of DM promoting a 'middle-class support policy' (*Mittelstandpolitik*). Among other things, this assistance is intended to encourage the growth of small businesses.[27]

Briefly considering the future, it must be said that the SPD and their coalition partners (FDP) are not entirely agreed about the legal reforms still necessary.[28] The former see stricter control over large monopolistic enterprises as a desirable policy aim, whereas the latter are anxious to avoid any bureaucratic excesses which may arise in attempting to accomplish such an aim. Their Cabinet has adopted the 1976 Monopolies Commission Report which advocated increased powers for the Cartel Office to break up large monopolies and limiting the holdings of banks in nonbanking enterprises to 5 per cent. Legislative proposals along these lines will be introduced during 1978.

Promotion of Economic Stability and Growth Act (StWG)

During the sixties, particularly after 1967, the German economy began to exhibit economic fluctuations. Giersch has shown that average annual growth rates fell to about half of those achieved during the fifties.[29] In 1967, there was, by German standards, quite a serious recession. Professor Schiller's 1967 Act was therefore designed to arrest these trends.[30] Section 1 of the Act sets the economic policy aims for both the Federal and Länder Governments of achieving price stability, a high level of employment, external equilibrium and constant economic growth within the context of a market economy. These are, of course, macro-economic goals, but there are important provisions in the Act for direct micro intervention together with some fairly rudimentary economic 'planning' arrangements.

As a result, the interventionist role of the Federal Government, in association with the Länder Governments, became rather more formally institutionalised. Machinery which would facilitate the Government's attempts to influence the decision-making processes of the various economic agents—employers' associations, trade unions, public authorities and public opinion—was introduced.

Section 9 of the Act calls for a reviewable five-year finance plan, while Section 2 requires the Federal Government to table every January in both Houses an account of its economic and financial policies, together with its own projections for the coming year in these areas. Moreover, this Section also requires the Federal Government to similarly table its reactions to the annual report of the five-man Council of Economic Advisers which appears during November. The Council itself had been established by a special law in 1963, when there was a negative deviation from the average growth rate. It is not attached to a particular Ministry and the academics who compose it produce forecasts which are no more reliable than those produced elsewhere. Its recommendations are often challenged by the Federal Government. As this chapter was being written, for example, the Council had proposed that money wage increases be kept to 3.5 per cent, although the Metalworkers' trade union had already claimed twice that amount even though the steel industry was making losses. Generally speaking, the recent pronouncement of the 'Five Wise Men', as the Council is colloquially known, has received support from employers' associations but met with opposition from the trade unions.[31]

Section 3 of the Act provides for the preparation of 'orientation' data which are presented to the representatives of economic interest groups, notably employers' associations and trade unions. This body is collectively known as 'Concerted Action'. It has been mainly regarded as a forum for extolling wage restraint as a means of ensuring full employment and price stability.[32] Concerted action was thought to be 'dead' as early as 1970/71, but it survived until the trade unions (temporarily?) boycotted its fortieth session (1977) in protest against the employers challenging the extended Co-determination Act in the Constitutional Court.[33] Section 12 provides for micro subsidies to industry and this topic will be examined in a separate section below. The Act heralded for many the end of the social market economy and the advent of a new type of economic policy, although Zweig does not see the change in this light: he somewhat surprisingly argues that the Act was an extension of the social market principle.[34]

Regional and Agricultural Policy

Two points should be made by way of introduction to this subsection. First, perhaps the most significant determinant of regional policy during the social market economy era has been the existence of an alternative economic *dirigisme* in the German Democratic Republic and, to a lesser extent, Czechoslovakia. The principal example of this is the insular West Berlin, although it will be necessary to examine the problems emanating from the so-called frontier corridor (*Zonenrandgebiet*). Secondly, government policy designed to improve the structure of agriculture is seen as part of the total regional development programme.

West Berlin

West Berlin is still *de jure* occupied and governed by the USA, UK and France. *De facto* it tends to be treated both politically and economically as the eleventh state of a Federal Republic. The gradual emergence of this position has been fraught with conflict between the Western and Eastern powers, notably the 1948 blockade and air lift, and the building of the wall which now divides the Eastern and Western sectors of the city in 1961. This latter development robbed the newly re-industrialised Western sector of its valuable source of labour from the East. In this political atmosphere migration of young workers from other parts of the Federal Republic to West Berlin has had to be encouraged by promotional campaigns which publicise the tax free 8 per cent supplement to earnings, DM22 allowance per child, free travel and removal expenses available to the *Neuberliner.* Apart from the legal (until 1973) and even illegal immigration of foreign workers, however, the young migrants do not tend to remain very long.[35] Indeed, 21 per cent of the population is over 65 compared to 13 per cent in the rest of the Federal Republic. Moreover, the total population has tended to decline throughout the sixties and seventies, particularly since the 1967 recession: the annual death rate is now 38,000 compared to a birth rate of 18,000, 5,000 of whom are foreigners.

Industrialists, particularly in electronic and electrical engineering, have been reluctant to expand their activities in the city. Real investment actually fell during the 1970s and what there was tended to be capital rather than labour using. Publicity is regularly given to the 'host of financial and tax reliefs' available to companies which assist in developing trade with Berlin. The city is projected as Germany's largest industrial conurbation, where large international concerns co-exist with newly established small companies.

In order to first encourage industrial investment to rebuild the city's industrial capacity in the fifties and then to maintain a viable labour force with employment opportunities after 1961, the Federal Government, and indeed the Allies, have pumped vast subsidies into the city. Between 1949 and 1958 DM9.4 billion were provided by West Germany together with DM4.1 billion from the Marshall Aid Programme.[36] During the same period tax concessions to West Berlin business concerns amounted to about DM2.3 billion, in addition to depreciation allowances. Today, as well as the normal Federal contribution to the city's budget of just under half of the total annual outlay (DM7 billion), additional direct payments to the city from Bonn account for a further DM3.5 billion.[37] In spite, or because, of all this, West Berlin's proportional contribution to national income is at least equal to that of the other Länder.

The Frontier Corridor

The frontier zone is about 40 kilometres wide, running the whole length of the eastern side of the country. Introduced as a regional development area in 1953, the basic notion was to avoid a no-man's land developing between West and East Germany. The area was generally isolated from both markets and raw materials. The rural south region would probably have qualified for help in any case. But some areas in the north, including the Salzgitter iron and steel complex and the Volkswagen works at Wolfsburg, are highly industrialised. These part state-owned undertakings are to be further analysed below. The highest levels of investment grants and preferential income tax rates are generally found in the corridor.[38] Small businesses in the zone have received millions of DM in special assistance for repaying loans.[39]

Other Regional Policies

In common with other governments in the industrialised market economies, the Federal Government has developed an increasingly comprehensive regional policy during the social market economy era. With currently well over one-third of the total population and almost two-thirds of the land area affected by one or other of its regional programmes, the Federal Republic is directly comparable with the United Kingdom where similar proportions obtain.[40] The joint Federal/Länder committee responsible for the Sixth Regional Plan to 'improve the economic structure of the regions', chaired by the Minister of Economics, announced that in 1977 DM588 million had been set aside for employment creation grants, together with DM666 million in investment allowances.[41] The origin of this joint committee is in itself of interest. A community tasks institute (*Gemeinschaftsaufgabe*) was created by the 1968 Finance Reform. Two of its functions are the improvement of the economic structure of the regions, and the improvement of the structure of agriculture and coastal protection. A joint committee to co-ordinate the former was established in 1972 and the latter in 1973.

The Emergency Areas (*Notstandsgebiete*), designated in 1951, were established in order to cope with the influx of post-war refugees and areas which had taken the brunt of the Allied invasion. These areas tended to be in the extreme north and west of the country, plus some of the border areas already discussed above. In 1953 they were renamed Restoration Areas (*Sanierungsgebiete*). This term was intended to imply that regional aid was envisaged as a temporary aberration to assist the areas to overcome their disadvantages in terms of fully competing in the social market economy. However, by the 1960s depressed coal mining areas in the Saar and Ruhr, as well as cities such as Kiel and Wilhelms-haven, caused the introduction of a permanent set of criteria for assessing whether an area should be granted development status. *Per capita* income was one such criterion. The areas first became known as *Sonder-gebiete* and, from 1966, Federal Development Areas (*Bundesausbaugebiete*). Moreover, all regional aid is defined and co-ordinated respectively by the 1965 Regional Development Act (*Raumordungsgesezt*) and the 1969 Reg-ional Action Programme. Finally, Federal development towns (*Bundes-bauorte*) and conurbations of rapid growth and industrial concentration (*Verdichtungsräume*) exist in order to plan, as the case may be, economic take-off or continued rational economic expansion.

Agriculture

The economic problems of West German agriculture seem to be almost intractable.[42] In its use of land, labour and capital, it is inefficient. These difficulties stem only partly from the fact that with industrialisation the proportion of total spending devoted to agricultural produce tends to fall—as spectacular as the re-industrialisation of Germany may have been. For although the derived demand for farmers has fallen accordingly and although the farming population has been reduced by a half during the social market economy era, there still tend to be far too many small-holdings owned by farming families whose major source of income is usually local industry. As a result, one-third of the EEC's farms under 27 acres are situated in West Germany.[43] These small farms also tend to be worked on a highly mechanised basis—hence the uneconomic use of capital equipment.[44] At the end of September 1977, West German inter-vention stores contained a third of the Community's butter, two-thirds of the skimmed milk powder and 40 per cent of the beef, the great bulk of which was all believed to be of domestic origin. Both the Federal Minister of Finance and *The Economist* have stressed that it is not just the taxpayer who meets the cost of supporting agriculture. *The Econ-omist* has reported that German farm prices are 40 per cent higher than the British. Germany's inefficient farmers, the argument continued, are encouraged by such a pricing situation to produce more, while Britain's efficient farmers are induced to produce less. Moreover, excessive food prices in the Federal Republic cost the housewife in excess of DM1 billion a year, as well as the DM1 billion in taxes to contribute to the agricultural support section of the German budget. Resources have been diverted from industry and there may have been a consequential short-fall of 500,000 jobs.[45]

Agricultural subsidies at the Federal level alone have been rising since Germany first regained sovereignty. They reached the DM1 billion mark by 1957, over DM2 billion in 1967 and in 1977 were in excess of DM3 billion.[46] Since 1969 compensatory payments have acted as a protect-ive tariff against imports from the rest of the EEC: it is estimated that by 1977 these payments will reach DM4.7 billion. To these must be added tax concessions, Marshall Aid in the 1950s and financial assist-ance from state Governments. In short, the total assistance to West German agriculture in 1977 will be in excess of DM10 billion.[47]

The four main schemes involving government intervention and affect-ing agricultural reform are, first, the early piecemeal efforts at consolid-ating land which operated until 1953. Secondly, the more thorough-going Land Consolidation Act (*Flurbereinigungsgesetz*) was passed in 1953.[48] This Act specifies the roles of both governments and farmers in a national agricultural plan with the intention that scattered and frag-mented holdings may be brought together. In the 1970s the annual cost of land consolidation alone has been well over DM300 million. Thirdly, relocation of farmsteads away from congested village centres (*Aussiedlung*) has also been an extremely costly exercise. Finally, land has been pur-chased for reallocation to remaining land-holders (*Aufstockung*). To these measures should be added the annual Green Plan for agriculture.

Subsidies and Tax Concessions

The extent of regional and agricultural subsidies has already been exam-ined, but there are other principles and areas involved. In this section, therefore, the analysis begins with a general introduction and then pro-ceeds to look at the remaining areas of intervention by subsidy: the rail-ways, shipbuilding, coal-mining and housing.

General Principles

Tax concessions played a very important role in inducing investment during the post-war re-industrialisation of West Germany. It was seen above that financial assistance to agriculture and the regions generally has also been growing in significance. Taken together, 'invisible' tax con-cessions and 'visible' financial assistance of all types (grants, loans and interest remissions) are technically regarded in West Germany as constituting subsidies.[49] Subsidies so defined are still generally used throughout the economy. In 1977, the total Federal, Länder and local authorities' outlay on subsidies was expected to be DM32.8 billion under Section 12 of the 1967 StWG Act, plus a further DM50 billion mainly for the Federal Railways, research outside of higher education and agricultural payments.

The need for micro intervention of this nature is, then, laid down in Section 12 of the StWG. The basic policy aims of such intervention should be consistent with Section 1 of the Act referred to above. The Federal Government is also required by Section 12 of the StWG to lay a biennial Subsidies Report (*Subventionsbericht*) before both Houses. These Reports deal with Government financial assistance of all types with the exception of assistance to the Federal Railways and Post Office, as well as EEC agricultural payments. In addition, an evaluation of tax concessions is attempted. Neither financial assistance nor tax concessions were rigorously defined in the Act. Since the Third Report, financial assistance has been defined as:[50]

Financial assistance consists of monetary payments made by the Federal Government to (places or organisations) outside of the Federal Authorities in order to
1. maintain production or economic activity in plants or sectors, or to assist in the adaptation to new conditions
2. encourage increases in productivity and economic growth in industrial establishments and economic sectors
3. reduce the cost of certain goods and activities, as well as stimulate the propensity to save, in areas of the market process crucial to private households.

Many conceptual problems have been encountered by the officials responsible for drafting the reports. Moreover, in practice, it has been difficult to distinguish between some forms of financial assistance and tax concessions, as well as distinguishing between maintenance and adaptation in the first heading of the above quotation.

As early as the sixties, Reuss referred to the rise in the magnitude of subsidies, although the StWG requires the Federal Government to regularly suggest means of reducing them.[51] There have been only limited areas where this has proved possible.[52] When it comes to resource allocation, it is hoped that state intervention will be the exception and market competition the rule.

The Federal Railways and Post Office

Most of the rail system was nationalised and rapidly enlarged at the end of the nineteenth century. However, if present trends continue, the economic position of the Federal Railways will become an acute problem area. Along with transport policy as a whole, they have never really been subjected to the social market discipline. Indeed, transport policy has displayed an intervention spiral.[53] With 400,000 employees, for whom a no-redundancy agreement was recently negotiated, the annual losses of the Federal Railway system rose from DM400 million in 1963 to nearly DM2,700 million in 1973; by 1976, losses were approaching DM4 billion.[54] Over the last few years there have been persistent rumours that the rail network was to be cut by a half. It is twice as large as that of the United Kingdom, a country of comparable size. A system which generally ran West to East until 1945 has had to be transformed into one which runs North to South. In the meantime, the Federal Government continues to subsidise the system. Rail fares are heavily subsidised; indeed, some passengers pay as little as 10 per cent of their full travel costs. Investment spending is also high. For example, DM780 million were recently invested in a giant marshalling yard near Hamburg. Upgrading of the somewhat poorly constructed track is needed. The support of the railways in 1977 will cost an estimated DM11.3 billion and in 1978 DM13.5 billion.

By way of comparison, the Federal Post Office has also been something of a loss maker, although not on the scale of the railways and in spite of the similarities in the size of the labour force. In 1963, the loss was DM250 million, in 1973 over DM450 million. By 1976, however, an overall surplus of over DM1 billion was recorded. The profitability of the telecommunications side was responsible and losses are still being sustained by the postal business—particularly parcels. Turnover was nearly 6 per cent up on 1975 at nearly DM30 billion and personnel costs have fallen as a proportion of total costs. In terms of turnover, therefore, the Post Office is significantly larger than the country's largest industrial undertaking (VEBA) which is partially state-owned and will be analysed below.

Shipbuilding

In common with other industrialised market economies, the German shipbuilding industry has received various forms of state assistance to protect it from international competition. Indeed, Langer's painstaking research has revealed that of the twelve methods of intervention employed in the eleven most important shipbuilding nations, seven are used in the

Federal Republic.[55] These seven methods are: tariff-free imports of shipbuilding materials, corporation tax refunds, favourable export credit terms, export credit insurance, investment assistance, support of shipbuilding research and grants to shipowners purchasing German built vessels. The degree of assistance afforded to shipbuilding has had effects on the industry's export and investment patterns. Further, there are implications for regional policy.

In the export field, the industry has the economy's highest export dependence ratio. Whereas in the early seventies industry as a whole exported 20 per cent of its output and capital goods industries 30 per cent, shipbuilding exported 46 per cent. However, shipbuilding occupied an inferior position in terms of its share in total export turnover: the first four industries—machine tools, motor vehicles, chemicals and electrical engineering products—had shares ranging from 20 per cent down to 10 per cent; shipbuilding's contribution was under 2 per cent and in 1972 it occupied the eleventh position. Export subsidies have been paid on a mainly *ad hoc* basis which has tended to conserve the industry's structure. In 1976, the Eighth Shipbuilding Assistance Programme changed the conditions on which export finance is based. Reuss shows that investment in the shipbuilding industry provided a liberal tax shelter which resulted in the industry becoming overcapitalised as early as 1952.[56] Excess capacity has continued to grow, but subsidies have also been increased. Investment grants have, however, tended to raise long-run productivity. Moreover, the industry is concentrated in the north of the country and regional planners have been very mindful of this. In Bremen over 19 per cent of total employment is in the shipbuilding industry; in Schleswig-Holstein the proportion is 12 per cent and in Hamburg nearly 9 per cent. Both the Federal and Länder Governments are coming under increasing pressure to maintain employment levels and introduce regional development plans. For example, a DM1 billion infra-structure investment plan is being implemented by Lower Saxony and the Federal authorities, yet only the northern reaches of this Land has shipbuilding capacity.[57] Further, concern was expressed when the Bremen firm VFW-Fokker announced its intention to cease the development of a short-haul jet passenger aircraft. This concern was not just because of the DM1 billion subsidy contributed towards the development costs, nor because of the methods of monitoring development costs and investigating the marketing prospects, but also because of the 'threat to employment'. (2,500 jobs in Bremen, and 4,500 in Hamburg, are nevertheless assured by the success of the middle range Airbus 300. The Hamburg authorities have a 20 per cent stake in this project. Bavaria also has a similar holding.)

Because of the current international excess capacity and intense inter-national competition, the shipbuilding industry was in 1977 running out of orders. Following tradition, the West German Government has placed its orders in West German yards and raised the subsidy to German ship-owners buying domestically produced ships from 12.5 per cent to 17.5 per cent.[58] But the replacement of German merchant vessels is generally unnecessary as the fleet is quite modern. In any case, wage costs in the yards tend to be relatively high.[59] The upward trend in the exchange rate of the DM also deters buyers from both home and abroad.[60] This can all be illustrated by the fact that registered tonnage ordered in 1972 was well over 1 million, but by 1976 it had fallen to 314,000. Of these tonnages, only 2.2 per cent went to foreign yards in 1972, but by 1976 the proportion had risen to 53.5 per cent.

Coal-Mining

The coal-mining industry has received large subsidies. Coal has been un-favourably compared in Germany to textiles, in the sense that the latter industry received no direct subsidies and yet efficiently adjusted to foreign competition. This example is used by those who advocate com-petition rather than government intervention as a means of inducing adjustment in industry, although the argument can be misleading if one looks at the degree of indirect tariff and import quota protection afford-ed to the German textile industry.[61]

During the early period of the social market economy, the coal-mining industry proved to be a serious bottleneck in the recovery programme. Massive intervention programmes of all types were mounted.[62] After 1957, however, over production of coal became something of a problem. By 1967 pit head stocks had reached over 22 million tonnes, excluding emergency stocks of 4 million tonnes. Some of the surplus was exported but state aid continued. The fall in demand for coal was partly attribut-able to the substitution of mineral oil in the primary energy sector: the oil equivalent of hard coal demand fell from 50 per cent of total primary energy consumption in 1963 to 22 per cent in 1973. Even following the steep increase in oil prices in 1973/74, the coal industry continued to receive state aid. Indeed, financial assistance in each of these years alone had reached an average of over DM1 billion. German steel industry spokesmen have for many years complained about the relative cost dis-advantage incurred as a result of the nation's coal policy which requires them to purchase their coking coal in the domestic market. This policy, they argue, has prevented them from using cheaper foreign sources of supply. As a result, the argument continues, the German coal miners' potential bargaining power has been unnecessarily increased. Given the present international plight of the steel industry, however, one is bound to ask how long it will be before such arguments could be equally applied to German steel itself. But in 1974 the Federal Government indicated that it intended maintaining a capacity of 94 million tonnes in the hard coal industry.[63] The industry has been pursuing a process of rationalisation: enterprises have been re-organised and highly mechanised production is being concentrated on economic seams. There has been a continual decline in employment in the industry which now stands at just over 200,000. It will be seen in the next section that a small section of the industry is state-owned.

But the problems of the industry have been exacerbated by the increased mechanisation and falling manpower. First, capacity utilisation is below the level of actual capacity by a margin of about 10 million tonnes a year. Maintenance costs of the under-utilised capacity almost equal the costs which would be incurred were capacity to be fully utilised. However, the former adds to losses, whereas the latter would have increased income. Secondly, the fall in manpower from over 600,000 in 1957 to 200,000 in 1977 has been accompanied by an increase in productivity per man shift—from 4,500 kg. to 18,000 kg. Coal thus remains a relatively costly primary energy source which is in excess supply. The price of domestic coking coal is thought to be DM40 per tonne higher than alternative foreign sources of supply, while in the case of coal used for the generation of electricity the difference between the price per tonne on the world and domestic markets may be as high as DM90 per tonne.[64] A fall in both general energy demand and the demand for coking coal by the steel industry led to stocks exceeding 33 million tonnes in 1977. Between 1978 and 1987 the annual supply to the electricity generating industry will also equal 33 million tonnes. Supply costs will not, however, be fully covered. Electricity consumers will pay a 4.5 per cent levy (*Kohlepfennig*) to compensate the coal industry for some of its losses. The levy will raise DM2 billion in 1978 in order to fulfil 'conservation, structural and, particularly, employment policy aims'. In addition, the industry will receive financial assistance amounting to DM1.4 billion from Federal and Länder sources. When tax concessions are taken into account, the total subsidy in 1978 will reach DM5.1 billion. Between 1978-82 the industry will also receive a DM582 million annual investment subsidy from the Federal Government.[65]

Housing

Intervention in the housing sector was originally necessitated during the early social market era by war damage and the flood of refugees and expelled persons who arrived from East Germany and the former eastern territories of the Third Reich. The shortage of housing was estimated in 1951 to be 4.8 million units. Subsidies have been subsequently provided to encourage the building of new houses and the modernisation of existing dwellings. Over 5 per cent of GNP was consequently expended on housing. Reuss sees this 'as largely the result of massive government intervention', while Hallett prefers to term it a combination of 'state intervention and private initiative'.[66] The state intervention referred to has consisted of both financial assistance and tax concessions. Approximately two-thirds of the total cost of investment in housing was met from these sources in the fifties and early sixties. Tax concessions and savings premia were made available to private individuals, firms or housing associations who could demonstrate that they were reducing the housing shortage by constructing buildings of all descriptions—flats, 'two-family houses', middle-class housing and so on. Low-income housing was financed by interest-free loans.

Although the housing shortage had generally been eradicated by the seventies, the total housing subsidies paid by the Federal authorities alone still exceed DM2 billion a year. Reuss concluded as early as 1962 that West German housing standards had lost contact with the market. On the other hand, the construction industry has been particularly badly hit by recession during the seventies and it is difficult to see how state intervention can be withdrawn without once again exacerbating unemployment in the industry.

Government Participation in Banking and Business Enterprises

Banking

The banking interests of the Federal and Länder Governments, as well as those of local authorities, require some emphasis. This is because these interests represent extremely important sections of banking activity in the Federal Republic. Indeed, outside of the field of commercial lending, which in a voting sense is dominated by the big three profit-orientated commercial banks, state enterprise banking, as defined, is of great significance. Each city and Land has its own bank; there is also a central bank at the Federal level. In addition, however, the Federal Government has majority holdings in no fewer than five publicly owned banks. These banks are concerned with financing house building, agricultural rationalisation, loans to small businesses and the resettlement of refugees and the war wounded.[67] They are currently responsible to a number of ministries but they may eventually all be merged into one huge undertaking.[68] By far the largest of these five banks is a development bank (*Kreditanstalt für Wiederaufbau* – KW) in which the Federal Government holds an 80 per cent share of the DM1 billion nominal capital. The Länder own the remaining 20 per cent of the nominal capital, but the bank's chairman is the Federal Minister of Finance.

The KW was originally formed in order to channel the Marshall Aid loans into reconstruction projects. As will be seen in the next paragraph, the Federal Government's ability to create credit is limited by the powers of the Federal central bank. The KW therefore became a banker's bank – a source of additional funds for the commercial banks. They also guaranteed those applications which they recommended to the KW. Shonfield sees this arrangement as an example of the collaboration of the public authorities with the investment experts on the commercial banking scene. He also maintains that the first general manager of KW, who later returned to head one of the re-constituted big three commercial banks but maintained a powerful link with the KW, did much to establish its profitability and connections with the private banks.[69] As well as having a Board of Directors, the bank has an advisory body which consists of several Federal and Länder ministers, as well as trade unionists, industrialists and representatives of other economic institutions.

Since the mid-fifties, the KW has become increasingly involved in regional development schemes. Gradually investment in small and medium-sized businesses which were situated in development regions completely replaced the original assistance to bottleneck sectors. The KW has in these terms become the nation's second bank, offering low-interest investment funds as one method of overcoming the post-1973 high levels of unemployment.

The current central banking system consists of the Federal central bank (*Deutsche Bundesbank*) and its local agencies in each Länder (*Landeszentralbanken*).[70] The central bank council (*Zentralbankrat*) consists of members of its subordinate executive board, together with the presidents of the Landeszentralbanken. The board of each of the Landeszentralbanken consists of its president, vice-president and, typically, up to two additional members.

The most significant feature of the Bundesbank is its considerable degree of autonomy with respect to note issue, open market operations and general credit policy – in short, its control over the supply of money. The president, vice-president and eight additional board members are all appointed by the President of the Federal Republic. Members of the Federal cabinet are allowed to attend meetings of the board, but they cannot vote. Section 12 of the Act which founded the Bundesbank (*Gesetz über die Deutsche Bundesbank, 1957*) requires the bank 'to support the economic policy of the Federal Government' which clearly involves interventionist policies.[71] On the other hand, Section 3 of the Act requires the somewhat conflicting achievement of exchange rate stability, to which the Bundesbank has accorded a high degree of priority.

The next level of public sector banking to be considered is that of the so-called *Landesbanken*. These banks should not be confused with the *Landeszentralbanken* mentioned above. They are owned by the various Länder governments and therefore operate at a regional level. They have three functions which are sometimes contradictory. First of all, they act as house banks to the Länder governments. They are not permitted to issue bank notes, but are responsible for providing finance for the considerable spending undertaken by the Länder on such projects as roads, schools and hospitals. Secondly, they act as clearing and investment institutions for the 600-odd municipally-owned savings banks (*Sparkassen*). The savings banks also have an interest in Landesbanken. The balance sheets of the savings banks total as much as those of the commercial banks. If one adds the funds held at each of the eleven central levels (*Girozentralen*), then the aggregate balance sheets are almost double those of the commercial banking sector.[72] During the social market era, the Landesbanken and Girozentralen have tended to amalgamate. Even by international standards, the resultant Landesbanken-Girozentralen tend to be enormous undertakings.[73]

It is in their third function where the Landesbanken-Girozentralen have come into direct competition with the commercial banks and, for that matter, the trade union-owned *Bank für Gemeinwirtschaft*. Their investments in industry and even in property and exchange rate speculation have on occasions led to losses and controversy.[74] Moreover, the association of savings banks and giros has been critical of the allegedly adverse effects of Bundesbank exchange rate policies on the West German economy.[75]

Participation in Industrial Enterprises

The analysis can now turn to the industrial side. On a narrow definition, that is a share of more than 50 per cent of nominal or voting capital, the West German state-owned enterprises contributed 10 per cent to national income, 20 per cent of total gross investment and 8 per cent of total

employment. Streit calculates.the relative importance of state ownership to be similar to that of the United Kingdom.[76] On the other hand,
an OECD study in 1964 commented that West German government-
owned enterprises acted in a commercially-orientated manner, although
in his introduction to the 1976 annual report on government participation (*Beteiligungen des Bundes*), the Minister of Finance added that
public enterprises had to create employment where possible.[77] This was
in contrast to the private sector where productivity increases often
result in redundancies.

Some efforts have been made to reduce state ownership of industry.
In 1959, the mining and smelting company Preussag was partially denationalised, although 22 per cent of its shares were purchased by the
state-owned VEBA—an organisation which will be analysed below. The
sale of the remainder of the shares was a huge success and their post-
sale value rose rapidly. In 1961, 60 per cent of Volkswagen was denationalised. This time shares were offered at a social discount: the
Savings Premium Act was invoked to enable those on annual incomes
of less than DM16,000 to purchase shares with a 20 per cent concession,
provided they were not resold for a period of five years. Demand was
again enormous and each applicant was limited to two or three shares,
on which there was a large capital gain. In 1965, VEBA (*Vereinigte
Elektrizitäts und Bergwerks Aktiengesellschaft* or United Electricity
and Mining Company) offered part of its stock on the private market.
On this occasion, the social discount applied to those on incomes of
less than DM14,000. This release was not a success and share prices
slumped after the sale.[78]

At the end of 1976, as will be seen from Table 6.1, the Federal Government directly participated in 90 public and private business undertakings. The supervisory boards of these enterprises tend to contain
bankers from both commercial and state-owned banks, trade union
officials, industrialists and government representatives. Their total
nominal capital was DM7.9 billion and the federal holding was DM4.4
billion. It will also be seen that, in terms of capital employed, the 19
undertakings for which the Finance Ministry was responsible were the
most significant: out of their total nominal capital of DM4.9 billion,
DM2.6 billion was state-owned. Table 6.1 also shows that the Transport
Ministry came next with 20 holdings worth DM1.6 billion, about half
of which was state-owned (only the special assets of the railways, such
as their small holding in the state air line, are included). In the same year
(not shown in the Table), the total number of private companies and
special assets in which the Federal Government had either an indirect

Table 6.1: Federal Direct Participation in Private and Public Companies in 1976

Ministry	Number of companies by responsible ministry	Of which Federal holding exceeded 50%	Nominal capital (DM'000)	Federal share in nominal capital (DM'000)
Finance	19	12	4 904 610	2 564 278
Transport	20	9	1 625 014	873 757
Urban and Rural Planning	18	6	581 894	217 935
Food, Agriculture and Forestry	6	2	149 620	110 611
Economic Co-operation	5	4	604 355	604 084
Research and Technology	11	9	2 473	2 170
Defence	2	1	204	52
Interior	4	1	86	52
Justice	1	1	50	35
Economics	1	1	20	20
Education and Science	1	—	33	11
Press and Information	2	—	270	85
	90	46	7 868 629	4 373 090

Source: Beteiligungen des Bundes 1976 (Bundesministerium der Finanzen, Bonn, 1977), p. 1. (Writer's translation)

Table 6.2: The Six Principal Finance Ministry Undertakings (1976)

Undertaking	Nominal Capital DM million	Federal holding (nominal) DM million	%	External turnover 1976 DM million	Employees 31.12.1976	Capital investment 1976 DM million
1. Majority federal holding						
Salzgitter AG	350.0	350.0	100	6 620[a]	53 639	583
VIAG	442.0	369.1	83.5	3 558	21 736	220
Saarbergwerke AG[b]	350.0	259.0	74	3 806	29 169	258
Industrieverwaltungs-GmbH	50.0	50.0	100	326	3 779	28
Total 1	1 192.0	1 028.1		14 310	108 323	1 089
2. Minority federal holding						
VEBA AG	1 404.0	614.3	43.8	27 229	67 084	1 623
Volkswagenwerk AG[c]	900.0	180.0	20	21 423	183 238	1 042
Total 2	2 304.0	794.3		48 652	250 322	2 665
Grand totals	3 496.0	1 822.4		62 962	358 645	3 754

Notes:
[a] Turnover 1975/76 (30/9).
[b] Remaining 26 per cent of share capital owned by the Saarland government.
[c] 20 per cent of the remaining share capital owned by the Lower Saxony Land government.
Source: Beteiligungen des Bundes 1976 (Bundesministerium der Finanzen, Bonn, 1977), pp. 3 and 5. (Writer's translation)

or direct participation of at least 25 per cent of capital employed was 915. According to the annual participation reports, the gross income of the Federal Government from its business interest averages over DM100 million each year. Significantly, the report also emphasises that profitability is not the primary aim of many government enterprises.

Table 6.2 gives a general overview of the six major industrial concerns for which the Finance Ministry is responsible, five of which rank among West Germany's top fifty companies in terms of turnover and net value added. These are examined in order of turnover below—that is: VEBA, Volkswagen, Salzgitter, Saarbergwerke and VIAG. It will be seen from Table 6.2 that the six firms had nearly 359,000 employees and a turnover of DM63 billion in 1976.

VEBA

VEBA has already been mentioned above and it is now apposite to examine this concern in a little more depth. In both 1975 and 1976, VEBA was the Federal Republic's largest undertaking: its turnover in 1976 was DM27 billion and its employees numbered over 67,000.[79] The Federal holding in its DM1,400 million share capital amounts to nearly 44 per cent, the remaining shares being held by about 1.2 million shareholders in 1975, although the number fell to 1 million in 1976. A series of shareholders' meetings, to which visitors are also invited, is held in five large cities. The group has interests in energy, mineral oil and chemicals, together with relatively minor holdings in commerce and transport. VEBA's energy companies generate electricity from coal, oil, natural gas and nuclear energy. VEBA-Chemie is a multi-product oil and chemical concern which manufactures petrochemicals as well as specialised products such as fertilisers. In mineral oil, the group has interests in both exploration, including the North Sea, and distribution.

Developments in the group's energy interests, particularly mineral oil, have caused some criticism. In 1974 the Cartel Office turned down a proposed merger between VEBA and a similar company (Gelsenberg AG), on the grounds that the Federal Government would itself be in breach of the GWB by virtue of its majority holding. The Economics Minister overruled this decision on the grounds that the merger would be in the interests of ensuring long-run mineral oil supplies. He referred to the 1973 Energy Plan of the Federal Government which advocated the establishment of a viable West German-owned mineral oil company capable of participating in international activities and forging links with oil producing countries. The Federal Government continued to purchase shares in Gelsenberg. By January 1975, VEBA possessed about 96 per cent of Gelsenberg shares.

The Monopolies Commission launched a special investigation into the merger.[80] It accepted the Cartel Office's interpretation of the GWB, adding that exceptions could not be made even where the Federal Government happened to be the majority shareholder. On the other hand, the Commission also accepted the Minister's arguments in so far as they applied to mineral oil, although a rider added that emulating the international cartel structure of the major oil companies would undermine the market principles within the Federal Republic. The Commission now seems to be convinced that VEBA's long-term strategy is one of taking over small and medium-sized companies.

VEBA has not succeeded in mounting an international foothold in production with one of the existing oil giants, although the Group's publicity material states that its 'broad base makes it a good partner for joint venture projects on a national and international scale'.[81] Large losses have been incurred on the mineral oil side which have been offset by the profitability of other companies in the Group, notably electricity supply. On the other hand, it should be noted that the electricity supply industry, particularly the giant Rheinisch-Westfälischen Elektrizitätswerk which supplies 40 per cent of the economy's electricity, has been accused by the Cartel Office of exploiting its monopoly power. VEBA's controversial chairman has called for increased state intervention and 'co-operation' among the European oil companies.[82] Proposed links with Iran and Norway have been reported.

VW

The success of Volkswagen during the social market era is perhaps the most widely acclaimed feature of the re-construction of the German economy. For most of the period the famous Beetle lay at the heart of that success: about 20 million have been produced, two-thirds of them in Germany. It was seen above that 60 per cent of Volkswagen was denationalised in 1961. The remaining 40 per cent of the share capital is equally divided between the Federal Government and the Land of Lower Saxony. Volkswagen has generally been able to maintain a lead over its nearest home rival—the General Motors' Opel subsidiary. At the end of 1976 Ford, the third producer at the popular end of the market, was over 100,000 units below Opel and Volkswagen at 342,000 units.

In March 1977, all three companies were warned against increasing their prices by the Cartel Office. The warning was given in writing—an unprecedented step. VW ignored the warning. Domestic sales were booming at the time and 1976 had been a very profitable year, although per-

sonnel costs were increasing. The DM1 billion profit level of 1976 was a
marked improvement over the DM157 million loss in 1975. In terms of
turnover it lifted VW from seventh to fifth position in the 1976 national
league table. In terms of net value added, the company was in fourth
position, compared to VEBA's eleventh position. However, partly as a
result of the increase in labour costs, VW has become a multi-national
corporation. Beetles are now produced in Mexico, Brazil, Nigeria and
South Africa, but no longer in Germany. The Golf ('Rabbit') is to be
assembled in the USA. Hence, the new generation of more sophisticated
Volkswagen and Audi (its wholly-owned subsidiary) cars will tend to be
produced more for the domestic market than has hitherto been the case.

Salzgitter

The wholly state owned Salzgitter company stands in contrast to VW.
Its steel producing plant at Salzgitter may be fairly near to VW's headquarters at Wolfsburg—they are both on the Lower Saxony border with
the German Democratic Republic—but in terms of economic performance Salzgitter has been handicapped by its relative high costs. These
high costs are partly attributable to the fact that the works were built
in the thirties in order to exploit the low-grade iron ores of Lower
Saxony, whereas the Ruhr based part of the industry is able to use the
large quantities of rich foreign ore shipped into Rotterdam. Another
factor in these relative high costs is that even after a merger, the group's
output remained well below the optimum capacity for a single integrated
works. Indeed, the merger was intended to improve 'the prospects for
one of the largest loss makers among the nationalised industries'.[83] Since
1974 the steel producing capacity has been further affected by the international slump in demand for steel. Salzgitter produces about 10 per
cent of the Federal Republic's pig-iron and steel.

The problems of the Salzgitter company do not end at steel-making
and its associated activities. The company also has a 75 per cent holding
in a Kiel shipbuilding company—the other 25 per cent being owned by
the Land of Schleswig-Holstein. The general problems facing the shipbuilding industry were outlined above. Howaldtswerke-Deutsche Werft
AG Hamburg und Kiel (the subsidiary in question) is a microcosm of
these problems: decreasing employment and a fairly rapidly declining
order book. The group's total loss in 1976 was DM47.5 million; in 1975
there had been a total group surplus of DM16 million and in 1974 the
total surplus had been DM52.7 million. Relatively smaller energy and
machinery undertakings have tended to compensate for steel losses.

Saarbergwerke

Virtually all the Ruhr coal industry – and for that matter most of the
coal produced in the economy – is now the responsibility of the privately-
owned Ruhrkohle AG. This company was formed by law in the late
1960s as a result of a somewhat desperate measure to rationalise the
coal industry. Interestingly enough, it resembles in structure the nationalised Saarbergwerke AG, in which the Federal Government has a 74 per
cent stake and Saarland a 26 per cent holding. The resemblance lies in
the fact that both companies were charged with the responsibility of
rationalising the coal industry in their areas. Saarbergwerke now produces roughly a half of the tonnage it produced in the mid-fifties; in 1974-
76 an average of about 9 million tonnes was being produced annually –
10 per cent of the total national capacity. Saarbergwerke also produces
coke, gas and electricity. It also has interests in commercial activities, as
well as being responsible for the supply of drinking water. In 1976 its
profit stood at DM13.1 million, mainly as a result of an 18 per cent
increase in turnover. In 1975 it had incurred a loss of DM5.7 million.

VIAG

The final company of any real significance in Table 6.2 is Vereinigte
Industrie-Unternehmungen AG (VIAG). This undertaking is a holding
company with interests in electricity supply (generated from both hydro
and steam power), electro-chemicals and aluminium smelting. Its electricity
supply operations tend to be concentrated in the south-east, while its
aluminium interests are located in Berlin and Bonn. In 1975 the group
made considerable losses in its aluminium business which it attributed to
exchange rate changes. These losses were mitigated by the profitability of
electricity supply, as in the case of VEBA above. Nevertheless, the loss
of the group totalled DM22 million in 1975. A general recovery of the
economy during 1976, however, resulted in a profit of DM66 million.
The basic purpose of VIAG is described as the 'merging, co-ordination
and financing of undertakings, particularly in the electricity supply and
electro-chemical sectors'. Two significant points can be made in this
respect. First, the KW Bank has a minority holding (16.48 per cent) in
the group – the remaining stock belonging to the Federal Government.
Secondly, the group tends to have participative holdings with either Land
governments or other electricity supply companies.

   Space does not permit a detailed analysis of the business and commercial interests of the other federal ministries mentioned in Table 6.1.
In some cases, these interests tend to follow the patterns established
fairly extensively in the industrialised market economies. For example,

the Transport Ministry owns the state airline (Lufthansa), as well as having holdings in the principal airports. The appropriate Länder and municipal authorities are fellow shareholders in the airport business which has expanded considerably during the social market era. The Ministry for Economic Co-operation is responsible for handling loans to developing countries. Finally, the Urban and Rural Planning Ministry is responsible for a number of the regional and housing projects mentioned earlier.

Conclusion

All that has been said does not, of course, gainsay the very real economic achievements of the Federal Republic: *per capita* income is among the highest in the industrialised world, while the inflation rate is among the lowest. Economic growth has been until recently unambiguously export-led. Further, in spite of the huge privately and publicly owned companies, the small business flourishes in the Federal Republic to a far greater extent than, for example, in the United Kingdom. Finally, perhaps the general organisation of working life and some of the methods chosen to channel vast tax concessions and generous financial assistance to the areas listed above have all contributed to at least a medium term success story.

There are nevertheless important exceptions to the social market economy rule. Research findings have been cited which indicate that in transport, agriculture, housing, shipbuilding and even, in a sense, banking, the discipline of market forces has played a subordinate role to state intervention in terms of resource allocation.[84] The degree of cross-subsidisation in the energy sector—particularly where electricity supply profits are concerned—does not support the more extreme claims of some social market proponents. Moreover, in some areas where state intervention has been minimal, the influence of large business concentrations and the commercial banks has probably had important economic effects. The logic of intervention, especially since 1973, is quite clear and it is significant that the analysis ends on this note: it has been frequently shown that the avoidance of ever-increasing unemployment levels has become a primary policy reason for the growth of government economic intervention.

Notes

1. *Financial Times*, 24 October 1977, p. 18; N. Johnson, *Government in the*

Federal Republic of Germany (The Pergamon Press, Oxford, 1973), pp. 120-6; *The Times*, 16 September 1977.

2. A. Grosser, *Germany in Our Time* (Penguin Books Ltd, Harmondsworth, 1974), pp. 159-60.

3. Quoted by A.S. Milward, *The German Economy at War* (The Athlone Press, University of London, 1965), p. 35.

4. R.H. Bowen, 'The Roles of Government and Private Enterprise in German Industrial Growth', *Journal of Economic History* (1950 (Supplement)), p. 71.

5. J.E. Barker, *Modern Germany* (John Murray, London, 1919), pp. 259, 266 and 270.

6. A.P.L. Gordon, *The Problem of Trust and Monopoly Control* (George Routledge and Sons Ltd, London, 1928), pp. 29-30 and 56.

7. R. Dahrendorf, *Gesellschaft und Demokratie in Deutschland* (Deutscher Taschenbuch Verlag, 1974), pp. 42-53 (also available in English); G. Stolper *et al.*, *Deutsche Wirtschaft seit 1870* (J.C.B. Mohr (Paul Siebeck), Tübingen, 1966), pp. 50 and 119 (also available in English).

8. G. Denton *et al.*, *Economic Planning and Policies in Britain, France and Germany* (Allen and Unwin, London, 1968), p. 40; L. Erhard, *Prosperity through Competition* (Thames and Hudson, London, 1962), pp. 1 and 184.

9. W. Hirsch-Weber, *Gewerkschaften in der Politik* (Westdeutscher Verlag, Köln und Oploden, 1959), pp. 62 and 104; W. Kendall, *The Labour Movement in Europe* (Allen Lane, The Penguin Press Ltd, Harmondsworth, 1974), p. 136; for an exception to the general agreement between the CDU and SDP on national-isation, see F. Hartmann, *Geschichte der Gewerkschaftsbewegung nach 1945 in Niedersachsen* (Universität Gottigen, Seminar von der Politik, 1972), pp. 128-9.

10. K. Adenauer, *Memoirs 1945-53* (Weidenfeld and Nicolson, London, 1966), pp. 164-5, 175-7 and 180.

11. W. Kendall, p. 139.

12. D. Cassel *et al.* (eds.), *25 Jahre Markwirtschaft in der Bundesrepublik Deutschland* (Gustav Fischer Verlag, Stuttgart, 1972), p. 303ff; E. Helmstädter *et al.*, *Wirtschaftskunde der Bundesrepublik Deutschland* (Eugen Diederichs Verlag, Düsseldorf, 1975), p. 215ff; K. Zweig, *Germany through Inflation and Recession* (The Centre for Policy Studies, London, 1976), pp. 4 and 47.

13. *Die Zeit*, 7/77, p. 18.

14. Gordon, pp. 106, 110-12 and Appendix A (p. 171ff) which contains a trans-lation of the 1923 Act; Stolper, pp. 122-3.

15. G.P. Dyas and H.T. Thanheiser, *The Emerging European Enterprise* (Mac-millan, London, 1976), p. 52.

16. Ibid., p. 54.

17. H. Grebing, *The History of the German Labour Movement* (Oswald Wolff, London, 1969), p. 174; Kendall, p. 136; D. Schuster, *Die deutschen Gewerksch-aften Seit 1945* (W. Kohlhammer, Stuttgart, 1973), pp. 10 and 22.

18. M.E. Streit in R.T. Griffiths (ed.), *Government, Business and Labour in European Capitalism* (Europotentials Press, London, 1977), p. 123.

19. Ibid.; Denton *et al.*, pp. 58-9.

20. M. Blacksell in H.D. Clout (ed.), *Regional Development in Western Europe* (John Wiley and Sons, London, 1975), p. 178.

21. G. Mann, *The History of Germany since 1789* (Penguin Books Ltd, Harmonds-worth, 1974), pp. 589, 603 and 862-3.

22. *Die Zeit*, 29/76, p. 18.

23. Denton *et al.*, p. 61.

24. Gordon, p. 139.

25. Dahrendorf, p. 44; Dyas and Thanheiser, pp. 56-8; A. Shonfield, *Modern Capitalism* (Oxford UP, London, 1965), pp. 247 and 261; Stolper, pp. 30ff.

188   *The Federal Republic of Germany*

26. W. Hesselbach, *Public, Trade Union and Co-operative Enterprise in Germany* (Frank Cass, London, 1976).
27. Denton *et al.,* pp. 63-5; F.G. Reuss, *Fiscal Policy for Growth without Inflation* (The John Hopkins Press, Baltimore, 1963), pp. 213-18.
28. *Financial Times,* 24 October 1977, p. 20.
29. H. Giersch, Wicksell-Vorlesungen 1970: 'Wachstum, Konjunktur und Wechsel kurse', *Kontroverse Fragen der Wirtschaftspolitik* (R. Piper and Co. Verlag, München, 1971), p. 15 (also available in English).
30. Gesetz zur Förderung der Stabilität und des Wachstums der Wirtschaft (*Bundesgesetzblatt,* Bonn, Jahrgang 1967, Teil 1, Nr. 32).
31. Deutsche Bundesbank, *Auszüge aus Presseartikeln* (Frankfurt), 80/77.
32. Cassel *et al.,* p. 256; Streit in Griffiths, p. 128.
33. Cassel *et al.,* pp. 251 and 253-4; *Die Zeit,* 29/77, pp. 1 and 17.
34. Zweig, p. 13; cf. Streit, p. 128 and Cassel, p. 251.
35. D. Burtenshaw, *Economic Geography of West Germany* (Macmillan, London, 1974), p. 151.
36. Reuss, pp. 209 and 211; cf. *Sechster Subventionsbericht,* Bundestagdrucksache 8/1195 (Bundesministerium der Finanzen, Bonn), pp. 25-7.
37. *The Times,* 22 June 1977, p. ix.
38. Blacksell, pp. 184-185; Burtenshaw, p. 205.
39. Reuss, p. 217.
40. Blacksell, p. 182; *Die Zeit,* 52/77, p. 9.
41. Deutsche Bundesbank, *Auszüge,* 34/77, p. 3; EEC *Report on the Regional Problems in the Enlarged Community* (EEC, Brussels, 1973), pp. 229-33.
42. G. Schmitt in Cassel *et al.*
43. *The Times,* 22 June 1977, p. viii.
44. *Financial Times,* 24 October 1977, p. 22.
45. *The Economist,* 5 November 1977, pp. 54-6.
46. D. Albrecht and K. Wesselkock, 'Subventionen und Subventionspolitik', *Schriftenreihe des Bundesministeriums für Wirtschaft und Finanzen,* Heft 19 (Wilhelm Stollfuss Verlag, Bonn, 1971), p. 26; Blacksell, p. 181; Reuss, p. 193; *Sechster Subventionsbericht,* pp. 21-2.
47. *Die Zeit,* 52/77, p. 9.
48. Burtenshaw, pp. 176 and 181.
49. Albrecht and Wesselkock, p. 8; Reuss, p. 188.
50. Albrecht and Wesselkock, p. 12; *Fünfter Subventionsbericht,* Bundestagdrucksache 7/4203 (Bundesministerium der Finanzen, Bonn), p. 5.
51. Reuss, pp. 189-91.
52. Albrecht and Wesselkock, p. 20.
53. R. Willeke in Cassel *et al.,* p. 316.
54. *Die Zeit,* 28/74, 1977, p. 25, and 37/77, pp. 20-21; *The Economist,* 9 April 1977.
55. J. Langer, *Ziele und Auswirkungen der Subventionierung der Werftindustrie in der Bundesrepublik Deutschland* (Veröffentlichung des HWWA-Instituts, Hamburg, 1974), chapter 3, particularly pp. 188-9, 222-35 and 277-81.
56. Reuss, p. 202.
57. *The Times,* 14 November 1977.
58. *Financial Times,* 24 October 1977, p. 24.
59. Because of increased holiday pay and other 'indirect' benefits throughout the economy, German total labour costs have increased dramatically in the 1970s. They are now the highest in the major economies (Deutsche Bundesbank, *Auszüge,* 16/78, p. 11).
60. Between 1969 and 1977 the DM rose 139 per cent against sterling, 90 per cent against the dollar and 26 per cent against the yen. (*Report,* German Embassy,

London, 4 April 1978, p. 2).

61. A.D. Neu in W.M. Corden and G. Fels (eds.), *Public Assistance to Industry* (Macmillan, London, 1976), p. 165.

62. Reuss, pp. 203-6.

63. *Fünfter Subventionsbericht*, pp. 15 and 20.

64. *Die Zeit*, 18/78, p. 19.

65. *The Times* and *Financial Times*, 27 April 1978.

66. G. Hallett, *The Social Economy of West Germany* (Macmillan, London, 1973), chapter 9; Reuss, pp. 196ff and 208.

67. Bundesministerium der Finanzen, *Beteiligungen des Bundes* (Bonn, 1975 and 1976), pp. 167-9 (1975) and pp. 170-2, 241, 251, 283 and 343 (1976).

68. *Die Zeit*, 16/78, p. 32.

69. Shonfield, p. 276ff.

70. M.C. Schnitzer and J.W. Nordyke, *Comparative Economic Systems* (South-Western Publishing Co., Cincinnati, Second Edition, 1977), pp. 324-5.

71. Reuss, pp. 52-3 and 289.

72. *Monthly Reports of the Deutsche Bundesbank* (Frankfurt), tables 9 and 10.

73. M. Schnitzer, *East and West Germany* (Praeger Publishers, New York, 1973), pp. 148-9.

74. *Financial Times*, 14 October 1974, p. 34 and 24 October 1977, p. 22; *The Times*, 16 June 1976, p. vi and 24 December 1977, p. 15; *Die Zeit*, 1/78, p. 18.

75. Deutsche Bundesbank, *Auszüge*, 85/77, p. 3.

76. Streit in Griffiths, p. 125; Denton *et al.*, pp. 222-3.

77. Bundesministerium der Finanzen, *Beteiligungen des Bundes*; OECD quoted by Denton *et al.*, p. 224.

78. H.-J. Arndt, *West Germany: Politics of Non Planning* (Syracuse UP, National Planning Series, No. 8, 1966), pp. 92-93; Denton *et al.*, pp. 65-6; Reuss, pp. 207-8.

79. *Die Zeit*, 37/77, p. 20.

80. Monopolkommission (Sondergutachten 2), *Wettbewerbliche und Strukturelle Aspekte einer Zusammenfassung von Unternehmen in Energiebereich (VEBA/ Gelsenberg)* (Nomos Verlagsgesellschaft, Baden-Baden, 1975).

81. *Der Spiegel*, 12/77, pp. 78 and 81-2.

82. *Die Zeit*, 40/77, p. 17.

83. Burtenshaw, pp. 96 and 103-4.

84. Since this chapter was prepared, an important publication has appeared. (D. Albrecht, 'Subventionen: Problematik und Entwicklungen', *Schriftenreihe des Bundesministeriums der Finanzen*, Heft 25 (Wilhelm Stollfuss Verlag, Bonn, 1978). In a Preface, the Federal Minister of Finance welcomes the growing realisation that subsidies are a legitimate economic and social policy instrument. He expresses some concern, however, about the extent of subsidisation, but confesses that although there is general agreement that subsidies should be reduced, there is always trenchant opposition from interest groups when concrete micro proposals for reductions are made. The author of this lucid publication (a ministerial adviser) adds two further points (pp. 48-9): first, he draws attention to the dissatisfaction with some effects of market forces and, secondly, he suggests that the political implications of growing subsidisation (see pp. 160-2 above) may have caused some public disquiet. Subsidies are therefore seen as a means of promoting self-help.

7 GOVERNMENT INTERVENTION IN THE ECONOMY OF FRANCE

J. R. Hough*

Introduction

> A major factor distinguishing France from other Western industrial
> societies has been the role played by government in the management
> of the economy . . . the direct way in which the French administration
> has intervened in industrial affairs has been in sharp contrast to the
> usual practice in the United States, England and Germany.[1]

Such was the conclusion of one of the most authoritative comparative
studies published in recent years. In some respects at least the intervention of the French government in the national economy over the
post-war period has differed markedly from the position in the other
countries dealt with in this volume, as regards both the extent and the
manner of such intervention. To quote further from the same study:

> Often, where the US market has oligopolistic competition, the French
> market has government management of the market, and where the
> US market is regulated, the French equivalent is government-owned.

In general the state can look with considerable satisfaction at the very
successful progress of the French economy since 1945, although the
various and sometimes conflicting policies followed have inevitably
given rise to criticisms: foremost among these has been the problem of
co-ordination and unification of policy. Thus an official OECD report
could refer to the need for: 'better co-ordination of the various political
and administrative bodies concerned in industrial policy' . . . and
'problems of co-ordination and compatibility between general economic
policy measures and those more specifically designed to develop industry'.
Another major study referred to 'the incoherence of industrial policy'.[3]

At this point brief mention should be made of the political background. More or less conservative coalition governments (dominated by
the Gaullist Party) have been in power since 1958 and this has led to a

*I am grateful to Professor Alain Bienaymé of the University of Paris—Dauphine
for his helpful comments on an earlier draft of this chapter.

190

period of reasonable stability with regard to the public sector/private sector economic mix. The threat of a left-wing government, though never far from the public mind, has not in fact become a reality.

Public Ownership

First and foremost among the methods used to intervene in the economy is that of direct participation in the ownership of industrial and commercial companies, this participation ranging from full-scale nationalisation to quite small holdings in a very large number of companies. Probably in no other Western industrial economy has direct state ownership or co-ownership of private enterprise been so extensive. Some nationalisations, of munitions factories and aircraft manufacturers, took place (primarily for strategic reasons) in the late 1930s but it was the post-war chaos that led to a major wave: from 1944 to 1947, the electricity, gas and coal industries, the Banque de France, four deposit banks, 32 insurance companies and the Renault car firm were all nationalised.

Further, in subsequent years 'public holdings',[4] i.e. majority or minority shareholdings, have been acquired in many companies, primarily where a company either covered an important sector of the economy or was important in the financial sector: thus the state effectively can control or influence the petroleum industry via ERAP (Enterprise for Research and Control of the Petroleum Industry), the chemical industry via EMC (Mining and Chemical Enterprise), and construction via SCET (Construction and Planning Company). As an indication of the extent of state ownership, ERAP has some 150 subsidiary companies. SNCF (French railways – rather surprisingly not a nationalised industry but a private sector company in which the state is the major shareholder), Air France, ORTF (radio and TV) and PTT (posts and telephones) are other major concerns all effectively under state control. The extent of the relative importance of 'public enterprises' (which the state either owns or effectively controls) in various industries is summarised in Table 7.1.[5]

The public sector in France is relatively larger than that in any other major industrialised country, being exceeded only by Austria. It has been estimated[6] that the state is the majority shareholder, either directly or via holding companies, in some 500 industrial and commercial companies; it is also a minority shareholder in over 600 others, many of which have received loans from one or other of the various official funds (discussed below) which frequently require, as a condition of the loan, a minority participation in the share capital and representation on the board of directors.

There is an interesting borderline between activities which are, or are

Table 7.1: The Public Sector in France

Importance of public enterprise production in the total production	Position	Industries concerned
More than 80%	Monopoly	Manufactured tobacco, matches, coal lignite and compressed coal dust, distributed gas, electricity, natural gas, telecommunication services.
Between 40% and 80%	Very important	Coked products, electrical and mechanical auto equipment, products of aeronautic industry, armaments and ammunitions, various minerals, transports by land, air and sea.
Between 20% and 40%	Important	Crude oil, automobile, inorganic chemistry, health services.
Between 5% and 20%	Secondary	Household appliances, organic chemistry, public works and buildings, transportation auxiliaries, housing service, services rendered to enterprises.

not, permissible for public sector concerns, as the result of a series of case law decisions. Thus Gaz de France was not permitted to run a commercial service for the repair and maintenance of gas installations, since this was held to be unfair to private sector firms, SNCF have been permitted to run buses but only on restricted routes, military bakeries have been permitted to indulge in limited competition with private bakers, EMC, the state-owned chemical company, has taken the view that it was not permitted to expand into chemical by-products, and local authorities have been permitted to run cinemas, casinos, petrol stations and camping sites. Within manufacturing industry the most direct competition between the public sector and the private sector occurs in the production of motor-cars, the state-owned Renault being not merely a major domestic supplier but also very important for its export sales. Similarly state-owned and private sector banks and insurance companies operate side by side.

The extent to which the French government in fact 'intervenes' in the operation of the various companies indicated above is not entirely clear: on the one hand many of their top managers and other executives have been transferred from senior positions in the civil service and often take with them specific instructions or strategies to be followed, and the concerns undoubtedly have to adhere to the general framework of government policies, such as economic planning (considered below). For example, the purchasing policy and power of Electricité de France have been used to enforce the reorganisation of the heavy electrical equipment industry. On the other hand, in their day-to-day operations the firms are left fairly free to run themselves much like any company in the private sector. Renault, for example, appears to have almost complete freedom to innovate, expand and modernise, with none of the bureaucracy or red-tape sometimes associated with state-owned organisations. Indeed, many state-controlled firms seem to have been well able to resist pressure from the relevant government departments to move out of the Paris area and re-locate their activities in the poorer regions of France. On the other hand, the success of the recent 'contractual' approach to certain economic policies, considered below, has undoubtedly been aided by its ready 'acceptance' by state-controlled firms.

The Financial Sector

It is in the financial sector that the state's intervention has been more extensive than in any other part of the economy, and this has been of crucial importance for the state's control over economic developments. As one commentator wrote:[7]

... the state reigns supreme in this domain: collecting savings through the nationalised banks, the nationalised insurance companies, postal checks, the savings 'Caisses' and government issues on the financial markets, it distributes them through the 'Crédit National', the 'Crédit Hotelier' (hotels, etc.), the Crédit Foncier (housing), the 'Fonds de Développement Economique et Social', etc. It leaves for private initiative, but a few merchant banks and the financial markets ...

There is thus a direct link with the government's credit policy which is geared to providing the necessary finance to implement the provisions of the current Plan. Dyas and Thanheiser[8] conclude that the government has indirectly been the primary source of funds for much of French private investment, through (i) its direct ownership of the major financial institutions, and (ii) its selective control of financial markets through preferred discount procedures for specific-purpose loans directed by special funds attached to the Ministry of Finance. The same authors consider that this preponderance of the state as a lender and borrower of funds has been one of the major causes of the continued under-development of the French financial markets.

Direct participation by the state in the financial sector has initially stemmed from the fact that in most years (although not 1975 or 1976) the central government has had a working surplus on its accounts which has been available for lending. Further, household savings in France are mostly channelled into the 'Caisses d'Epargne' (savings banks) or the postal cheque system or Bons du Tresor (savings certificates) all of which channel funds, directly or indirectly, to the government: these have been used to lend on concessionary terms to the nationalised industries, to certain sectors of social importance, notably housing, and to firms for regional policy purposes. Since the mid-1960s, official policy has been to curtail direct lending by the Treasury.[9] (In 1975 the Treasury directly financed only some 5 per cent of total investment.[10]) Instead, financial flows now tend to be channelled through the specialist financial institutions, the most important of which are the Caisse des Dépots et Consignations, the Crédit Foncier and the Crédit National.

Pre-eminent among these is the Caisse des Dépots et Consignations which is a quite remarkable, if not unique, institution. Founded in 1816, it has grown and diversified steadily over the ensuing 160 years and has seen a particularly rapid period of expansion since the end of the second world war. It now undertakes a wide variety of functions over the fields of finance, banking and insurance and has total assets of Frs. 400 billion (as at 31 December 1977). Whilst it is true that this figure has no great significance since the CDC does not have direct control over some of the funds which pass through its hands,[11] it does emphasise that the CDC is of far greater size and importance than any similar institution in France (at the same date the total assets of Crédit Foncier and Crédit National were some Frs. 70 billion and Frs. 5 billion respectively). The Caisse des Dépots is responsible for the administration and investment of many separate funds, including numerous pension funds, but the bulk of the money which it has freedom to place now comes from the deposits of the Caisses d'Epargne and some private sector investment funds: the CDC uses such resources to make loans for housing and to local authorities, to invest on the Paris Bourse in both government stock and blue chip securities and to place on the short-term money market.[12] The former of these has grown dramatically in importance in the 1970s with the late development of interest in owner-occupation of dwellings: loans are channelled both through Caisses d'Epargne but also, more importantly, through the special fund for subsidised low cost housing, the Caisse des Prêts aux Organismes d'habitations à loyer moderé. Loans are also made for a wide variety of investment projects, to local authorities, public utilities, and other borrowers. The Caisse des Dépots works in close conjunction with the Ministry of Finance and the latter has a large say both in the total volume of financing in any one year and in the allocation of funds between different sectors of the economy. The Ministry can also directly influence interest rates on loans and associated capital subsidies or remissions of interest.[13] Therefore, the theoretical independence and autonomy of the Caisses des Dépots, which was stressed in a recent official report, is in practice subject to fairly close supervision from the Ministry of Finance.

The other two important financial institutions mentioned above can be dealt with more briefly. The Crédit Foncier specialises in housing finance and grants loans both to builders and to people seeking to purchase their own homes. It borrows from the general public via bond issues, from insurance companies, and to a lesser extent from the Caisse des Dépots. The Crédit National, on the other hand, is geared towards providing funds for industrial investment, export credit, and approved industrial research, with money raised by bond issues and by grants from the official Economic and Social Development Fund.

Competition Policy

There do not exist in France any direct equivalents of the UK's NEDC, Monopolies Commission or Restrictive Practices Court. The functions of the former, and many more, are carried out by the Commissariat Général du Plan which is, of course, of far greater importance and which will be considered below. Policy against monopolies and restrictive practices has not been so extensive in France as in the UK even though there has been a general trend towards greater competition over the post-war period. Competition policy has been directed by the Commission Technique des ententes et positions dominantes (recently re-named the Commission Technique de la Concurrence), operating under the aegis of the Ministry of Economy and Finance, which is now governed by an Ordinance of September 1967, replacing earlier provisions of 1953. Inter-firm agreements are prohibited if they 'prevent, restrict, or falsify the effect of competition' but may be permitted if they are deemed to favour economic progress. Abuse of a 'dominant position' may also be declared illegal: the existence of a market monopoly is not in itself considered wrong, merely its abuse, and this is defined as:

> Activity of a firm or a group of firms occupying a dominant position in the domestic market, characterised by a monopoly situation or by

an evident concentration of economic power, when these activities
have as their object, or may have the effect of, interfering with the
normal functioning of the market.[14]

Both definitions are, therefore, delightfully vague and the Commission
has had considerable freedom to place its own interpretation on them.
Apart from its educative role, it has in fact taken an extremely liberal
attitude: in pursuit of the former it has issued a series of reports and
has emphasised that its long-term aim is control via having a better-
informed public rather than by any coercive measures. In investigating
individual cases, the Commission has been anxious that its work should
not impede the government's policy of industrial concentration (considered essential for sustained economic growth and for the success of
the Plan) and it has taken the view that since oligopolies were becoming
more numerous it should seek means of justifying them.[15] In order for
there to be a 'dominant position', the Commission stated that there
must be 'stable, important and direct' financial links between the firms
in question and that something more than merely defending a dominant
position was needed to constitute abuse. Thus in 1969 high selling prices
for cement were accepted on account of the industry's special need for
self-financing of investment.

The most common infractions have been minimum prices, rigid
quotas, cartels, compensations and penalties of various kinds, but after
the effective commencement of the policy on anti-competition practices
in 1955, the first legal prosecution did not take place until 1966 and the
second not until 1969. In all Le Pors concludes that the Commission
appears to have achieved rather little: from 1966 to 1974 it investigated
a total of only 101 cases, mostly of minor economic importance.[16] One
must bear in mind that 84 of these cases were not permitted to continue
in their previous form (19 of these being permitted after modification
or restriction) and it seems likely that, as in the United Kingdom, the
threat of legal action was sufficient to ensure co-operation. Over all, however, relatively little seems to have been achieved and inter-firm agreements are still widespread. The report of the Committee on Competition
for the sixth Plan concluded that the nature of competition must vary
from one sector to another, so the emergence of a unified or more coherent national policy seems unlikely. (It should be remembered here
that numerous small firms persist in France.) Professor Chardonnet concludes that 'save in certain highly concentrated sections, pricing agreements are rare in France . . . and as for restrictive practices they are
forbidden by law'.[17] On balance, this seems to be less supported by the

evidence than the conclusion of Dyas and Thanheiser that 'discussions and negotiations between competitors are a fact of life'.[18]

Monopolisation has never been so extensive in France as in many other developed countries and this is given as the reason why no organisation exists for the control of monopolies, on the lines of those in the USA, Canada, UK, Japan or West Germany.[19] Proposals for control at the European level are, however, now well advanced after being discussed at the European summit conference of October 1972.

The educative role has recently been taken up by a new body, the Institut National de la Consommation, as the vogue of consumer protection has affected France much as in other countries:[20] forms of non-price competition, labelling and advertising will all receive closer attention in the future.

Externally, there is still considerable protection for French producers from such institutions as the European Coal and Steel Community, the European tin-plate Convention, and the administered price and quota systems for agricultural products and the food-processing industry but extensive liberalisation of trade within the EEC has taken place since the signing of the Treaty of Rome. French tariff barriers, formerly the highest in Europe with an average rate of over 18 per cent, plus a whole series of additional regulations, quotas and customs controls, have disappeared for intra-European trade and there has been a massive expansion of imported manufactured and semi-manufactured goods (perhaps quadrupling in 10 years from 1959 to 1969). There can be little doubt that the marked increase in foreign competition provided a sharp incentive towards increased productivity and effectiveness on the part of French firms.

Industrial Policy

Throughout the post-war period there has been concern that the average size of French industrial and commercial firms was too small in comparison with those in neighbouring countries and since the early 1960s the government has pursued an active policy of encouraging mergers and industrial concentration. Further nationalisations have been ruled out but there have been substantial tax concessions for companies merging or acquiring subsidiaries, an aim of the policy also being that unprofitable or badly-managed firms should be taken over.[21] To date major restructuring of whole sectors of industry has been achieved in only a few sectors, notably chemicals and metals but there have been significant regroupings in the chemical, aviation, shipbuilding and motor industries and also in banking and insurance. Significant mergers achieved have

been those of Saint-Gobin with Pont-à-Mousson, Péchiney with Ugine
Kuhlmann and Evian and Kronenbourg with BSN (Boussois-Souchon-
Neuvesel), and the setting up of the Creusot-Loire group and perhaps the
most famous recent case was that of the Peugeot-Citroën link.

Such developments have more recently been aided by the setting-up
in 1970 of the Institut de Développement Industriel (Industrial Development Institute), modelled on the United Kingdom's IRC (Industrial Reorganisation Corporation), a rare example of France following the economic example of Britain. The IDI operates as an autonomous body with
a governing board comprising largely industrialists from the private
sector, its capital being derived 49 per cent from the state, 51 per cent
from banks and financial institutions. It seeks to aid primarily rapidly-
growing medium-sized firms by (i) providing additional capital either
by taking a shareholding or by granting a loan normally for a maximum
of five years, and (ii) giving advice after in-depth sectoral studies. With
regard to this latter, the IDI takes the initiative, not waiting for industrialists to approach it but going ahead with studies especially of those sectors
given priority under the current Plan. Regarding the provision of capital,
funds have been made available to many smaller and medium-sized firms,
often via the IDI taking a minority shareholding which is sold to the
other shareholders at the termination of the loan. Such participation
has never exceeded the 24 per cent stake it took in Compagnie Internationale pour l'Informatique, the IDI's policy being not to take control of the companies it is aiding. The work of the IDI has been hampered by shortage of funds and it has not achieved the status that the IRC
has enjoyed in Britain: the IDI has capital of only Frs. 500 million,
nearly half of which has been used for a major restructuring of the paper
industry and to aid Compagnie Internationale pour l'Informatique, in the
computer field. Further expansion of the IDI in the near future seems
unlikely in view of the fact that it has been seen as competing with the
banks which are its shareholders, and in view of the government's stated
policy of encouraging credit to be provided via the normal private sector
market mechanism rather than by the intervention of the state.

The work of both the Institut de Développement Industriel and the
Commission Technique de la Concurrence must be seen as an integral
part of the French government's active industrial policy, which has been
set out in detail in successive Plans. The focus of this policy has been to
increase industrial competitiveness in order to achieve the sustained high
rate of economic growth to which France has now become accustomed,
to significantly increase France's industrial exports which have tended
to lag behind those of her competitor countries, and more recently, to

create more jobs with a view to reducing unemployment. To this end productive investment has been encouraged by both tax incentives and preferential credit terms. The government has also taken steps to remove legal or other hindrances to expansion, such as the law which required a 'comité d'entreprise', with employees' elected representatives, to be set up in any company which had fifty or more employees. One company with which the writer is familiar remained with a staff of 49 for some years before eventually dividing itself into two fictitious legal entities enabling it to expand to a staff of 98, to escape the provisions of such laws. Professor Chardonnet's view is that industrial concentration is still discouraged, e.g. by the fact that on the occasion of a merger the taxes to be paid, notably stamp duties, cost more in France than in any other EEC country.[22]

Unfortunately, there can be little doubt that the achievement of a coherent and unified industrial policy has been impeded by the differing viewpoints of the plethora of ministries and other governmental or semi-official bodies. Figure 7.1 shows in diagrammatic form the various ministries and their specific industrial responsibilities as in 1974. There have been some more recent changes but as the OECD Report put it

> There is no doubt that as regards the political and administrative organisation of the government, elements subsist which can only be explained in historical terms.[23]

In recent years The Interministerial Committee for Industrial Policy has attempted to achieve greater co-ordination and the re-vamped Ministry for Industrial and Scientific Development (MDIS) has since 1969 assumed overall responsibility for industrial and scientific development, especially with regard to gearing scientific research to the needs of industry, to utilising the fruits of research and to aiding the adoption of improved management techniques. Much of this Ministry's detailed work with industry is routed through its Directorate of Technology, Industrial Development and Mines which is largely decentralised to the level of the twenty-two economic planning regions. Here it liaises closely with the prefect of each region and with his 'commission administrative regionale' (CAR). Since 1970 any major industrial development has also had to be cleared with the Ministry for the Protection of Nature and the Environment which has overall responsibility for the care of the environment and for general living conditions.

In connection with industrial and scientific research MDIS acts as a co-ordinating body, supervising the work of the General Delegation for

Figure 7.1

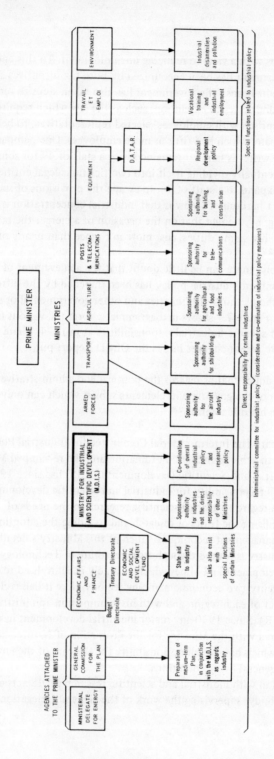

Source: The Industrial Policy of France, OECD (1974).

Scientific and Technical Research (DGRST), the Consultative Committee for Scientific and Industrial Research (CCRST) and the Interministerial Committee for Scientific and Technical Research (CIRST), as well as the principal public sector research bodies, CNES (for space activities), CNEXO (for the exploitation of ocean resources) and CEA (for atomic energy). The practical uses of industrially-orientated research are stimulated by the Agence Nationale pour la Valorisation de la Recherche (ANVAR) which advises on economic applications of new ideas, protection via patents, and tax concessions for research work, as well as publishing details of current research programmes. The OECD report[24] lists a further eleven national bodies concerned with the furthering of research, so in this field too there is an evident problem of overlap between the work of many different agencies.

Not the least of the ways in which the state can influence industry is through the use of the state's own purchasing power. The state's purchases now total over 7 per cent of Gross Domestic Product and in the 1970s the government has increasingly been seeking to use the power this implies: the threat of withdrawal of custom from a company has frequently proved sufficient to ensure a more 'co-operative' attitude. The prime example has been the re-structuring of the electrical and electro-mechanical equipment industry, two-thirds of the production of which is purchased by Electricité de France; through the latter, the government could virtually dictate the future shape of the industry.

After the 1978 elections, the government announced a revised industrial policy with greater emphasis on efficiency, profitability and 'getting rid of dead wood'. Firms will be expected to be more independent, government financial aid will be cut, and price controls lifted, in an effort to restore France to the path of high economic growth.

Manpower and Unemployment

In Plan 6 and even more in Plan 7 there has been renewed emphasis on manpower policy. Influenced by the sharp rise in the official unemployment statistics in the 1970s, the government has stressed the need to achieve a higher level of re-training and greater mobility of industrial manpower. Under a national inter-industry agreement signed in July 1970, employers and trade unions agreed on the right of workers to continuous training (there is an obvious connection with the new concept of 'l'éducation permanente' or 'recurrent education'). The government passed an Act the following year laying down the conditions on which firms were obliged to agree to continuous training and it also earmarked substantial budget grants to be allocated through the Fonds pour la Formation Professionnelle et la Promotion Sociale. Professional and other advice was to be available through the Association pour la Formation Professionelle des Adults (AFPA).

Stress was placed on the need for a better organisation of the labour market and the Agence Nationale pour l'Emploi, officially designated 'the main instrument for official intervention in the labour market', was expanded both to fulfil this new role and to give better geographical coverage with the opening of new regional offices throughout France. With the new Délégation à l'Emploi, set up in 1975, official policy placed special emphasis on the creation of additional industrial jobs for women and for school-leavers and began to limit the intake of foreign workers into France. The sum of Frs. 12 billion was earmarked to be spent by 1976 on schemes to improve occupational training and employment conditions. There are now three separate organisations, all set up in 1970, providing information and research relating to the labour market: the Centre d'Études de l'Emploi (CEE), to study the general functioning of the labour market, draw up employment forecasts for different industrial sectors and levels of qualification, and to make detailed regional studies; the Centre d'Études et de Recherches sur les Qualifications (CEREQ), to study the employment situation in the various professions and to examine links between the output from the education system and the needs of industry; the Office National d'Information sur les Enseignements et les Professions (ONISEP), to disseminate information regarding professional qualifications and the future needs of the professions.[25] in its first two years of existence this body distributed some 2,500,000 leaflets throughout France in an effort to give wider publicity relating to the professions.

In 1974 a series of new measures gave increased compensation for redundancy, new incentives to employers for employing young people; extra grants for further education and studies of the problems of earlier retirement and reduction of the working week. Immigration of foreign workers was effectively halted on 1 July 1974 and in June 1975 a 'prime d'incitation à la création d'emplois' was introduced: this undertook, as a temporary measure, to pay a subsidy of Frs. 500 per month for six months to employers of young people in certain fields. Following the publication of the Sudreau Report which advocated greater action by the state in the fields of professional training and health care at work, and to strengthen the factory inspectorate, the government has passed a series of decrees and has set up a Secretariat of State for the Condition of Manual Workers, all concerned with improving various aspects of industrial working conditions but 'Les Cahiers Français' of March/April 1977 was able to conclude that to date relatively little had been achieved in practice.

A major problem in assessing the labour situation in France is that the available statistics relating to unemployment are unfortunately very inadequate; indeed, there is no one statistical series which can be taken as a sufficient indicator of the unemployment situation. Unemployment statistics do, of course, present difficulties in other countries but at least one can usually think of any deficiences as being fairly consistent over time; even this has not been so in France. The number of people unemployed may be indicated in the following ways:

(i)   those in receipt of financial aid from the state or from semi-public bodies such as ASSEDIC (but there is a considerable problem of overlap since in November 1974 59 per cent of those receiving state aid from ASSEDIC also received direct aid from the state);

(ii)   those registered with the Agence Nationale pour l'Emploi, who are summed in the 'Demandes d'Emplois en fin de Mois' (DEFM). These statistics are readily available since they are published each month by the Ministry of Work and are therefore widely used. Only during the 1970s, however, has the Agence Nationale pour l'Emploi opened regional offices throughout France so that its statistics began fully to reflect the true national situation. As one authoritative survey put it: 'A few years ago these figures were much criticised since the offices of the Agence did not extend to many geographical areas. Today this is no longer the case since the Agence has opened many more offices, and many more people now register'.[26]

(iii)   Survey enquiries via annual interviews of a sample of the population, in which people declare whether they are seeking a job, the resulting statistics being termed 'Population Disponible à la recherche d'emploi' (PDRE). Similarly, the 'Population Marginale Disponible à la recherche d'un emploi' (PMDRE) includes 'Marginal' cases such as those seeking part-time work and those who say they seek work but in fact have taken no steps to obtain a job.

Some indication of the state of confusion may be gained from the following figures for March 1974:

Recipients of state unemployment aid	150,800
Recipients of ASSEDIC aid	156,500

DEFM	438,900
PDRE	440,400
PDRE and PMDRE (often termed 'chomeurs' – the unemployed)	781,800

An official study[27] of the relationship between the above statistical series found that PDRE was usually greater than DEFM, with a fairly stable ratio over time of 1.6, due largely to the fact that certain people, especially women and young workers, do not register with the Agency: the ratio became distorted, however, because during times of high unemployment a greater proportion of those out-of-work do register, whereas some of those included in DEFM are omitted from PDRE, e.g. if the sample survey misses them. A breakdown of the DEFM figure of 438,900 quoted above shows some 277,000 included in PDRE, 63,000 included in PMDRE, and some 99,000 not included in either, largely people who have obtained a job and not told the Agency. One measure of total unemployment is 'PDRE + 50 per cent of DEFM' which gives some idea of the degree of approximation involved. In his excellent short book on unemployment in France, J.M. Fahy[28] concluded that, 'the various measures in use gave, for December 1974, figures varying from 195,700 (ASSEDIC) to 1,100,000 ("PDRE + 50% of DEFM") without it being possible to say where the correct figure really lies'. Unemployment is now a major problem in France as in other countries: the total of unemployed rose steeply in the early 1970s, although there is even doubt about the size of this rise since the increases in the published figures coincided with the opening of the Agency's regional offices; it reached well over one million and seems likely to fall only slowly for some years to come.[29] The direct effect on government policies, in terms of both the labour market policies considered above and macroeconomic policy referred to below, has been clear and unequivocal.

The Contractual Approach and Finance

One of the most significant innovations in the field of economic policy in France in recent years has been the introduction of a 'contractual' approach to relations between the government and other parties. The 'contract', usually expressed in a formal written document, entails apparent obligations for both parties although such a veneer cannot hide the fact that the government is the dominant power. One special report[30] saw the move towards 'une économie concertée et même contractuelle' as 'une transformation profonde du capitalisme' but other writers have been more sceptical. In connection with price controls 'contrats de

stabilité' were first introduced in 1965 to replace the previous strict
control of prices by a system under which firms could raise prices of
certain products if they compensated by reducing prices of other products. By 1966 these gave way to 'contrats de programme' which covered
not merely prices but also investment, professional training, regional re-
location and productivity: price increases were only permitted if firms
gave undertakings regarding investment, productivity improvements,
and other matters: eventually the whole of industrial production was
covered by such controls. With the escalation of inflation in 1971 a
stricter system of 'contrats anti-hausse' was introduced, price increases
for manufactured products being limited to 1.5 per cent for a period of
six months, with no increases at all permitted for services. For its part
the state undertook that there would be no increases in public sector
charges bearing directly on firms' costs. By 1972 further reinforcement
termed 'programmation annuelle' covered most medium- and large-size
firms and permitted price increases primarily to offset rises in the costs
of raw materials; by 1974 under the 'accords de programmation annuelle
contrôlée' even the latter were severely restricted, firms were compelled
to reduce prices after any fall in costs of raw materials, and a 100 per
cent tax was introduced on any increase in profits: the veneer of a contractual agreement had by now worn rather thin. Opposition to such
price controls has recently been expressed more strongly, including by a
number of leading economists. Many price controls were lifted in 1978.

Perhaps on more validly contractual lines have been the 'contrats de
progrès' and 'programmes d'action concertée'. The former were agreements to control wage increases in the public sector; increases in workers'
real wages, over and above rises to offset the current rate of inflation,
were granted in exchange for productivity agreements. The 'programmes
d'action concertée' have consisted essentially of plans for the modernisation and reorganisation of certain industries through joint action by
industrialists and the public authorities. Commencing with that for the
iron and steel industry in 1966, and going on to those for data-processing
equipment (the 'plan calcul'), engineering, industrial electronics, furnit-
ure and toys, these plans have involved rationalisation via the closing
down or conversion of out-of-date factories, and the redeployment and
retraining of personnel, in return for government grants. A parallel
approach for public sector companies gave them greater autonomy and
less detailed governmental control, as recommended by the Nora report
of 1967. Commencing in 1969 the state has drawn up 'contrats de programme' with the major nationalised industries the prime aim of which
has been to give the latter greater financial responsibility. Drawn up

initially for periods of four or five years, and subsequently renewed, each has required the industry in question to become at least self-sufficient financially, save where the state required it to maintain a public service run at a loss, for which it would receive direct compensation (for example, unprofitable local railway lines): this was directly in line with the recommendations of the Nora report. Each 'contrat de programme' has set out the intentions of the authorities regarding capital acquisitions, loans, productivity, profitability and future trends in tariffs and wages. Tariffs had to be raised to cover current running costs plus 'that part of Investment which cannot be financed by loans'[31] and not surprisingly the subsequent price increases have given rise to considerable public criticism and press comment.[32] Renewed interest in this approach, including the drawing up of new contracts for Air France and Charbonnages de France, was reported early in 1978.[33]

The change in policy can be illustrated by reference to Electricité de France and SNCF (the French railways). In the case of Electricité de France the nationalisation law of 1946 required it to base its tariffs on marginal costs (nearly twenty years before such a requirement was introduced in the United Kingdom with the 1967 White Paper on the financial problems of the nationalised industries) and by 1960 this had developed into a sophisticated system of variations in tariffs for each of twenty-three regions, five times of the year, and five hours of the day, reflecting variations in marginal costs. The recent tariff increases have tended to increase the tariff differentials to the extent that the local electricity tariff is now one factor to be taken into consideration by any firm contemplating re-location in one of the regions. Electricité de France achieved a successful turn-round from a deficit to a working surplus by 1974, aided by the trend towards generation from nuclear energy. By 1976 the cost of one kilowatt-hour of electricity was 11.9 centimes from fossil fuels, but only 7.5 centimes from nuclear energy.[34] There is still some concern, however, that the level of consumption of electricity in France is much lower than in other comparable countries (domestic consumption per household in 1974 was 1686 KWH in France, against 4776 KWH in Britain) and is currently growing much more slowly. In the case of SNCF, large deficits had been recorded for many years and the aim specified in the 'contrat de programme', of ending these by 1974, could not be achieved. Many small unprofitable local lines were terminated, some 7,000 kilometres of track, about one-fifth of the total, being closed by 1973, and much-needed administrative reforms were carried out. For example, until 1970 SNCF still comprised six regional units, based on the previous private railway companies, five of these regional units having their head offices in Paris. With the rapid growth of freight traffic in the 1970s and the bringing into use of high-speed passenger trains on several major lines (well in advance of what British Rail has achieved), the financial position of SNCF has improved considerably: the working deficit was reduced steadily each year from 1970 to 1973 and a revised plan arrived at achieving a balance by around 1977.[35]

As part of its policy of making the nationalised industries become more self-reliant financially, the government is gradually reducing the direct provision of funds to them for investment and is requiring them to borrow on the capital market and from other sources. Government funds have traditionally been channelled through FDES (Fund for Social and Economic Development): it provided the nationalised industries with Frs. 1,110m. out of their total Investment of Frs. 12,454m in 1972 but by 1974 this had fallen to Frs. 440 m out of a total of Frs. 15,161 m. By early 1978 the total annual deficit of the nationalised industries was running at the rate of Frs. 30,000 m and was still increasing.

FDES has existed since 1950 to give loans at low rates of interest both to the public and the private sectors, essentially to provide the finance required to aid the implementation of the Plan. It has subsequently provided funds for firms re-locating outside Paris, for conversions of older factories, for agricultural modernisation and, more recently, for tertiary sector investment. Loans have usually been made available over periods of ten to fifteen years, at a rate of interest of 6 per cent and there has also been a provision that where FDES encouraged a firm to obtain a loan elsewhere, often on the money markets, the Fund would refund any interest paid in excess of the 6 per cent rate. The pattern developed of small firms borrowing direct from the Fund but larger firms being encouraged to borrow elsewhere so as not to exhaust the Fund's resources. Much of its aid was geared to the provision of grants and loans for regional policy purposes. FDES has had considerable publicity and is sometimes seen as a prime mover in the generation of industrial investment and expansion. In fact, however, its role has been declining steadily since 1961, save for a period of temporary increases over 1967-70 relating to the reorganisation of the steel industry, and it now only grants loans in exceptional circumstances such as the loan of one billion Francs to Citroën when the latter was in difficulties in 1974. Otherwise the provision of such loans is now seen as the province of the banking and financial sector (expressed in the slogan 'la débudgetisation des investissements'). Total loans granted by

FDES were some 2.7 billion Francs in 1974, i.e. about one-tenth of the
total loans emanating from the Caisse des Dépots et Consignations. When
this figure is compared with that of nearly 4.0 billion Francs for 1968,
it is evident that there has been a considerable decline even in current
Francs, the decline in real purchasing power being of course very much
greater. FDES does still grant the 'primes' for regional development,
currently totalling some Frs. 3 billion per annum. Calculations in an EEC
survey in 1969[36] showed that loans from government to industry,
expressed as a percentage of GNP, were lower in France than in any of
the other five EEC countries; financial grants or subsidies, however, were
higher in France than in any of the other countries except Luxemburg.

Economic Planning

To foreign observers perhaps the main point of interest in the French
economy is its sustained and apparently successful experience of economic planning, an experience which distinguishes France from any other
Western developed country. So devastated was France at the end of
World War II that a systematic and co-ordinated plan for post-war reconstruction seemed essential and the new planning office (Commissariat
Général Du Plan) under Monsieur Jean Monnet was given the task of
defining priorities and outlining courses of action. Plan 1 was a simple
document concentrating on the basic needs of coal, steel, electricity,
cement, transport and agricultural machinery.

Succeeding plans gradually became more ambitious and complex:
Plan 3 (1958-61) is often referred to as the first fully coherent and
integrated national programme, effectively covering the whole economy;
Plan 4 (1962-65) and 5 (1966-70) were even wider in scope since their
objectives included a greater social and regional emphasis. Plan 5 may in
fact be seen as the high-water mark of planning in France, subsequent
plans representing something of a retreat from the attempt to co-ordinate
virtually all aspects of social and economic policy over a five-year period.

Plan 7, which covers 1976-80, has four main themes:[37]

(i)   to provide the economic conditions necessary for full employ-
        ment and social progress (with references to demographic growth
        and control, education, and a modern competitive industry).

(ii)   to raise the quality of life (with references to better working
        conditions, quality of housing, town planning, and prevention of
        environmental pollution).

(iii)   to reduce inequalities (particularly of incomes, and also regard-
        ing access to various public services, including health and education),
        and

(iv)   to achieve greater regional devolution.

In pursuit of these themes, the plan sets out twenty-five detailed 'programmes', implementation of which is 'guaranteed' by the government: these cover such diverse headings as the telephone system, urban transport, re-training of labour, new towns, and energy policy.[38] Whilst all this represents a complex and carefully integrated approach to social and economic policy, it is not so detailed or precise as was Plan 5.

Much has been written on the decline of economic planning in France in recent years, one commentary, for example, seeing it as now 'relatively unambitious by the standards of the early 1960s'.[39] It is undeniable that in the 1960s there grew a feeling of disenchantment with the planning process and with what it was achieving: on the one hand the needs of short-term demand management policy caused the longer-run targets of the plan to be set on one side on a number of occasions, particularly in 1963 and 1968, whilst on the other a comparison of the plan's forecasts with the out-turn achieved sometimes indicated significant discrepancies. Critics of economic planning could easily attribute the undeniable success of the economy to the sustained impetus from post-war reconstruction, to the release of resources out of the relatively declining agricultural sector and to the competitive effect of the European Economic Community rather than to the planning process. Certainly after the major social unrest of 1968 economic planning was seen in a less favourable light.

Deleau and Malgrange emphasise that from Plan 6 onwards the planners abandoned the attempt at 'concertation', i.e. at globally coordinating the economic decisions of private firms via a kind of huge Leontief input-output table,[40] and they comment: 'The VIth Plan proved the end of previous ambitions about the operational scope of French Planning'.

In a recent lecture[41] Monsieur Jean Ripert, the head of the Commissariat General du Plan, acknowledged the relative decline in status of the CGP over the last ten years or so but stressed the need for the planning process to continue if a consistent and realistic approach to policy was to be achieved. He saw the current emphasis as being on 'consultation' rather than 'concertation', a view that fits in with the conclusion of Holmes and Estrin that: 'French Planning is becoming a framework for medium-term government economic policy'.[42]

Some of the more basic details relating to economic planning in France are given elsewhere[43] and need not be repeated here but it should be emphasised that comparisons between the apparently planned economy of France and an apparently unplanned one such as the United Kingdom are partly misleading since a number of policies (for example, energy policy, regional economic policy, policy on monopolies and restrictive practices, long-term forecasts of public expenditure and tax incentives for a variety of purposes such as industrial investment) are, with variations, common to both, but in the former they are all included in the plan. It should also be borne in mind that French planning is rather more than 'indicative' in view of the whole battery of financial and other incentives provided for firms to comply with its provisions.

As to whether economic planning can take the credit for the remarkable success of the French economy since 1945, no formal conclusion is possible. Published statistics showing usually a close relationship between the forecasts of successive plans and the out-turn achieved are not conclusive: there may be wide disparities at the level of individual firms or even industries and in the absence of detailed micro-economic studies of how individual firms' decisions have been affected by the planning process the case cannot be proved either way.[44] There is, of course, a prima facie case for attributing at least part of the quite exceptional success of the economy to the planning process, since they have coincided in time, after a long previous period of economic stagnation in France.

Regional Economic Policy

Regional imbalance has been a persistent economic problem throughout the post-war period and only in the 1970s could it be said that some of the most acute of the problems, at least, were nearing solution, whilst at the same time new ones had arisen.

Traditionally France's industries, and much of her commercial life, have been geographically concentrated, with much being located in the triangle formed by Paris, Lille (in the north) and Strasbourg (in the east); other prominent centres were Lyons, which has expanded rapidly since 1945, Marseilles, Bordeaux and a number of other relatively isolated towns. Much of the remainder of France, and notably the west and south-west, had little or no industry, relatively low standards of living, poor housing stock, and undue reliance on an inefficient and unproductive agricultural sector. When Professor Gravier in 1947 published his famous book *Paris et le desert français*, not only was the title most significant (the west and south-west of France being the 'desert'), but national interest was raised, perhaps for the first time, in the serious problem of regional imbalance.

By 1950 the government had produced an official report on the regional disparities and had set up a fund to encourage local industrial

development and in 1953 it provided further aid for engineering firms
to establish themselves in the poorer regions. Over all, however, the
effect was small and regional imbalance was continuing to grow worse.
Not until 1955 was serious action taken, by the establishment of 'zones
critiques' which were to receive favourable treatment, the introduction
both of controls on further industrial development in the Paris region
and of a series of incentives (investment grants, loans, interest subsidies,
tax concessions and grants for manpower re-training and mobility) for
firms 'decentralising' from Paris out to one of the poorer regions, and,
soon afterwards, by dividing France into 22 economic planning regions,
each of which was to have its own development plan. Progress continued
to be slow and further government measures[45] were required from time
to time throughout the 1960s and early 1970s.

By the mid-1970s the map of France showing the incentives available
to an industrialist considering moving a plant to, or setting up a new
plant in, one of the regions resembled a patchwork quilt, with eight
separate levels of assistance, but broadly the further west or south-west
one goes the larger the incentives become.[46] To act as counterweights
to the attractions of Paris, eight provincial cities or conurbations (Lille-
Roubaix, Nancy-Metz, Strasbourg, Lyons-St Etienne, Marseilles-Aix,
Toulouse, Bordeaux and Nantes-St Nazaire) have been designated as
'métropoles d'equilibre' (regional capitals) and have been encouraged to
develop social infrastructure as well as cultural and artistic centres.
Added to this now is a complementary policy of developing medium-
sized towns.

Perhaps the prime concern of successive French governments in paying more serious attention to regional economic policy has been the
drift of population from the regions to Paris. Unattracted by what was
available to them locally, often released from farming as this slowly
began to become more mechanised, and influenced by their period away
from home on military service, the younger, more mobile, and better
educated elements of the local population in many of the poorer regions
have tended to seek to move, often to Paris. The national census figures
for 1954, 1962, 1968 and 1975 show pronounced internal migration
movements with, in the earlier part of the period, a net inflow into the
Paris region of some 100,000 people a year, declining by the 1970s to
a figure of some 12,000 per year. The western and south-western regions
(Brittany, Pays de la Loire and Aquitaine are good examples) saw serious
net outflows of population in the 1950s and early 1960s but with this
being largely halted by the 1970s (and even reversed in the case of Brittany). The 1975 census figures, in particular, gave considerable cause

for satisfaction in connection with the westerly regions; regrettably, however, they also showed that the position in the north-eastern corner of
France was worsening steadily: as some of the older industries (notably
coal, shipbuilding, steel and textiles) declined, the relatively ageing and
unskilled labour force did not prove attractive to new employers and
local rates of unemployment, and of emigration to other parts of France,
began to grow. All the evidence indicates that the Lille area in particular
now has deep-rooted problems that are liable to persist for some years
and which it will not be easy to cure.

As firms have been encouraged to move out of the Paris region (or
'decentralise'), the evidence indicates that they have been content to
move to bordering regions (e.g. Centre), where few financial incentives
operate, rather than to those regions in most need. Probably, therefore,
it has been the curb on developments in the Paris region, rather than the
range of financial inducements available, which has had the most effect.
The peak of such moves, both in terms of number of firms moving and in
terms of number of jobs affected, was reached in 1961 but has continued
at a steady, albeit declining, flow subsequently.

Over all, whilst a more even geographical spread of economic activity
has certainly been achieved, and the relative concentration on Paris
lessened, some of the remoter regions (especially Aquitaine, Limousin,
and Auvergne) remain relatively poor and with little prospect of much
economic improvement in the near future. With the problems of the
north-eastern corner of France currently worsening, the regional problem
is far from solved. Perhaps the greatest success has been achieved in Brittany, whose economic position has been transformed.[47] A major problem
for an economist is that there is no single way of assessing a lessening of
regional inequalities and recourse has to be had to a variety of statistical
indicators.[48] To assess real standards of living, for example, one can use
figures of the number of cars, or televisions, or washing-machines, or
refrigerators, per head of population in each region to show that since
the 1950s many of the other regions have been catching up on, and in
some instances have overtaken, Paris. All this is in contrast to the regional problem in the United Kingdom which has always related primarily
to high local rates of unemployment: regional policy was seen to be
working if it enabled a developing region's unemployment rates to be
brought closer to the national average. Only since the mid 1970s have
the unemployment rates for the French regions started to show note-
worthy disparities but the difficulties in connection with French unemployment statistics, mentioned above, must be borne in mind.

Other Policies

Space constraints permit only a brief reference to other elements of economic policy.

As can be seen by reference to Plan 7 and its supporting documents, there is now much interest in France in energy conservation and in protection of the environment and a series of edicts relating to each, rather similar to those in comparable countries, have appeared within the last few years.

This essay has not attempted to deal with general macro-economic policy, in the sense of aggregate demand management, but mention should be made of the fact that such policy differs significantly from those in many other developed countries.[49]

Notes

1. G.P. Dyas & H.T. Thanheiser, *The Emerging European Enterprise, Strategy and Structure in French and German Industry* (Macmillan, London, 1976).
2. OECD, *The Industrial Policy of France* (1974).
3. Jean Chardonnet, *La Politique Economique Interieure Française* (Dalloz, Paris, 1976).
4. For this expression and for considerable further detail see R. Drago, 'France', Chapter 1 in W. Friedmann (ed.), *Public and Private Enterprise in Mixed Economies* (Stevens, 1974).
5. Taken from R. Drago, op.cit.
6. By Chardonnet, op.cit. This position appears to be relatively static at present although *The Economist*, 19 February 1977 reported details of nine major industrial groups liable to be nationalised if ever a socialist/communist government were to come to power.
7. L. Stoleru, in 'L'Imperatif Industriel', 1969, quoted in Dyas and Thanheiser, op.cit. The private financial sector has developed further in the 1970s.
8. Ibid.
9. Chapter 3, 'France', in E.V. Morgan, R. Harrington and G. Zis, *Capital Markets in the EEC* (Financial Times, 1974).
10. From M. Perouse (Directeur Général of the Caisse des Depots): 'The Process of Decision-Making for the Financing of Investment in France' (Transcript of lecture given at the London School of Economics, 5 November 1976).
11. Report on 'La Caisse des Dépots et Consignations' published in 'Notes et Etudes Documentaires', No. 3996-8, 20 June 1973.
12. M. Perouse, 'Les Caisses d'épargne, la caisse des dépôts et la financement de l'économie' (Communication présentée a l'Académie des Sciences Morales et Politiques, 27 September 1976).
13. Report, op.cit.
14. A. Le Pors, 'Les Transferts État-Industrie en France et dans les Pays Occidentaux', in Notes et Études Documentaires, No. 4303/5, 12/7/1976.
15. Ibid.
16. Ibid.
17. Ibid.

18. Ibid.
19. A. Le Pors.
20. J. Chardonnet.
21. J. Chardonnet.
22. Ibid.
23. Ibid.
24. Ibid.
25. For fuller details see Les Cahiers Français, No. 175, March/April 1976.
26. 'Le Nouvel Observateur', Faits et Chiffres, 1975.
27. 'Economie et Statistique', 1975.
28. J.M. Fahy, Le Chomage en France ('Que Sais-Je?' series, PUF).
29. See the forecasts in 'L'Économie Française en 1980', Économie et Statistique, No. 84, December 1976.
30. Les Cahiers Français, No. 180, March/April 1977.
31. P. Comte, 'Les Contrats de Programme', Notes et Études Documentaires, No. 4167/8, 26/2/1975.
32. For a controversial left-wing view of recent developments see H. Segré, 'Les Entreprises Publiques, la crise et le VIIᵉ Plan', Economie et Politique, November 1976.
33. *Financial Times*, London, 26 January 1978.
34. Special report on 'Electricité de France', Notes et Études Documentaires, No. 4329/31, 2/11/1976.
35. P. Comte.
36. Quoted in A. Le Pors.
37. *New from France*, June 1975 (French Embassy, London).
38. *New from France*, September 1976 (French Embassy, London).
39. P. Holmes and S. Estrin, *French Planning Today*, University of Sussex Economics Seminar Paper Series 76/14 (page 33).
40. M. Deleau and P. Malgrange, *Recent Trends in French Planning* (CEPREMAP, Paris, No. 7511 bis). (This paper gives a good exposition of technical aspects of the planning process and of the econometric model used).
41. Given at London School of Economics, 22 October 1976.
42. Ibid. (page 8).
43. For example, J.R. Hough, 'French Economic Policy', *National Westminster Bank Review*, May 1976.
44. See D. Liggins, *National Economic Planning in France* (Saxon House, 1975), and J.R. Hough, op.cit.
45. For details of these developments see K. Allen and M.C. MacLennan, *Regional Problems and Policies in France and Italy* (1970).
46. Full details are given in J. De Lanversin, *L'Aménagement Du Territoire Et La Régionalisation* (1970).
47. See H. Krier, 'Les Incidences du Marché Commun sur developpement economique d'une region – le cas de la Bretagne', in *Revue d'Economie Politique*, March/April 1974, No. 3.
48. For a good general discussion of what has been achieved in the French regions, see H. Clout (ed.), *Regional Development in Western Europe* (Wiley, 1975).
49. See J.R. Hough, op.cit.

NOTES ON CONTRIBUTORS

G.C. Allen is Emeritus Professor of Political Economy, University of London.

R.H. Allan is Co-ordinator of the Industrial Economics Programme, University of Melbourne.

J.P. Nieuwenhuysen is Reader in Economics, University of Melbourne.

N.R. Norman is Senior Lecturer in Economics, University of Melbourne (on leave as Research Director, Australian Industries Development Association, Melbourne).

James W. McKie is Professor of Economics, University of Texas at Austin.

H.G. Jones was formerly Senior Research Fellow, University of Strathclyde.

Peter Maunder is Senior Lecturer in Economics, Loughborough University.

Eric Owen-Smith is Senior Lecturer in Economics, Loughborough University.

J.R. Hough is Senior Lecturer in Education and Economics, Loughborough University.

NAME INDEX

Adenauer, Konrad 162
Allen, G.C. 9
Attlee, Clement 134-5

Bacon, Roger 131
Barker, J.E. 161
Benn, Tony 139
Bevan, Aneurin 135
Biedenkopf, Professor Kurt H. 162
Bowen, R.H. 161
Brittan, Samuel 136, 156
Bullock, Lord 154-5
Butz, Earl 84

Callaghan, James 134, 154
Carter, President Jimmy 96
Chardonnet, Professor J. 196, 199
Churchill, Sir Winston 134
Corden, Dr Max 156

Dahrendorf, Ralf 161
Deleau, M. 209
Dyas, G.P. 193, 197

Eden, Sir Anthony 134
Eisenhower, President Dwight 90
Eltis, Walter 131
Erhard, Professor Ludwig 161, 163
Estrin, S. 209
Eucken, Professor Walter 161

Fahy, J.M. 204
Fälldin, Thorbjörn 124, 127

Giersch, H. 165
Gordon, A.P.L. 161
Gravier, Professor J.F. 210

Hallett, Dr Graham 176
Hayden, W.G. 46
Heath, Edward 134, 136, 140, 144, 147
Hesselbach, W. 165
Heurgren, Sven 122
Holmes, P. 209
Hough, J.R. 9
Humphrey, H. 95

Isaac, J.E. 49

James, H.G. 9

Kaldor, Professor Nicholas 143
Kerr, Sir John 42

Langer, J. 172-3
Le Pors, A. 196
Lord, Alan 142-3
Lowe, A.V. 130

Macmillan, Sir Harold 134, 136-7, 145
Malgrange, P. 209
Matsukata, Prince 19
McKie, James W. 10
Meidner, Dr Rudolf 110, 121-2
Monnet, Jean 208
Morrison, Herbert (Baron Morrison of Lambeth) 136

Nader, Ralph 12, 82
Nieuwenhuysen, J. 9-10

Owen Smith, Eric 9

Phelps Brown, Sir Henry 49

Reuss, F.G. 171, 176
Ripert, J. 209
Ryder, Lord 10, 139, 148-9

Schiller, Professor Karl 165
Shonfield, Andrew 177
Stolper, G. 161
Streit, Manheim 179

Tanaka, K. 29
Thanheiser, H.T. 193, 197
The Economist 143, 147, 155, 169

Vernon, Raymond 10, 130

Watt, David 155
Whitlam, Gough 42, 58
Wilsher, Peter 155

Wilson, Sir Harold 13, 135-6, 138-40, 146, 149, 154

Young, Stephen 130

Zweig, K. 166

SUBJECT INDEX

Advisory, Conciliation and Arbitration Service (UK) 154
Agence Nationale pour la Valorisation de la Recherche 201
Agence Nationale pour l'Emploi 202-3
Agricultural Act 1947 (UK) 151
Agricultural Marketing Service (US) 98
Agricultural Stabilization and Conservation Service (US) 97
Agriculture:
  Australia 41, 54
  US 84, 95
  Sweden 111, 113
  UK 151
  W. Germany 169-71
Aircraft industry:
  Japan 30
  US 88-90
  UK 130, 133, 147, 150-1
  W. Germany 186
  France 191
Air France 191, 206
Aix 211
Aluminum Company of America (Alcoa) 75
Aluminium industry:
  US 75
  UK 146-7
  W. Germany 185
Amakudari (Japan) 37
American Telephone and Telegraph 75
Amtrak (US) 85
Animal and Plant Health Inspection Service (US) 97
Anti-Monopoly Law (Japan) 26
Anti-trust policy in US 74-8
Aquitaine 211-12
Arbitration Wage System in Australia 48-51, 56-7
Armaments industry in US 88-90
Associated Electrical Industries (UK) 145
Association pour la Formation Professionelle des Adults 202

Australia:
  Macro-economic policies 41-7
  Intervention in labour and product markets 47-54
  Competition policy 55-6
  Foreign ownership and control 57-65
  Capital market 65-70
Australian Housing Corporation 67
Australian Industry Development Corporation 58, 64, 66
Australian Resources Development Bank 64, 66
Australian Wool Corporation 54
Auvergne 212

Banking and finance:
  Japan 20-3
  Australia 41, 65-9
  US 83
  Sweden 106, 113
  UK 138-40
  W. Germany 163, 176-8
  France 193-5, 197-8
Bank of England 135
Bank of Japan 23, 38
Bank für Gemeinwirtschaft 178
Banque de France 191
BASF (W. Germany) 163-4
Bavaria 173-4
Bayer (W. Germany) 163-4
Bonn 168, 185
Bordeaux 210-11
Bremen 173
British Leyland 13, 148-9, 155
British Motor Corporation 146, 148-9, 155
British Shipbuilders 147
Brittany 211
BSN (France) 198

Caisses d'Epargne 194
Caisse des Dépots et Consignations 194-5, 208
Capital Issues Committee (UK) 137
Capital Market in Australia 65-70
Cartel Office in W. Germany 164-5, 182-3

Cartels in W. Germany 162-4
Central Bank of Sweden 106
Centre d'Études de l'Emploi 202
Centre d'Études et de Recherches sur
  les Qualifications 202
Centre Party (Sweden) 101-2, 124-5,
  127
Charbonnages de France 206
Chemical industry:
    Australia 59, 61
    US 84
    W. Germany 161, 163-4, 173,
      182
    France 191-2, 197
Christian Democratic Party (W.
  (Germany) 162
Chrysley (UK) 147, 149, 155
Citroën 198, 207
Civil Aeronautics Board (US) 97
Clayton Act 1914 (US) 74
Clothing industry:
    Australia 59, 61
    US 84
    UK 149
Coal industry:
    US 92-3
    UK 133, 135-7, 144
    W. Germany 161, 163, 174-5
    France 191, 208, 212
Co-determination Act 1977 (Sweden)
  120
Co-determination Act (W. Germany)
  166
Colvilles Ltd (UK) 137
Commissariat Général du Plan 195,
  200
Commission Technique de la Concur-
  rence 195-6, 198
Committee to Review the Function-
  ing of Financial Institutions
  (Wilson Committee – UK) 139
Commodity boards (Australia) 54
Commodity Credit Corporation
  (US) 98
Commodity Futures Trading Com-
  mission (US) 96
Commonwealth Development Bank
  (Australia) 66
Commonwealth Trading and Savings
  Bank (Australia) 64
Communist Party (Sweden) 101-2
Compagnie Internationale pour
  l'Informatique 198
Companies (Foreign Takeovers) Act

1972 (Australia) 58
Competition policy:
    Japan 12, 22, 26-8
    Australia 12, 55, 63
    US 12, 74-8
    Sweden 13, 111, 123, 127-8
    UK 13, 152-3
    W. Germany 13, 162-5
    France 195-7
Comptroller of the Currency (US)
  96
Computer industry in UK 151
Concentration of industry:
    Japan 20-3, 26-8
    Australia 12, 59-64
    US 77-8
    UK 13, 152
    W. Germany 13-14, 163-4
    France 196-7
Conciliation and Arbitration Com-
  mission (Australia) 47-51
Concorde (UK) 133, 150
Conservative Party (Sweden) 101-2
Conservative Party (UK) 131, 134-8,
  142, 145-7, 149, 152-4
Consolidated Rail Corporation (US)
  84-5
Consultative Committee for Scientific
  and Technical Research (France)
  201
Consumer Product Safety Commission
  (US) 82, 97
Consumer Protection Advisory Com-
  mittee (UK) 153
Consumer protection in US 82
Corps of Engineers (US) 97
Cotton Industry Act 1959 (UK)
  145
Council of Economic Advisers (W.
  Germany) 166
Crédit Foncier 193-5
Crédit Hotelier 193
Crédit National 193-5
Creusot-Loire 198
Czechoslovakia 166

Délégation à l'Emploi 202
Democratic Party (US) 73
Department of Economic Affairs
  (UK) 138
Department of Energy (US) 92
Department of Justice (US) 75-7,
  97
Deutsche Bundesbank 177-8

Directorate of Technology, Industrial Development and Mines (France) 199

Director-General of Fair Trading (UK) 153

Distribution of Industry Act 1945 (UK) 140

Domestic electric appliance industry in UK 142-3

Economic Planning Agency (Japan) 32

Electricité de France 193, 201, 206

Electric Power Development Company (Japan) 35, 38

Electricity industry:
Japan 35-6
US 79, 86-8
Sweden 112
UK 135-7
W. Germany 175, 182-3, 185
France 191, 193, 201, 206, 208

Electronics industry:
Japan 30
France 205

Elliott Automation (UK) 151

EMC (Mining and Chemical Enterprise in France) 191

Emergency Areas (W. Germany) 168

Employment Act 1946 (US) 95

Employment and Training Act 1973 (UK) 154

Employment Protection Act 1975 (UK) 154

Energy policy:
US 90-3
Sweden 124, 127
UK 135-7
W. Germany 186
France 206

English-Electric Computers 151

Enterprise for Research and Control of the Petroleum Industry in France 191

Environmental Protection Agency (US) 81, 97

Equal Employment Opportunity Commission (US) 81, 97

Equal Pay Act 1970 (UK) 154

Equity Capital for Industry (UK) 139

European Coal and Steel Community 197

European Free Trade Area 146

Export Finance and Insurance Corporation (Australia) 66

Fair Trade Commission (Japan) 22, 26-7

Fair Trading Act 1973 (UK) 153

Farmers Home Administration (US) 97

Federal Aviation Administration (US) 97

Federal Communications Commission (US) 80-1, 97

Federal Crop Insurance Corporation (US) 97

Federal Deposit Insurance Corporation (US) 96

Federal Energy Administration (US) 97

Federal Home Loan Bank Board (US) 96

Federal Land Banks (US) 83

Federal Maritime Commission (US) 97

Federal National Mortgage Institution (US) 83

Federal Power Commission (US) 97

Federal Reserve Board (US) 96

Federal Trade Commission Act 1914 (US) 74

Federal Trade Commission (US) 76-7, 97

Finance Corporation for Industry (UK) 139

Finance for Industry (UK) 139

Financial Corporations Act 1974 (Australia) 65, 68-9

Fonds de Développement Economique et Social (FDES) 193, 207-8

Fonds pour la Formation Professionelle et la Promotion Sociale 202

Food and Drug Administration (US) 82, 97

Footwear:
Australia 59, 61
Sweden 119

Ford of W. Germany 183

Foreign Investment Review Board (Australia) 59-60, 68

Foreign ownership and control in Australia 57-65

Foreign Takeovers Act 1975 (Australia) 58-60, 68

Forestry in Sweden 101, 111-13, 124

France:
    Public ownership 191-3
    Intervention in financial sector
        193-5
    Competition policy 195-7
    Industrial policy 197-201
    Manpower policy 201-4
    Contracts with industry 204-8
    Planning 208-10
    Regional policy 210-12
Free Democratic Party (W. Germany)
    162, 164-5
Freight transport in US 79-80
Full Employment and Balanced
    Growth Act (US) 12, 95

Galbraith, John Kenneth 94-5
Gas industry:
    Japan 36
    US 91-2
    UK 135-6, 144
    W. Germany 182, 185
    France 191-2
GATT 25
Gaullist Party (France) 190
Gaz de France 191
Gelsenberg AG (W. Germany) 182-3
General Delegation for Scientific and
    Technical Research (France) 199-201
General Dynamics (US) 89
General Electric Company (UK) 145
General Electric Company (US) 89
General Motors 183
Ginko (Japan) 35, 38
Girozentralen 178
Green Plan for Agriculture (W.
    Germany) 170
Guest, Keen and Nettlefold (GKN)
    15

Hamburg 172-3
Health and Safety at Work 1974 (UK)
    154
Hoechst (W. Germany) 163-4
Homestead Act (US) 93
Housing:
    Australia 67
    US 83, 85-6, 95
    Sweden 127
    W. Germany 176
    France 193-5
Howaldtswerke Deutsche Werft AG

Hamburg und Kiel 184

IBM Ltd 75, 152
IG Farben (W. Germany) 163-4
Import-Export Bank (Japan) 25, 38
Industrial and Commercial Finance
    Corporation (UK) 139
Industrial Assistance Commission
    (Australia) 56
Industrial Development Act 1966
    (UK) 140
Industrial Development Advisory
    Board (UK) 146
Industrial Development Institute
    (France) 148
Industrial Expansion Act 1968 (UK)
    146
Industrial Relations Act 1971 (UK)
    154
Industrial Training Act 1964 (UK)
    153
Industrial Reorganization Corp-
    oration (UK) 14, 130, 145-6
Industrieverwaltungs – Gmblt (W.
    Germany) 181
Industry Act 1972 (UK) 147, 149-50
Industry Act 1975 (UK) 148, 150
Institut de Développement Industriel
    198
Institut National de la Consommation
    197
Intermediate Areas (UK) 141
Inter-ministerial Committee for
    Industrial Policy (France) 199
Inter-ministerial Committee for
    Scientific and Technical Research
    (France) 201
International Computers Ltd (UK)
    151
Interstate Commerce Commission
    (US) 97
IRI (Italy) 148
Iron and Steel Board (UK) 135
Investment Funds (Sweden) 106-8,
    111

Japan:
    Broad role of state 17-18
    The state in:
        Meiji era 18-21
        the Zaibatsu 20-3
        the US influence 22
        trade policy 24-5

Japan: the state in:
　competition policy 26-8
　regional policy 28-30
　state links with industry 30-2
　planning 32-3
　public corporations 34-8
Japan Airline Manufacturing Company
　35, 38
Japan Airlines 35, 38
Japan Atomic Energy Corporation
　34, 37
Japan Monopoly Corporation 34, 37
Japan National Railways Corporation
　34, 37
Jigyodan (Japan) 35-6, 38

Kiel 169, 184
Kinko (Japan) 35, 38
Kockums (Sweden) 113, 125-7
Kodan (Japan) 34-5, 38
Koko (Japan) 35, 38
Kosha (Japan) 34-5, 37
Kreditanstalt für Wiederaufbau 177
Kronenbourg 198

Labour Court (Sweden) 105, 117-18
Labour Market Board (Sweden) 13,
　102, 106-11, 115
Labour market policies:
　Australia 48-57
　US 81
　Sweden 13, 105-12, 115-22
　UK 133-4, 153-5
　France 201-4
Labour Party (Australia) 41-3, 45-7,
　50-3, 58, 64
Labour Party (UK) 131, 134-6, 138-
　41, 144, 146-50, 152-4
Land Consolidation Act 1953 (W.
　Germany) 170
Länder governments in W. Germany
　160, 165, 168, 171, 173, 175-8,
　183, 185-6
Land reform (Japan) 22
Landesbanken (W. Germany) 178
Landeszentralbanken (W. Germany)
　177-8
Leyland Motors (UK) 146, 148-9,
　155
Liberal Party (Australia) 41-2, 47,
　52
Liberal Party (Sweden) 101-2
Liberal Party (UK) 134
Licensing in US 80

Lille 210-12
Limousin 212
LO (Sweden) 110, 116-22
Location of Offices Bureau (UK)
　141
Lockheed (US) 15, 89
London Passenger Transport Board
　36
Lower Saxony 173, 181, 184
Lufthansa (W. Germany) 186
Lyons 210-11

Machine-tool industry:
　Japan 30
　UK 149
　W. Germany 173
Manpower Services Commission (UK)
　154
Market Court (Sweden) 105, 122-3
Marketing schemes in Australia 53-4
Marseilles 210
Marshall Aid 166, 170
McDonnell-Douglas (US) 89
Mergers:
　Japan 22, 26
　Australia 58, 62-3
　US 76-8
　Sweden 111, 120
　UK 145-6, 151-2
　W. Germany 164
　France 197-8
Meriden motor-cycle co-operative (UK)
　150
Metalworkers' union (W. Germany)
　166
Metz 211
Mining:
　Australia 54, 58-60, 62, 64-6
　Sweden 101, 107, 113
Mining Enforcement and Safety Admin-
　istration (US) 97
Ministry of:
　Defence (W. Germany) 180
　Economic Affairs in W. Germany
　　163-4, 180, 182-3
　Economic Co-operation (W. Ger-
　　many) 180, 186
　Economy and Finance (France)
　　195, 200
　Education and Science (W. Ger-
　　many) 180
　Finance (France) 193, 195, 200
　Finance (W. Germany) 169, 179-
　　80

Ministry of (cont.):
Food, Agriculture and Forestry (W. Germany) 180
Industrial and Scientific Development (France) 199-200
Interior (W. Germany) 180
International Trade and Industry (Japan) 26-8, 30, 32-3
Justice (W. Germany) 180
Press and Information (W. Germany) 180
Protection of Nature and Environment (France) 199-200
Research and Technology (W. Germany) 180
Rural and Urban Planning (W. Germany) 180, 186
Transport (W. Germany) 180, 186
Monopolies and Mergers Act 1965 (UK) 152
Monopolies and Restrictive Practices (Inquiry and Control) Act 1948 (UK) 152
Monopolies Commission (UK) 146
Monopolies Commission (W. Germany) 164, 183
Motor vehicle industry:
Australia 44-5, 61
US 84
Sweden 120, 122, 124
UK 140, 142, 146, 148-50
W. Germany 173
France 191-3, 197

Nancy 211
Nantes 211
National Aeronautical and Space Administration (US) 83
National Board for Prices and Incomes (UK) 144
National Board of Education (Sweden) 108
National Complaints Board (Sweden) 123
National Consumers' Council (UK) 153
National Country Party (Australia) 41-2, 47, 52
National Debt Inspectorate (Sweden) 123
National Economic Development Council (UK) 138
National Energy Plan (US) 91
National Enterprise Board (UK) 10,

13, 130, 133, 139, 148, 150
National Farmers' Union (UK) 151
National Food Administration (Sweden) 123
National Highway Traffic Safety Administration (US) 97
National Industrial Relations Court (UK) 154
National Labour Relations Board (US) 97
National Pension Fund (Sweden) 107, 114-15
National Price and Control Office (Sweden) 123
National Research Development Corporation (UK) 150-1
National Social Insurance Court (Sweden) 115
Nationalisation:
Japan 34-8
Australia 64-5
Sweden 112-13
UK 134-7
France 191
'New industrial strategy' (UK) 138
Nippon Telegraph and Telephone Corporation (Japan) 34, 37
Nora Report (France) 205-6
Nuclear Regulatory Commission (US) 97

Occupational Health and Safety Administration (US) 81, 97
OECD 190, 199, 201
Office of Federal Contract Compliance (US) 97
Office National d'Information sur les Enseignments et les Professions 202
Ombudsmen in Sweden 13, 103, 122-3
OPEC 91
Opel (W. Germany) 183
Oriental Development Company (Japan) 20
Overseas investment in Australia 57-60, 63-4
Overseas Trading Corporation (Australia) 66

Paris 193, 207, 210-12
Paris Bourse 194
Pays de la Loire 211
Péchiney 198

Pension and Benefit Welfare Programs
    (US) 97
Petroleum industry:
    Japan 27
    Australia 60-1
    US 75, 90-3
    W. Germany 182-3
    France 191-2
Peugeot (France) 198
Planning:
    Japan 11, 32-3
    US 95
    UK 137-8, 140-1, 149-50
    W. Germany 14, 165-6
    France 208-10
Pont-à-Mousson 198
Postal services:
    Japan 34, 37
    Australia 65
    US 85
    W. Germany 172
    France 191
Preussag (W. Germany) 179
Price Commission (UK) 144
Prices Justification Tribunal
    (Australia) 48, 51-3
Prices policy:
    Australia 12, 51-3
    UK 136, 144
    France 204-5
Project Independence (US) 91
Promotion of Economic Stability
    and Growth Act (1967) (W.
    Germany) 14, 162, 165-6, 171
Public Corporations:
    Japan 34-8
    Australia 64-5
    US 12
    UK 134-7
    W. Germany 178-86
    France 14, 191-3
Public utilities in US 12, 77-80, 86-8
Purchase tax (UK) 142
Pure Food and Drug Act 1906 (US)
    82

Race Relations Act 1978 (UK) 154
Railways:
    Japan 20
    Australia 65
    US 84-5, 95
    Sweden 112
    UK 135
    W. Germany 171-2, 179

France 191-2, 206-7
Reconstruction Finance Bank (Japan)
    23
Redundancy Payments Act 1965
    (UK) 154
Regional Action Programme 1969
    (W. Germany) 169
Regional Development Act 1965
    (W. Germany) 169
Regional policy:
    Japan 12, 28-30
    Australia 54
    US 92-3
    Sweden 110-12
    UK 13, 132, 140-1
    W. Germany 14, 166-9
    France 14, 193, 210-12
Renault 191-3
Republican Party (US) 73
Resale Prices Act 1964 (UK) 144
Reserve Bank (Australia) 60, 66-9
Restoration Areas (W. Germany)
    168
Restrictive Trade Practices Act 1956
    (UK) 152
Rheinisch-Westfälischen Elektrizitäts-
    werk 183
Richard Thomas and Baldwins (UK)
    137
Riksdag (Sweden) 101-4, 106, 108,
    114, 116
Robinson-Patman Act 1936 (US)
    76
Rolls-Royce 15, 130, 134, 147
Rotterdam 184
Roubaix 211
Ruhr 169, 184-5
Ruhrohle AG (W. Germany) 185
Rural Electrification Administration
    (US) 97

Saar 169
Saarbergwerke AG (W. Germany)
    181-2, 185
Saarland 181, 185
Sachs AG (W. Germany) 15
SACO (Sweden) 104, 116
SAF (Sweden) 110, 116-22
Saint-Gobin 198
SALF (Sweden) 116
Saltsjöbaden Agreement (Sweden)
    117
Salzgitter AG 168, 181-2, 184
Schleswig-Holstein 173, 184

Sears, Roebuck (US) 77
Securities and Exchange Commission (US) 96
Security of Employment Act 1974 (Sweden) 119-20
Select Committee on Nationalized Industries (UK) 137
Selective employment tax (UK) 140, 143-4
Sex Discrimination Act 1975 (UK) 154
Sherman Act 1890 (US) 74-6
Shinko-Zaibatsu (Japan) 21
Shipbuilding industry:
    Japan 20
    Sweden 113, 125-7
    UK 133, 147
    W. Germany 161, 172-4
    France 197, 212
Shipbuilding Industry Board (UK) 147
Silk industry in Japan 20
SNCF (French railways) 191-2, 206-7
Social Democratic Party (W. Germany) 162, 164-5
Social Democratic Party (Sweden) 101-2, 105, 107, 122, 124-5
Social Market economy philosophy in W. Germany 161-2
Soil Conservation Service (US) 97
South Manchuria Railway Company (Japan) 20
Standard Oil Company (US) 75
Statsföretag (Sweden) 13, 112-13
Steel industry:
    Japan 20
    US 84
    Sweden 111-12, 125-6
    UK 135-7
    W. Germany 163, 175
    France 208, 212
Steelworks 80 (Sweden) 112
St Etienne 211
St Nazaire 211
Strasbourg 210-11
Strikes – data for seven countries 116
Subsidies Report (W. Germany) 171
Sudreau Report (France) 202
Sumitomo Kinsoku Kogyo (Japan) 31-2
Sunbelt (US) 92-3

Sweden:
    political background 101-3
    formulation of legislation 103-5
    role of Labour Market Board 105-9
    labour redeployment 110-12
    state ownership of industry and finance 112-14
    social policy 114-15
    industrial relations 115-22
    consumer protection 122-3
    environmental protection 124-5
Swedish Investment Bank 113

Tariff Board (Australia) 56
Tariff protection:
    Japan 24-5
    Australia 12, 47, 55-6
    US 84
    W. Germany 161
    France 197
TCO (Sweden) 116
Teito Rapid Transport Authority (Japan) 36
Television broadcasting in US 80-1
Temporary Employment Subsidy (UK) 15
Tennessee Valley Authority 86-8
Textile industry:
    Australia 59, 61
    Japan 20
    Sweden 109, 119
    UK 145, 149
    W. Germany 174
    France 212
Thomas Cook & Sons (UK) 147
Tokoku District Development Company (Japan) 35, 38
Tokusha Gaisha (Japan) 35, 38
Toulouse 211
Trade Association Law (Japan) 26
Trade Descriptions Act 1968 (UK) 153
Trade policy:
    Japan 24-5
    Australia 47, 55-6
    UK 133
    US 84
Trade Practices Act 1965 (Australia) 55
Trade Practices Act 1974 (Australia) 55, 63
Trade Practices Commission (Australia) 55

Trade Union and Labour Relations
   Act 1974 (UK) 154
Trade Union and Labour Relations
   (Amendment) Act 1976 (UK)
   154
Trans Australia Airlines 64
Treasury Deposits Bureau (Japan)
   20
Treasury (France) 194
Treaty of Rome 197
Trust Fund Bureau (Japan) 20, 35
Truth-in-Lending Law 1971 (US)
   82

Ugine Kuhlmann and Evian (France)
   198
Unemployment:
   Australia 43-4, 46, 49-50
   Sweden 108
   UK 137, 140-1
   W. Germany 186
   France 201-4
United Kingdom:
   extent of public sector 130-4
   nationalisation 134-7
   planning 137-8
   finance 138-40
   regional policy 140-1
   micro impact of macro policies
      142-5
   industrial policy 145-51
   agriculture 151
   competition and consumer
      protection policies 152-3
   labour market policies 153-5
   assessment 155-6
United States:
   role of government 72-4, 93-8
   anti-trust policy 74-8
   regulation of public utilities and
      licensing 78-81, 86-8
   consumer protection 81-2
   finance 83
   state support of industry 83-4
   agricultural policy 84
   transport policy 84-5
   trade policy 84
   Tennessee Valley Authority 86-
      8
   armaments industry 88-90
   energy policy 90-3
   regional policy 92-3
   planning 95
United States Railway Association 84

Upper Clyde Shipbuilders (UK) 147

VEBA AG (W. Germany) 164, 179,
   181-4
VFW-Fokker (W. Germany) 173
VIAG (W. Germany) 148, 181-2,
   185
Volkswagen AG 168, 179, 181-4
Volvo 119-20

West Berlin 14, 166-8, 185
West Germany:
   philosophy of state intervention
      160-2
   competition policy 162-5
   interventionist policies following
      1967 Act 165-6
   regional policy 166-9
   agricultural policy 169-70
   subsidies 170-1
   railways 172
   shipbuilding 172-4
   coal-mining 174-5
   housing 176
   banking 176-8
   state-owned enterprises 178-86
White Paper on Manufacturing Industry
   (Australia) 47
White Paper – The Regeneration of
   British Industry 150
White Paper on Industrial and Regional
   Development 1972 (UK) 147
Wilhelmshaven 169
Wolfsburg 168, 184

Yokohama Specie Bank (Japan) 20